TOUR DE FRANCE
LEGENDARY CLIMBS

First published in 2016 by
Carlton Books Limited
20 Mortimer Street
London W1T 3JW

A CIP catalogue record for this book is available from the British Library.

ISBN 978-1-78097-790-4

Editorial Director: Martin Corteel
Design Manager: Luke Griffin
Designer: Darren Jordan
Production: Maria Petalidou
Picture Research: Paul Langan

Printed in China

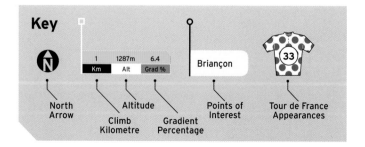

Opposite: **Wout Poels and Richie Porte lead Chris Froome past Dutch Corner during the 2015 Tour de France.**

TOUR DE FRANCE
LEGENDARY CLIMBS

RICHARD ABRAHAM

CARLTON
BOOKS

Designed with
Google Earth

Contents

Opposite: **The famous hairpins of Alpe d'Huez.**

Location maps

The most famous climbs of the Tour de France are located across five regions: the Alps, the Pyrenees, the Massif Central, the Vosges and Provence.

FRANCE

1. PROVENCE

MONT VENTOUX
Page 192

2. ALPS

COL DE JOUX PLANE
Page 84

COL DU GLANDON
Page 54

CORMET DE ROSELEND
Page 112

COL DE L'ISERAN
Page 92

COL DE LA MADELEINE
Page 64

COL DU GALBIER
Page 32

COL DE LA CROIX DE FER
Page 46

ALPE D'HUEZ
Page 20

COL D'IZOARD
Page 74

COL DE LA BONETTE
Page 102

3. VOSGES

BALLON D'ALSACE
Page 212

4. MASSIF CENTRAL

PUY DE DÔME
Page 202

5. PYRENEES

COL D'AUBISQUE
Page 134

HAUTACAM
Page 172

COL DU TOURMALET
Page 124

COL DE PEYRESOURDE
Page 180

LUZ ARDIDEN
Page 156

PLA D'ADET
Page 148

SUPERBAGNÈRES
Page 164

Introduction

The roar of the crowds, the thud of the helicopter blades in crescendo, the riders gasping for air, the hot sun and the chill mountain breeze, the fumes of the following vehicles and the rush of dust that they leave behind. This is the thrill of the Tour de France in the high mountains. Even at home, through the TV, it's enough to make hairs stand up on the backs of necks.

The high mountains represent the very best of the Tour de France, and the Tour is obsessed with them. Such is the fascination with these high mountains that the names of Alpe d'Huez, the Col du Galibier or the Col du Tourmalet have entered the lexicon of the world's biggest annual sporting event and fired the imaginations of the wider public. These landscapes are what set the Tour de France apart from any other sporting event. They are the reason millions of amateur riders make the pilgrimage to experience them for themselves. They are the reason we fall in love with it.

Ask anyone with an interest in cycling to name mountain peaks in France and many would struggle beyond Mont Blanc and Mont Ventoux. Ask them to name high passes in the Tour and they could reel off a long list with ease. In the words of the current director of the Tour de France, Christian Prudhomme, "Cycling is in love with the mountains."

The Tour de France ranks its climbs by difficulty, beginning at fourth category for the easiest and counting down. The greatest of these mountain climbs are given the classification of *hors catégorie* or "beyond classification". It is a rare distinction and a hallmark of a certain quality. The 20 climbs in this book represent the most spectacular, and the toughest, of the lot.

Physically speaking, they don't always have much in common. Some are long – the Col de l'Iseran is more than 47 kilometres from top to bottom – and others like the 10.7km Pla d'Adet are short. They are found right across France: 776 kilometres separate the Col d'Aubisque in the western Pyrenees from the Ballon d'Alsace in the Vosges, the furthest apart of the climbs that feature in this book. The Puy de Dôme is just 1,465m up, a little more than half the altitude of the Cime de la Bonette, the highest point ever reached by the Tour de France at 2,802m. Some are the sites where riders scrap it out for the stage win with just a few kilometres remaining. Others are obstacles to be scaled early on epic days in the mountains. There is always so much to play for: the stage, the overall, or simply survival.

What they do have in common is this: the greatest mountain climbs are where the riders will go deeper into their reserves of effort, willpower and suffering than ever before. This book brings together the mountain climbs with the richest history in the world's biggest bike race. Using exquisite high definition satellite imagery captured from Google Earth, it offers a unique new perspective on these iconic locations, illustrating the features that cement their legendary status and telling the stories of the riders of the Tour de France who on these slopes have ridden themselves into the history books.

Opposite: The travelling circus of fans, helicopters, riders and vehicles hits the high Alps during the 2012 Tour de France.

Below: Bradley Wiggins leads the peloton through the Pyrenees on his way to becoming the first British winner of the Tour de France.

1
HISTORY OF THE MOUNTAIN CLIMBS

The history of the Tour de France in the mountains is one of intrigue, excess, risk taking and constant innovation. The early pioneers of the race immediately realized the potential of these jaw-dropping arenas and, within less than a decade of its first edition, the race had established itself in the high passes of the Alps and Pyrenees. With such breathtaking natural terrain to play with, it couldn't help but make a success of them.

Opposite: Octave Lapize pushes his bike on his way to winning the Tour's first ever mountain stage, in 1910.

The Early Years

From the beginning, the mountain climbs of the Tour de France captured the public's imagination with tales of daring, adversity and adventure. Their debut in 1910 was an instant hit and, within a few decades, climbs such as the Col du Tourmalet and Col du Galibier had woven themselves into the fabric of the Tour.

Opposite: Early Tour climbs such as the Col d'Izoard often featured rugged roads.

Below: Cool water from spectators' bottles offers brief respite from the hot, arduous mountain climbs.

If there were ever a day for the Tour de France founder Henri Desgrange not to pull a sickie, Thursday, 21 July 1910, was it. The editor of *L'Auto* newspaper had introduced his debut high mountain experiment into that year's Tour and now, just as the riders were about to leave Bagnères de Luchon in the cold Pyrenean mountain air at 3.30am, he wasn't there to see it.

He was, perhaps understandably, more than a little afraid of the potential monster that he had created. He had introduced his Tour to the concept of a categorized "mountain climb" five years earlier when the race went over the Ballon d'Alsace and later the Côte de Laffrey and Col Bayard. But this was something else altogether.

Having planned a route that tackled five unpaved and altogether wild mountain passes, including the 2,115m Col du Tourmalet, Desgrange was now wracked with last-minute anxiety that he might be sending his so-called "convicts of the road" to their doom. He'd been convinced to do so by his deputy Joseph Steinès, who had driven to the Tourmalet earlier in the year and been creatively economical with truth when he sent his report back. "Perfectly fine," he said, neglecting to mention the snowstorm, the hypothermia and the near death experience when he fell into an icy stream.

In the end, however, Desgrange had nothing to worry about. The spring snows had melted, the mountain bears didn't attack, and the riders made it to Bayonne intact, even if the effort pushed them beyond the bounds of anything they'd done so far. "Assassins!" was the accusation Octave Lapize directed at his task-masters as he crossed the Col

d'Aubisque, the fourth of the day's five climbs, in an episode which has attained legendary status in the Tour's long history.

And therein lies the secret of the mountain climbs in the Tour de France. Even from day one, here were places where tales and deeds of riders could seamlessly pass into legend. Places where exoticism, adventure and human endurance could be blended by the sorcerers of the first ever newspaper reports (with more than a sprinkling of poetic embellishment) into epic tales. After all, photographs were at a premium, TV hadn't been invented and they had papers to sell. It is no coincidence that every director of the Tour in its 111-year history had started out in journalism.

The Tour of 1910 was the last time that Desgrange or any organizer would ever downplay or understate the exploits in the mountains. Desgrange himself, with some vigour, would publish his odes to the mountains, once fervently warning riders "to redouble their prudence, all through the mountains, because horses, mules, donkeys, oxen, sheep, cows, goats, pigs can all be wandering untethered on the road".

Racing in the mountains in those early years tended to be a very lonely, personal endeavour. Tour winners like Lapize, Gustav Garrigou, Philippe Thys and Firmin Lambot had only two gears – one sprocket on either side of their rear wheel – and weren't allowed to receive outside help. They couldn't

procure spares on the road, and had to finish with what they started with. A puncture at the wrong time could mean hours lost. Big gaps very quickly opened up between riders.

The Tour and the public loved it, and the Alps made their race debut less than a year later, including the 2,556m Col du Galibier. The following years saw classic mountain stages such as those from Bagnères de Luchon to Bayonne or from Nice to Grenoble cement themselves as Tour de France staples.

Of course the Tour de France has never just been about pure sport. And from the very first passage of the Ballon d'Alsace on the German border, "right under the eye of the enemy", the high mountains have played an integral role in fulfilling the race's true purpose, whether that be helping to unify a French nation, acting as a giant worldwide billboard for the country, making money for the organizers, teams and riders, or simply flogging more papers.

Whether it was by tweaking the route to favour or disadvantage certain riders, or by periodically refreshing the competition with the introduction of the King of the Mountains classification in 1933 (first won by "The Flea" Vicente Trueba) or the first mountain time trial over the Col de l'Iseran in 1939, the high mountains came to define the Tour.

Within a couple of decades of that fateful day in 1910, the race had a stock of well-known and well-loved climbs that it could simply plug in and play. The high mountains had exceeded even Desgrange's lofty expectations. They had become the forefront, the very essence, of the Tour de France.

The Golden Era

When the Tour de France emerged from the Second World War it wasn't ready simply to continue on from where it left off. Since *L'Auto* had met its demise during the conflict, the Tour and its new owners, *L'Equipe* (run by former *Auto* editor Jacques Goddet and new only in name), were ready to start afresh.

France and the rest of the world were ready for a fresh start, too. As television and colour photography began to take off, the old mountain climbs and the old imagery simply couldn't cut the mustard. What was needed for the first post-war Tour in 1947 was novelty and innovation, not nostalgia for a past that nobody particularly wanted to remember.

The late 1940s and 1950s were thus an era of monumental change for the Tour, in which the mountains were at the cutting edge. The baking hot, bleached white peak of Mont Ventoux arrived on the scene in 1951, and the following year's Tour saw the introduction of summit finishes for the very first time in a race which was dominated by Fausto Coppi. The Italian won the first ever stages at Sestrières, Puy de Dôme and on a climb that would later come to be synonymous with the Tour: Alpe d'Huez.

Just as Coppi and his arch-rival Gino Bartali had done for Italy, Louison Bobet became a national hero for 1950s France with three consecutive Tour wins between 1953 and 1955. Then along came another in Jacques Anquetil, the first man to win five Tours. They both did so with commanding performances in the high mountains, which during the 1960s went higher than ever. The Cime de la Bonette, which at 2,802m remains the highest the Tour has ever been, was crossed in 1962. The first rider over the top was Federico Bahamontes, a Spaniard known as the "Eagle of Toledo" and one of the greatest pure climbers of all time.

It wasn't always about the winners. Raymond Poulidor, affectionately known as "Poupou", captured home nation hearts in a career spent duelling with Anquetil and then, in the late 1960s and 1970s, with a new Belgian on the scene called Eddy Merckx. Poulidor had the misfortune of coming up against two of the greatest riders the Tour has ever known, but the sight of "the eternal second" giving it a good go on climbs like the Puy de Dôme and Pla d'Adet earned him the adoration of his public, which continues even to this day.

During Merckx's era of domination new climbs were featured as well as old favourites. He had cemented his 1969 debut Tour win with stage victories on the Ballon d'Alsace and then, with his masterclass to Mourenx, over the same four Pyrenean climbs that featured on that first ever mountain stage in 1910. On the other hand the Pyrenean resort of Pla d'Adet, where in 1974 he fought to hold off Poulidor's challenge, was brand new to the Tour that year.

In fact the Tour owed much of its wanderlust to the creation and promotional drive of ski stations and winter resorts in the Alps and Pyrenees. Plenty – including Pla d'Adet, Superbagnères and Luz Ardiden – have since written themselves into a recurring role in the Tour de France, which began to favour shorter stages, longer transfers, and a creative flourish of split stages, time trials and team time trials.

As well as new places, new concepts were introduced, such as the polka dot jersey for the King of the Mountains competition. Now one of the most iconic and celebrated items of sporting clothing, it gained its slightly comical aesthetic from the original sponsor of the competition, chocolate brand Poulain, whose wrappers featured red polka dots. It didn't seem to bother Lucien Van Impe, one of the sport's great pure climbers and wearer of the first polka dot jersey in 1975, whose career saw him winning six mountains classifications, the overall 1976 Tour and nine mountain stages between 1972 and 1983.

Such competitions spawned new terminology in the race and added an extra dimension to the mountain climbs of the Tour. The *hors catégorie* classification for the very toughest climbs was introduced in 1979 as riders like Van Impe began to specifically target the mountains. The following decade also enjoyed the first successes by riders from outside Europe – from Australia, Colombia and the USA – as live colour television coverage saw the Tour enter into the living rooms of millions of people right around the world.

It entered the final decade of the twentieth century with back-to-back wins for an American, Greg LeMond. However it was another, very different American who would come to dominate and define the next époque of the Tour de France.

The Modern Tour

The Tour's mountain tales in the two decades either side of the millennium have been sullied by the misdeeds of a lost generation. But there are signs that the sport has finally turned a corner.

It started as whispers and rumours. Slowly but surely, the Tour de France began to seem different. Not only were different riders grabbing centre stage, they were doing so in a different way. Something had changed.

"In 1993, I knew that I was in great form," double Tour winner in the 1980s, Laurent Fignon, recalled to *Cycle Sport* magazine in 2005, "... but in the blink of an eye, 30 riders had come past me, and I believed I was in good form, 30 riders, just like that. And after that I was riding with people I did not believe

I would ever be riding with in the mountains. People who were riding on EPO."

Performance enhancing drugs have always been a part of cycling. Starting with the basic amphetamines and painkillers employed by the earliest riders of the Tour de France to ensure they were able to push their bodies beyond the natural limits of endurance, drug taking has to a greater or lesser extent been an undercurrent of the sport for as long as it has existed. Well before Fignon's time it had even claimed lives; after British rider Tom Simpson

collapsed and died on the upper slopes of Mont Ventoux in 1967, French coroners determined that amphetamines, alcohol and heat exhaustion had proved a fatal combination.

Yet this was something new. Average speeds began to creep up, and riders began to climb the Tour's highest and most foreboding mountains in record quick times. At the time these exploits were explained away by citing better training methods, better nutrition and better equipment, but as time went on a stink began to emanate from the sport. The most pungent whiffs came blowing across the summits and passes of the Tour de France.

The technological breakthrough that brought about such a change was synthetic erythropoietin, or EPO. Combining it with steroids and hormones like synthetic testosterone, and later the gruesome activity of blood transfusions, trainers had discovered ways, as the saying was at the time, to turn donkeys into racehorses.

In 1997 Marco Pantani rode up Alpe d'Huez in 37 minutes and 35 seconds. Although precise times vary, it was more than five minutes (12%) quicker than the riders just ten years before him. While some riders still rode and won clean, the extent of cheating, lies and deceit even threatened the very continuation of the Tour. The race reached its nadir in 1998 when a string of police raids, expulsions and rider protests threatened to bring the whole thing grinding to a halt before it reached Paris. The sport's integrity was flaking away like bark from a rotting log.

In 2013 Lance Armstrong, the rider who rose to the highest of heights during the

1990s and 2000s, came crashing back down to earth. There are now 10 summit finishes, and seven Tours de France, with no winner at all: organizers decided that awarding them to another rider would prove a waste of time.

Sadly Armstrong's first retirement in 2005 did little to end the farcical scenes as riders like Floyd Landis, Alexandre Vinokourov, Michael Rasmussen and Riccardo Ricco used the Tour's high mountains to demonstrate their chemically enhanced superpowers.

Thanks to their physical difficulty and hence popularity as a domain of the doper, the Tour's great mountains got an unfair deal in this sordid era. Their reputations, while not entirely clear of mischief and scandal to begin with, were undeniably stained.

However, there are signs that the sport has since changed again. Whether pre-empting a new era of the sport or simply responding to the demand for a fresh start, the nature of the high mountains in the Tour de France has begun to change too.

As riders become more closely matched, a trend indicative of increased professionalism, stronger teams and probably also lower levels of doping, the high mountains have become even more closely fought than ever. No longer do riders gain or lose minutes on mountain stages; today's Tours are won by seconds pinched here and there.

Far from declining in significance, if anything the mountains of the Tour de France are more important than ever. As the Tour seeks to look back to its past and carve for itself a new future, its greatest mountain climbs will undoubtedly sit right at the heart of it once again.

2
CLASSIC CLIMBS OF THE ALPS

The Alps are the true mountain giants of the Tour de France. They are the biggest, the longest and the highest mountains that cycle races have ever climbed. From the 48km road to the Col de l'Iseran, to the Cime de la Bonette that sits over 2,850m up in the clouds, the high passes of the Alps are the rooftop of the Tour. The drama that has taken place here for more than 100 years has seldom failed to live up to these grandest of settings.

Opposite: Vast valleys and soaring, snow-capped peaks define the landscape of the Alps and dwarf the riders of the Tour de France.

Alpe d'Huez

1850m

Length: 13.8km
Start: 744m
Ascent: 1017m

Featuring the most famous set of hairpin bends in the world, Alpe d'Huez is the very epitome of the Tour de France in the mountains. From the 1950s to the present day, the "Hollywood climb" of cycling has seen some of the most dramatic and iconic moments in Tour history.

> **The Alpe! It's like all the Alps encapsulated in one mountain.**
> *Gérard Ejnès, author and journalist*

Alpe d'Huez is to the Tour de France what Wembley Stadium is to football, what Monte Carlo is to Formula One motor racing, what Wimbledon is to tennis and what Lord's is to cricket. It is Glastonbury, the storming of the Bastille, a hall of fame, and so much more.

Even though the Tour moves around France from year to year and doesn't always include a trip here, the famous 21 hairpins from Bourg d'Oisans form the most famous arena in cycling. The only place that can even come close to rivalling Alpe d'Huez as a "home ground" for the Tour is the Champs-Elysées – which in over a century of the Tour has only hosted the finish since 1974.

The Alpe has been called "the Hollywood climb" of the Tour de France and like the Los Angeles Boulevard, where movie stars' handprints are set in the ground along the walk of fame, here the names of every one of the winners of the 29 stages to finish there are marked on one of the 21 hairpin bends.

Tourists and amateur riders swarm to ride the climb throughout the summer months. Each time that it features in the Tour de France hundreds of thousands of fans make a beeline to one of the 21 bends. Alpe d'Huez is the very best of the Tour: picnics made of fresh fruit and *jambon beurre* baguettes, long afternoons spent in the July sun catching the odd word of race reportage on a far-off tinny

radio, the slow crescendo leading to the thud of helicopter rotors and the race's arrival. Alpe d'Huez is frenzied fans whipped up into a trance-like state of excitement. It is colour, noise, heat, and drama.

Why does this climb have such a venerated role in the race? It's not the highest – just 1,815m at the top, almost a full vertical kilometre lower than the nearby Col du Galibier. At 13.8 kilometres it's not the longest either; nor does it have the same history as the likes of the Col du Tourmalet, having first been featured in 1952.

"I think it's a pretty dull climb," said 1992 stage winner Andy Hampsten. "Sure, there's all the history of it, but in my mind it's more of a cycling stadium than a beautiful road."

Perhaps it's due to the vast number of fans, including the thousands of orange-clad Dutch fans that congregate around hairpin seven or "Dutch Corner". Perhaps it's because it is named "Alpe", the clearest signal possible to the general public, telling them to expect winding roads, spectacular scenery and Toblerone-shaped snowy peaks. Perhaps it's even the fact that the hairpins are numbered to 21, which has a certain ring to it (21 is the card game and there are generally 21 stages in the modern Tour). Never mind that from bottom to top there are actually 22 hairpins (a bend between numbers six and seven isn't counted).

Crucially Alpe d'Huez was perfect for the modern-day Tour de France; it was bright, noisy, short (riders could climb it in a little over 40 minutes, ideal for a TV show) and action-packed. It is where fans cheer and jeer the riders; Lance Armstrong was almost pushed off his bike during the 2004 time trial, and the Alpe was where Chris Froome and his team-mates suffered the worst of their verbal abuse in 2015. The Sky team car made it to the top covered in beer, flour and all sorts else, with both wing mirrors smashed in. For good or ill, the climb was a far cry from the earlier long ascents where the empty mountain landscapes dwarfed the riders and the florid writing of the early reporters embellished tales of heroics and daring. This was cycling for the TV age. There have only been 12 years since 1976 when the Tour hasn't returned to Alpe d'Huez; in 1979 it hosted two consecutive stage finishes, and in 2013 riders climbed it twice in one stage, looping back round via the Col de Sarenne.

"Alpe d'Huez definitively transformed the way the *Grande Boucle* ran," said Tour commentator and author Jacques Augendre. "No other stage has had such drama."

Opposite: **Thousands of fans on Dutch Corner patiently await the arrival of the Tour on the grassy banks on Alpe d'Huez.**

Bourg d'Oisans

Hairpin one

1	848m	10.4
Km	Alt.	Grad. %

4	1123m	9.0
Km	Alt.	Grad. %

7	1370m	9.3
Km	Alt.	Grad. %

6	1277m	7.4
Km	Alt.	Grad. %

La Garde

Dutch Corner

START ▶	744m
	Alt.

2	948m	10.0
Km	Alt.	Grad. %

3	1033m	8.5
Km	Alt.	Grad. %

5	1203m	8.0
Km	Alt.	Grad. %

Altitude meters

2000

1500

1000

500

0

Start 1 2 3 4 5 6 7 8 9 10 11 12 13 Finish

Kilometers

Flamme rouge

13	1822m	4.9
Km	Alt.	Grad. %

FINISH ■   1850m
Alt.

10	1632m	11.5
Km	Alt.	Grad. %

8	1452m	8.2
Km	Alt.	Grad. %

9	1517m	6.5
Km	Alt.	Grad. %

Huez

11	1723m	9.1
Km	Alt.	Grad. %

12	1773m	5.0
Km	Alt.	Grad. %

Google Earth

Route to the Summit

Twenty-one hairpins and 13.8 kilometres; the route to Alpe d'Huez is a moment for every rider of the Tour de France to savour, even if the sections over 11% and the high-pressure atmosphere of jumped-up, screaming fans means they don't always enjoy it.

DUTCH CORNER

◀ Dutch Corner

Hairpin number 15 (or the seventh from the bottom) is cycling mecca for Dutch fans. It began when Joop Zoetemelk became the first Dutchman to win on the climb, doing so in 1976, and built as his countrymen won seven of the next 12 summit finishes on Alpe d'Huez. On race day at "Dutch Corner" the hot air is thick with the scent of beer, smoke, barbecue and suncream and the day's soundtrack is an endless Europop mix tape. Almost everything – clothing, wigs, facepaint – is orange. In the 1990s when Michael Boogerd was one of the best cyclists in the Netherlands, the corner would rock to the beat of "Boogy is de beste", whose title doesn't require much translation to get the gist of the song across. The proud people of the Netherlands have had to wait a while since the last Dutch winner to emerge through the airhorns and flares of the bend. That was Gert-Jan Theunisse, who won in 1989.

Left: Dutch Corner: an iconic place for fans from the Netherlands.

Hairpin one

The beginning part of the climb to Alpe d'Huez is also the hardest. From the left-hand turn at the start of the climb, the road doesn't drop below 10% for two kilometres. It's at this point that the hairpin bends are most spaced out, making the climb feel a lot longer and harder than it actually is. From this point on, each hairpin counts down from 21 and features a small plaque with the winners of stages on Alpe d'Huez. Bend 21 is Fausto Coppi (1952) and Lance Armstrong (2001); bend 20 is for Joop Zoetemelk (1976) and Iban Mayo (2003)

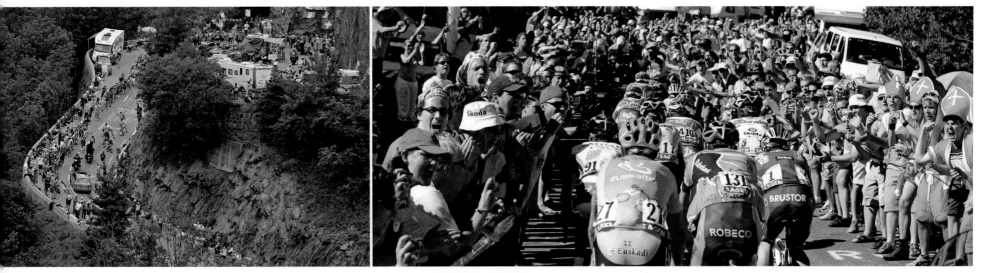

Opposite: **Fans line every inch of road on one of the 21 most famous hairpins bends on Earth.** Above left: **They flock to Alpe d'Huez in their thousands.** Above right: **A riot of orange: Dutch Corner on race day.**

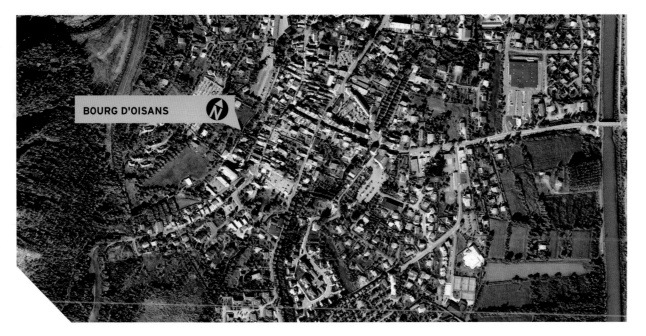

◀ Bourg d'Oisans

Alpe d'Huez is famous for being the finish of another grand cycling event: La Marmotte. One of the first of the big European cyclosportifs (mass participation amateur rides), the event attracts thousands of riders and is still regularly oversubscribed by thousands more. Beginning in the town at the foot of the climb, Le Bourg d'Oisans, the 175km route heads over the Col de la Croix de Fer and the Col du Galibier and then finishes on the top of Alpe d'Huez. It's a gruelling challenge, even for the serious amateur, and this particular route has never been attempted by the Tour de France. Bourg d'Oisans itself is a typical alpine small town; in winter it buzzes with ski shops and in the summer the bike shops take over. It sits on one of the main alpine arteries linking the city of Grenoble with the town of Briançon. The road to Alpe d'Huez crosses a pair of roundabouts before heading straight for the imposing rock face, at which point a sharp left turn takes riders under the inflatable gantry and immediately on to the climb

Left: **Bourg d'Oisans is the starting point for Alpe d'Huez.**

La Garde

The first small village on the climb from Bourg d'Oisans, La Garde sits on a straight section between hairpins 16 and 15. Its little bell tower marks the beginning of a slightly easier section of the climb, where gradients stick to roughly 8.5% for five kilometres. Looking ahead, riders can see the road zigzagging up the mountain and out of sight; with just three kilometres gone, there's still a lot of climbing left. However this section affords spectacular views down to the village and, below it, the valley floor.

Huez

The little settlement that gives the climb its name feels remarkably busy for somewhere situated at 1,400m altitude and nine kilometres up from the valley floor. At this point riders have waved goodbye to the views down to the River Romanche (for the time being) but can spot the grassy tops of the mountains around them emerging out of the forests. With four kilometres to the summit, Huez marks the beginning of the final tricky ramp, one which includes a kilometre at 11.5% average followed by another at 9%.

Flamme rouge

The one kilometre to go marker indicates the start of the temporary roadside barriers and represents the arrival to a safe haven for the riders of the Tour. The barriers help corral the enormous crowds, who before this point have left little more than a single corridor of tarmac available to ride through (making overtaking particularly tricky). At this point riders are grateful that the road turns to a gentle false flat of around 4%, setting up a high-speed finish. This is the last chance for riders hoping to avoid a short sprint finish to drop others.

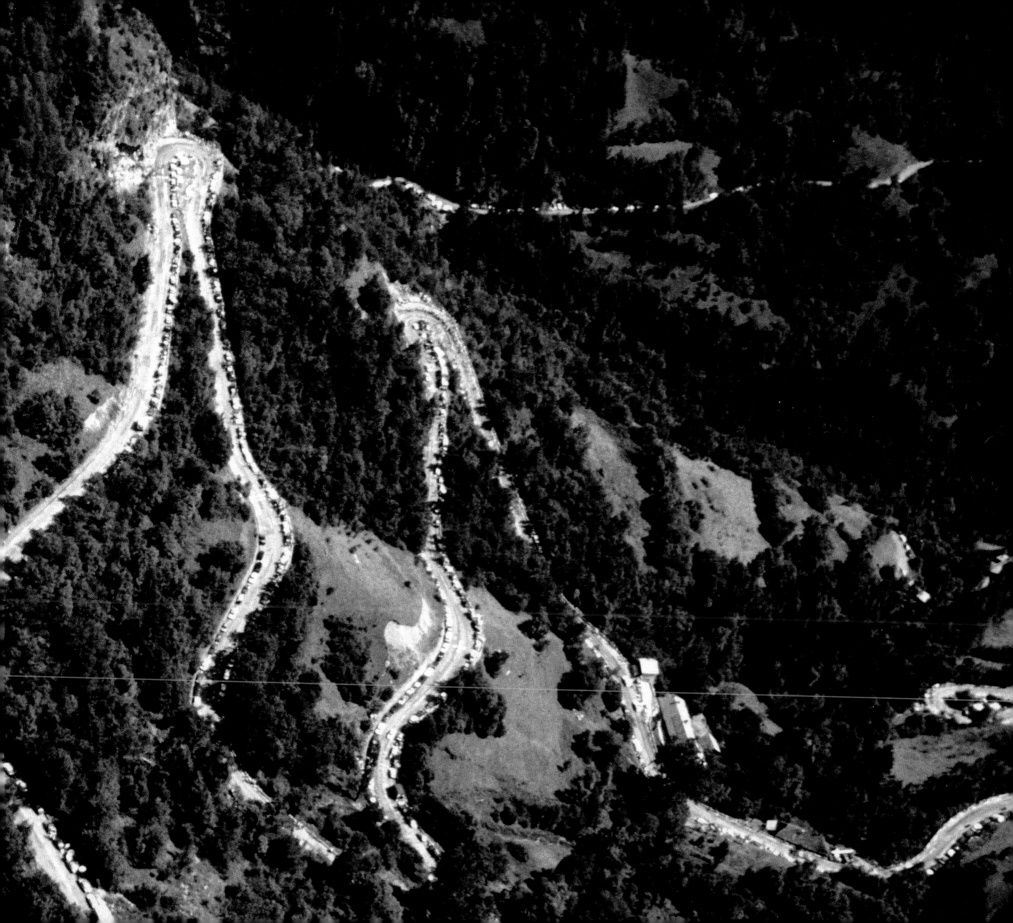

The Mountain Kings

Any one of the 29 showdowns on Alpe d'Huez could make it into the top four greatest Alpe hits, from Fausto Coppi's 1952 masterclass to Lance Armstrong's 2004 time trial win and Chris Froome's desperate ride that saved his 2015 Tour de France.

1979 Joop **ZOETEMELK**

The Dutchman was famously ascetic in his lifestyle and conservative in his racing, but Alpe d'Huez did wonders for Zoetemelk's reputation. He had already won on the Alpe in 1976, a victory which went a long way both to dissolving the notion that this perennial nearly man of the Tour de France was a bit of a wheelsucker and to restoring the credibility of Alpe d'Huez itself after a forgettable first visit in 1952. 1979 would see Zoetemelk win again, becoming the first double winner on the climb on a bizarre stage that started and finished in the alpine resort immediately after a stage finish there the previous day. This oddity was due to roadworks on the nearby Col d'Izoard, which required a last-minute change of route. After descending the climb, riders went over the Col de la Morte and Col d'Ornon before returning to where they had started. Zoetemelk managed to put 47 seconds into Bernard Hinault on this 18th stage, a win that resonated back in the Netherlands and sowed the seeds of the modern day riot of orange that is Dutch Corner. However he would go on to finish second in the Tour (for the fifth of six times in his career) behind Hinault, having conceded more than 13 minutes over the three weeks.

1986 Bernard **HINAULT**

The image of Bernard Hinault and Greg LeMond crossing the finish line of Alpe d'Huez hand in hand is one of the most enduring images of the Tour de France. Hinault, the five-time champion, had broken clear with his team-mate, successor and incumbent yellow jersey Greg LeMond earlier on in the stage and the two rode together up Alpe d'Huez. It was far more complicated than two team-mates helping each other out on the summit finish; LeMond believed he had been duped into helping Hinault win the Tour 12 months earlier, and the simmering rivalry between them was obvious as both men squeezed every last drop of energy out of each other. Indeed, when Hinault had attacked earlier on in the stage, more than a small part of him was hoping it would see him drop LeMond. As LeMond let Hinault cross the line first, with both men grinning from ear, it seemed that the American had all but sewn up the Tour de France while Hinault moved to second. However, for Hinault the Tour wasn't over and LeMond had to fight until the very last stage to make sure the yellow jersey was his. In 2013, the two men reunited for a recreation of the famous finish-line photo.

1997 Marco **PANTANI**

The mercurial Italian, nicknamed "The Pirate", still holds the record for the fastest ever ascent of Alpe d'Huez – 37 minutes 35 seconds – although like most of the achievements in his career and his era of cycling, it comes with an asterisk next to it. In 1997, Pantani forced the pace on the second hairpin from the bottom, riding a searing tempo in his distinctive, out of the saddle, low profile style. The little bald man in the iconic red, blue and yellow Mercatone Uno jersey (size extra-small) shelled riders from his wheel, with yellow jersey Jan Ullrich the last to let go with around 10km remaining. Despite having to push away fans crowding around him, Pantani continued alone to the finish where he flew up to the line snarling, pumped his hands into the air and let out a roar. It was a breathtaking display which marked Pantani's return from a serious injury sustained when he collided with a car in late 1995. But as Pantani's career declined (the Italian eventually died from a cocaine overdose in 2004) and his deceit unravelled, it became clear that his performance on Alpe d'Huez was almost certainly significantly enhanced by the use of EPO and other illegal substances.

1999 Guiseppe **GUERINI**

One of seven Italian stage winners on Alpe d'Huez, Guerini made an opportunistic attack from the lead group of favourites on the climb as the rivals for the overall classification were reluctant to take the fight to the yellow jersey of Lance Armstrong, who was leading the Tour for the first time in his career. The Italian was riding hell for leather with a slender lead and had just passed the flamme rouge gantry marking one kilometre to go when he collided with a spectator, sending both to the ground. It's a moment that regularly makes the cut whenever the best "Tour de France bloopers" are compiled; the fan is stood in the centre of the road looking through his camera as Guerini approaches. He moves right, Guerini moves left, but the fan suddenly moves in tandem with him and there is nothing either can do to avoid the collision. The fan helps Guerini remount (but is eventually pulled back by angry spectators around him) while Guerini presses on. Despite the drama, he managed to win the stage by 21 seconds from Pavel Tonkov, sealing his moment in the spotlight while the spectator presumably slinked off in shame to have his photographs developed.

Col de Sarenne

In 2013 the Tour pulled off something it had never before achieved, a stage featuring two consecutive ascents of Alpe d'Huez. It was spectacular testament to the Tour's power of capturing the imagination. It was a stage that made dreams come true, and which one person in particular will not soon forget.

It's the sort of stage that little French boys daydream about in class and scribble down in the back of their exercise books. A summit finish on Alpe d'Huez. Twice.

For a long time it appeared that the Tour's most famous summit finish would remain a fantasy, and that there would be no way of making this double Alpe d'Huez stage anything more than *une étape de rêve*. But Tour organizers discovered the road leading to the Col de Sarenne, a 9km addendum to Alpe d'Huez that descended out of town, climbed over the col and returned to the valley floor by a different route. In 2013 they added it to the route and the Tour would climb Alpe d'Huez twice.

The Sarenne is the chalk to Alpe d'Huez cheese. Wide, sweeping hairpins on the main climb are exchanged for a steep, narrow lane through a rugged, unspoilt alpine environment. Its inclusion had the desired effect of generating pre-race hype (and throughout the 2013 Tour itself commentators looked ahead to this final week showdown).

There were some protests from environmental campaigners, who argued that the Tour's passage would damage the natural environment of the Sarenne. There were protests from riders too, who looked at pictures of the gravelly track with its steep drops and didn't like it one bit. But a frisson of controversy, plus the fact that climbs as narrow and patently dangerous as the Sarenne are seldom passed by the Tour, was all part of the Sarenne story.

It is testament to the power of the Tour that the race made it happen, as it has done with mountainous obstacles for a century.

Spectators were limited from the roadside and the road was resurfaced, and on 18 July 2013, the Tour de France continued on through the streets of Alpe d'Huez towards the 1,999m, rugged and barren pass of the Col de Sarenne.

A stage win on Alpe d'Huez has life-changing consequences, even more so if you become the first (and so far only) stage winner after two consecutive ascents of the climb. Riding in the day's break, Christophe Riblon actually fell into a ditch on the technical descent of the Sarenne after encountering a patch of moisture on the new tarmac while carrying too much speed. However, the Frenchman remounted, caught his two breakaway companions and dispatched them one by one on the final ascent, finally ditching Tejay Van Garderen on the final little ramp before the climb flattens out in the ski station.

While the peloton behind him negotiated the descent largely unscathed, Riblon's win followed on from compatriot Pierre Rolland in 2011, and two years later Thibaut Pinot would make it a French hat-trick on Alpe d'Huez.

"Every time I watch it again I get goosebumps," Riblon said in 2014. "The commentary is brilliant, and when I see those images I feel like I'm on that bike again and I can relive those last few kilometres, when I raised my arms.

"It has changed my life completely. It's changed what people think of me, and it's given me real confidence. I hope that I'll remain the only person to win after two ascents of Alpe d'Huez for a long time. It's something exceptional."

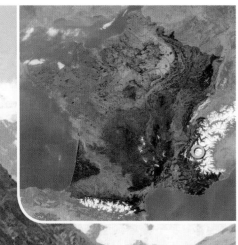

Col du Galibier

2645m

Length: 34.9km
Start: 721m
Ascent: 1924m

For a long time the Col du Galibier was the highest and the longest climb in the Tour de France. While it might have been surpassed in numerical terms by other ascents, for beauty and toughness the Galibier is still unrivalled.

" It's not like one of these climbs where you see the trees above you. You go up and sometimes you see a little corner of the road, but it's like you're riding into the sky. **"**

Andy Schleck

The Col du Galibier is not like other climbs. Sure, there are other roads that are higher, longer and steeper, but the scale of the Galibier is utterly mesmerizing. The pass doesn't just take you between two valleys – it feels like crossing into another world.

It is 34.9 kilometres long on the northern ascent from Saint Michel de Maurienne, climbing 1,924m. From Briançon in the southeast the road is 36.3km long, rising 1,441m. The summit is almost two miles above sea level, at 2,645m. In fact for a long time it was the highest climb and the highest point of the Tour de France. Even today there are only three places where the Tour has been higher: the Col Agnel (2,744m), the Col de l'Iseran (2,770m) and the Cime de la Bonette (2,802m).

The numbers, however, can only tell half of the story; the Galibier is a place you need to visit in order to truly understand it. Tour founder Henri Desgrange went through what can only have been a spiritual experience on the climb, which he added to his Tour for the first time in 1911. You can almost imagine him standing on a precipice overlooking the mountain panorama, clutching his hat to his chest and crying out his famous phrase: "Oh Laffrey! Oh Bayard! Oh Tourmalet! I would be failing in my duty not to proclaim that next to the Galibier you are pale cheap wine. In front of this giant I can do nothing more than raise my hat and salute."

"You don't find any other climb that is comparable to Galibier," said Andy Schleck, winner in 2011 of the only stage to finish on the summit. "The scenery and the small roads going to the top so high up is what makes it, for me, the most beautiful climb in France."

The Galibier is so high that standing guard on its flanks are two cols worthy of classification in their own right: the Col du Télégraphe and the Col du Lautaret. The Tour de France has crossed the Col du Galibier 58 times (on one extra occasion, in 1996, bad weather meant the passage was cancelled and neutralized). Of those passes 37 were from the north via the Télégraphe, including the first passage of the Tour in 1911, making it the most familiar route to the top. And just imagine the sense of anxious excitement that was felt by the riders and organizers on the morning of the first stage over the Galibier. In the early twentieth century the high mountains – particularly those above 2,000m – remained a remote and dangerous place for anyone, let alone bicycle riders. The modern-day equivalent would perhaps be something akin to taking the Tour de France to the Mount Everest base camp.

Indeed, there have been recent reminders of the physicality and scale of the Galibier. In 2015 a landslide in the Chambon Tunnel further down the valley of the Col du Lautaret meant the climb couldn't be crossed (the nearby Col de la Croix de Fer was used in its place). Bad weather in 2013 shortened the stage of the Giro d'Italia, the Tour of Italy, that ventured over the French border to an attempted summit finish, stopping in a blizzard at the Marco Pantani memorial. And in 1996, because of storms, teams had to drive around most of the stage over the cols of the Iseran and Galibier and instead contest a 46km sprint to Sestrières.

Today the climb remains one of the toughest in the race. Long straights offer no psychological respite and make it a road to be climbed with the head as much as the legs. Meanwhile the higher riders climb, the thinner the air gets; at the giddy heights of 2,500m near the summit the air is sharp and goes straight to your head like the local mountain *eau de vie*. Any serious effort pushes riders into an oxygen debt from which their lungs and blood have to battle to recover.

It is a climb that demands an effort above and beyond that required by other high mountain passes in the race. If you're looking for the very definition of *hors catégorie*, the Col du Galibier is it.

Opposite: **The breathtaking peaks of the Alps loom large over the riders of the Tour de France as they press on towards the upper slopes of the Col du Galibier.**

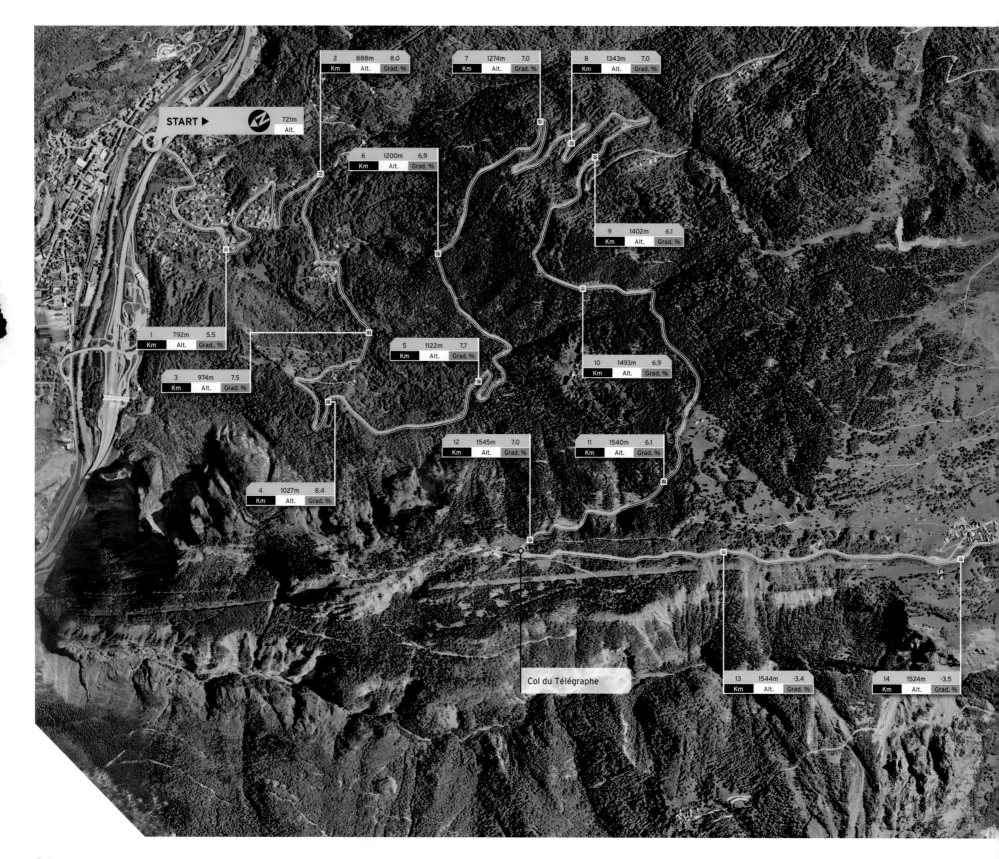

START ▶   721m Alt.

2	888m	8.0
Km	Alt.	Grad. %

7	1274m	7.0
Km	Alt.	Grad. %

8	1343m	7.0
Km	Alt.	Grad. %

6	1200m	6.9
Km	Alt.	Grad. %

9	1402m	6.1
Km	Alt.	Grad. %

1	792m	5.5
Km	Alt.	Grad.. %

3	974m	7.5
Km	Alt.	Grad. %

5	1122m	7.7
Km	Alt.	Grad. %

10	1493m	6.9
Km	Alt.	Grad. %

12	1545m	7.0
Km	Alt.	Grad. %

11	1540m	6.1
Km	Alt.	Grad. %

4	1027m	8.4
Km	Alt.	Grad. %

Col du Télégraphe

13	1544m	-3.4
Km	Alt.	Grad. %

14	1524m	-3.5
Km	Alt.	Grad. %

Valloire

15	1493m	-3.7
Km	Alt.	Grad. %

16	1441m	-3.3
Km	Alt.	Grad. %

17	1409m	-3.2
Km	Alt.	Grad. %

18	1471m	5.1
Km	Alt.	Grad. %

19	1532m	8.5
Km	Alt.	Grad. %

Google Earth

25	1811m	8.6
Km	Alt.	Grad. %

20	1564m	3.1
Km	Alt.	Grad. %

21	1589m	2.3
Km	Alt.	Grad. %

22	1632m	5.1
Km	Alt.	Grad. %

23	1694m	6.0
Km	Alt.	Grad. %

24	1757m	7.4
Km	Alt.	Grad. %

26	1917m	7.4
Km	Alt.	Grad. %

Plan Lachat

29	2135m	8.6
Km	Alt.	Grad. %

30	2228m	8.9
Km	Alt.	Grad. %

33	2451m	7.7
Km	Alt.	Grad. %

Memorial Marco Pantani

Tunnel

28	2068m	8.0
Km	Alt.	Grad. %

34	2545m	8.9
Km	Alt.	Grad. %

27	1971m	4.4
Km	Alt.	Grad. %

31	2299m	8.5
Km	Alt.	Grad. %

32	2376m	8.4
Km	Alt.	Grad. %

FINISH ■

	0000m
	Alt.

Desgrange memorial

Google Earth

Image © Landsat © Google 2014

Route to the Summit

The 34.9km route to the summit of the Col du Galibier is such a vast undertaking that riders of the Tour de France cannot help but notice the extreme changes in surroundings as the road heads higher, the air gets thinner and the weather gets wilder.

COL DU TÉLÉGRAPHE

◀ Col du Télégraphe

Standing guard on the northern side of the Col du Galibier is a mountain pass worthy of serious respect in its own right: the Col du Télégraphe. Looming over the town of Saint Michel de Maurienne, the 12km road climbs through thick woods in a series of regular bends at an average gradient of 7.1%. Outside the Tour the road is busy – buses and construction vehicles take advantage of the broad carriageway and wide bends – and the climb very much feels like the precursor to the more majestic slopes of the Galibier to the south. That is exactly what it is – the climb isn't categorized when it continues onto the Galibier. The imposing telegraph station and fort, which gives the col its name, was built in the time of Napoleon in order to relay semaphore messages through the mountains. Once clear of the suburbia that clings like barnacles onto the edge of the valley, the road reaches 1,566m, passes a little bar and drops down into the town of Valloire via a brief four kilometre descent.

Left: The guardian of the Galibier, the Col du Télégraphe.

Valloire

A bustling ski town full of souvenir shops selling whistling marmot stuffed toys, Valloire is where the climb turns from the subsidiary slopes of the Col du Télégraphe to the first ramps of the Col du Galibier. It starts off gently, rising out of town at no more than 5%. However, the road gradually steepens as it ascends away from the houses; the trees become stunted and then disappear altogether. Eight kilometres later and any signs of permanent habitation have been left behind, swapped for achingly pretty views across the high mountain gulleys.

Opposite: The tunnel was the only way across the Galibier until 1976. Above left: The Henri Desgrange memorial is inaugurated in 1949. Above right: A series of sweeping bends make the Galibier a fast and technical descent.

TUNNEL

Left: The tunnel leads riders under the Col du Galibier.

◀ Tunnel

Just as the road approaches the summit it decides, after 30km of climbing up over the mountain, to tunnel underneath it. In fact the oak doors to the dank 355m tunnel through the Galibier at 2,556m altitude used to be the only way through the pass; it was only in 1976 that the extra kilometre of road over the modern-day col was constructed to allow repairs to the then 85-year-old tunnel. The harsh conditions meant it took construction workers 26 years to finish the job and the tunnel only opened again in 2002. It remains closed to normal cyclists, but the Tour can opt to go through it or over it. The irony of a tunnel so high up the mountain wasn't lost on the earliest riders of the Tour. Emile Georget, the first rider over the pass in 1911 (and therefore in the history of the Tour) remarked that they should have just started tunnelling from the bottom and saved everyone the bother of spending hours slogging away at the mountain face in the first place.

Plan Lachat

The Col du Galibier can be considered as two drainpipes, and at Plan Lachat riders reach the end of the first one. In order to climb higher the road must ascend the near vertical edge of the pipe, at which point it enters the trough of another one perpendicular to it. In practical terms, Plan Lachat is where things get serious. The road crosses the Valloirette stream and onto a series of hairpin bends cut deep into the rock at an average of around 8%. Here is where riders pass the 2000m mark and the altitude begins to bite.

Marco Pantani memorial

Situated in a small, bowl-shaped depression in the upper mountain pastures 4.2 kilometres from the summit, the Marco Pantani memorial marks the spot where in 1998 the Italian climber launched what is probably his most famous attack, dropping Jan Ullrich in the gloom of the storm clouds and going on to win the stage at Les Deux Alpes. It's one of a number of memorials across Europe to this popular rider; this one is a simple transparent plaque with his outline drawn in the glass and tilted at the same angle as the road.

Desgrange memorial

Just a few hundred metres downhill from the southern entrance to the Galibier tunnel stands the Desgrange memorial, a solid stone column dedicated in 1949 to the memory of the Tour's founding father, who had died nine years earlier. Desgrange loved the fearsome Galibier and it is only fitting that this particular climb bears his monument. Each year the "Souvenir Henri Desgrange" prize is awarded to the rider first over the highest point of the race, which is often the Col du Galibier.

The Mountain Kings

The Col du Galibier is a stage set for the Tour's greatest heroes, where some of the great champions of the sport have pinned their colours to the mast and achieved the greatest exploits, both in their careers and in the Tour de France as a whole.

Previous pages: Seldom does one find views better than those from atop the Col du Galibier during the Tour de France.

Opposite top left: Emile Georget improvises refreshment on the Tour's first trip over the Galibier in 1911.

Opposite top right: One hundred years after Georget first crossed the pass, Andy Schleck wins the Tour's first ever Galibier summit finish in 2011.

Opposite bottom: Fausto Coppi grimaces with the effort as he soloes over the Galibier in 1952.

1911 Emile GEORGET

Emile Georget was the first man to the summit of the Galibier in the Tour's first serious alpine experiment in 1911; only he and two others managed to get their heavy, single-speed bikes up to the top without getting off and pushing. Even Georget had to stop on occasion to fill his water bottles in the cool mountain streams. It was a year after the Tour had first crossed the Pyrenees, but the Galibier was on a different scale altogether; riders had little chance of staying together over such huge passes and Georget finished the 366km stage from Chamonix to Grenoble after a mammoth 13 hours and 35 minutes. The first rider to cross the line behind him, Paul Duboc, did so over 15 minutes later. Georget was used to long-distance slogs – he also won the 1911 Paris–Brest–Paris, a 1,200km out and back race that took him over 50 hours to complete. However, the images and the romance of rides struggling into deserted mountain landscapes only served to bolster the Tour's resolve to make them do it; the Galibier returned to the Tour route every single year until 1948, and since then the Tour has only missed it out on 36 occasions.

1952 Fausto COPPI

When the 11th stage of the 1952 Tour rolled out of Bourg d'Oisans after its first ever summit finish at Alpe d'Huez, Fausto Coppi was already in the yellow jersey of race leader. However, his French rivals, incuding Raphaël Géminiani, were desperate to take it from his shoulders and attacked him from the gun. Coppi found an answer to every challenge over the first climb of the Col de la Croix de Fer and, as the race hit the opening slopes of the Galibier, simply took off on his own. His move had the effect of tearing the race to shreds; the closest to the Italian at the finish in Sestrières was over seven minutes behind him on the day and 19 minutes back overall. Coppi was built for climbing. He was nicknamed "The Heron" – when he was off the bike his long legs seemed to carry on up into his torso as if he'd pulled his trousers up too high. But on two wheels those levers propelled him with an almost effortless style, and his speciality was long-range, mountain attacks. The 1952 Tour was the last of his two victories; had the Second World War not ripped the middle out of his career, who knows how many he could have won?

1998 Marco PANTANI

Metaphorical storm clouds had already gathered around the 1998 Tour de France – the discovery of a boot load of performance enhancing drugs in the car of a Festina team carer just before the race had busted open the rampant and uncontrolled culture of doping. On the 15th stage from Grenoble to Les Deux Alpes the physical storm clouds arrived and the Tour rode up and into them over the Col du Galibier. The bright yellow and turquoise form of Marco Pantani came darting out of the freezing wet gloom on the upper slopes of the Galibier, leaving his rivals including the yellow jersey of defending champion Jan Ullrich to wallow behind him. Lit up by the vehicle headlights, Pantani skimmed up to the summit and pressed on down the Col du Lautaret to win alone on the summit finish at Les Deux Alpes. Ullrich was in such a panic that he made the mistake of not putting on a rain cape on the descent (Pantani had literally stopped on the side of the road to get his on) and the big German froze – both physically and psychologically. He lost almost six minutes on the Italian, conceded the yellow jersey and eventually the Tour.

2011 Andy SCHLECK

The Luxembourgeois rider knew he had to try something big ahead of the 18th stage of the 2011 Tour – his arrears on his key rivals and his weakness at time trialling meant he needed a large buffer going into the penultimate stage against the clock if he was to stand any chance of winning in Paris. His long-range attack, culminating with a solo victory on the first ever stage to finish on the summit of the Col du Galibier, was the stuff of Tour de France legend. With 60km to go Schleck attacked on the Col d'Izoard, bridging up with two team-mates who were able to help him on the long climb to the Col du Lautaret. As he approached the slopes of the Galibier he set off alone, battling into a headwind. Eddy Merckx, riding in an official car, pulled up along side him. "He spoke French to me, I remember that, and he said 'ça c'est incroyable,' which means what you're doing is unbelievable, and just keep going," Schleck recalled. Unfortunately his move wasn't enough and although he donned yellow after the following stage to Alpe d'Huez, it was the gritty Australian Cadel Evans who won overall.

Col du Lautaret

The guardian of the pass to the Col du Galibier, the Col du Lautaret is a *domestique* in mountain terms. Linking two disparate valleys and two ranges of the Alps, it is the key building block of the very toughest high mountain stages which visit the show-stopping *hors catégorie* climbs nearby.

The Col du Lautaret stands guard on the southern flank of the Col du Galibier like a shoulder of rock. At 2,058m, it is one of the 20 highest passes ever to have featured in the Tour de France, and higher than all but a handful in the Pyrenees. Yet the Lautaret is seldom categorized, since almost every time the race has passed the collection of chalets and buildings, it has done so on its way up or down the Galibier. The Lautaret sits in the physical and metaphorical shadow of its gargantuan neighbour.

Unlike the Col du Télégraphe which, like a hurdle, riders must jump up and over on the way to the Galibier via the northern road to Saint Michel de Maurienne, the Lautaret is a confluence of three roads. The main road runs roughly west to east with the turning to the Galibier heading north from the pass. Descending south from the Galibier via the sinuous road and past the enormous drops thus gives two options: turn left to Briançon or right to Bourg d'Oisans and Grenoble.

The climb itself is very different in character from anything else the Tour regular crosses in the Alps. It is long: 34.2 kilometres from Les Clapiers in the west and 27.7 from Briançon in the east, where it comprises 76% of the total distance of the Galibier from the southern side. For 364 days of the year (365 days when the Tour doesn't cross it in that edition) it is an arterial road that ultimately links Grenoble with Turin, and as such, away from the Tour, it is a wide main road, rather busy with lorries and vans.

Its purpose is the same for the Tour, too. Dissecting the mountains and marking the boundary between the northern and southern Alps, it links together parts of the Alps and gets riders quickly from A to B. From Briançon riders can continue to Sestrières or the Col d'Izoard; from Les Clapiers they can carry on to Les Deux Alpes, Alpe d'Huez, the Col de le Croix de Fer or Grenoble.

Although the climb starts abruptly in Les Clapiers, the hardest bit – two kilometres at 7.5% – is over with first. It continues at a gentle pace past the Barrage du Chambon, in and out of tunnels and criss-crossing from one rocky ledge to another before opening out into wide meadows. Occasionally the road descends for a kilometre or two – but it is a case of the most recent metres of altitude gained cruelly seeping out on a gentle downhill slope. It's a similar story from Briançon too; the gradient never exceeds 5.2% and averages just 3.1%.

It's really not a leg-breaking climb in the traditional sense; Tours are seldom won or lost on the slopes of the Lautaret. But the cumulative effect of its long slopes makes it a deceptively tough proposition for everyone. Descending isn't really all that much easier than climbing either – the shallow gradients and frequent uphill sections mean that the riders have to work just as hard.

Being neither here nor there, north nor south, perhaps the Col du Lautaret is suffering from a bit of an identity crisis. But ask riders of the Tour de France what they make of it and their opinion will be unanimous: it is very much an *hors catégorie* climb.

Col de la Croix de Fer

2067m

Length: 29.4km
Start: 730m
Ascent: 1337m

Perhaps underused in the Tour de France given its location in the heart of the Alps and its stunning aesthetics, the Col de la Croix de Fer blends the Pyrenean difficulty of an ever-changing gradient with a truly awe-inspiring alpine scale over almost thirty kilometres.

> ❝ On arrival at the bottom of the Croix de Fer I noticed the mountains. I was overwhelmed and it seemed impossible to me to be able to cross summits like these by bike. ❞
>
> *Bernard Hinault (1977)*

At the top of the Col de la Croix de Fer stands a beautifully simple iron cross. Little more than a piece of metal wire hammered into the outline of a crucifix, it is attached to a simple stone pillar propped up on a cairn, taking the colour of whatever blues, browns, whites or greens from the alpine palette are directly in front of the observer.

The Col de la Croix de Fer couldn't be more alpine in its location or its ambience. And as far as names go, they seldom come more evocative than that belonging to the "pass of the iron cross". The pass links Bourg d'Oisans and Saint Jean de Maurienne, two of the most important towns in the Alps when it comes to the Tour de France. The former sits in the Romanche valley at the foot of Alpe d'Huez and the latter, in the Arc valley, leads to the Col de la Madeleine, the Col de l'Iseran, and onwards to the northern Alps.

The pass is surrounded by the towering peaks of the Belledonne mountain chain and the Aiguilles de l'Argentière and has appeared in the Tour 18 times since 1947. Following a 20-year absence between 1966 and 1986, all but one of the 11 stages to take the 2,067m way of the cross have ended with summit finishes at the ski resorts and iconic alpine finishes of Alpe d'Huez or La Toussuire.

And yet its character is distinctly non-alpine. From Saint Jean de Maurienne, the 29.5km climb averages a gradient of 5.5% but rises and dips the whole way up as if it were in the middle of the Pyrenees. From a 10% average in the opening few kilometres there comes a 2.5km descent, a further 5km at 9%, another little descent, 7km of between 3% and 5% and then a final erratic push to the top at between 7% and 10%. From the southwest via Rochetaillé and the Barrage du Verney it's not much different. The The 29.4km route skirts alongside the enormous hydroelectric dams holding back the Verney and Grand Maison lakes, dipping in and out of gullies and stepping up the Eau d'Olle valley. Again a short descent is followed immediately by a leg-breaking ascent, this time a section of 11%.

It's these abrupt changes in steepness that make the Croix de Fer such a fearsome proposition in the Tour de France. Lightweight climbers can take these jolts in their stride, but they spell doom for bulkier riders less able to change tempo so quickly. The rises and falls take the road in and out of cool hollows, past raging torrents and up to bright, windswept plains; it's a climb where changes of temperature can be just as disruptive as changes in tempo.

It has made relatively few appearances in the race despite (and also because) of its location. Its sister col, the Glandon, is right next to it. 2.5km southwest of the Col de la Croix de Fer, the road splits and one fork heads back uphill to cross the Glandon and head towards La Chambre. It means there are effectively six different routes for the Tour to pass through these particular mountains, four of which include the Croix de Fer.

However, 2015 proved to be the year of this pass when the nearby Col du Galibier was ruled out of bounds due to a landslide. On stage 18 the race climbed the southwest side and turned left to the Glandon. The following day they went back up the same way, down to the fork and back up and over the Croix de Fer. The day after that it was back over the Croix de Fer from Saint Jean de Maurienne to a summit finish at Alpe d'Huez.

It was just reward for a sumptuous yet often under-appreciated alpine classic that has that essential combination of stunning scenery and arduous terrain that defines the Tour's mountain stages.

Opposite: The yellow jersey group basks in the sunshine as it approaches the upper slopes of the Col de la Croix de Fer during the 2008 Tour de France.

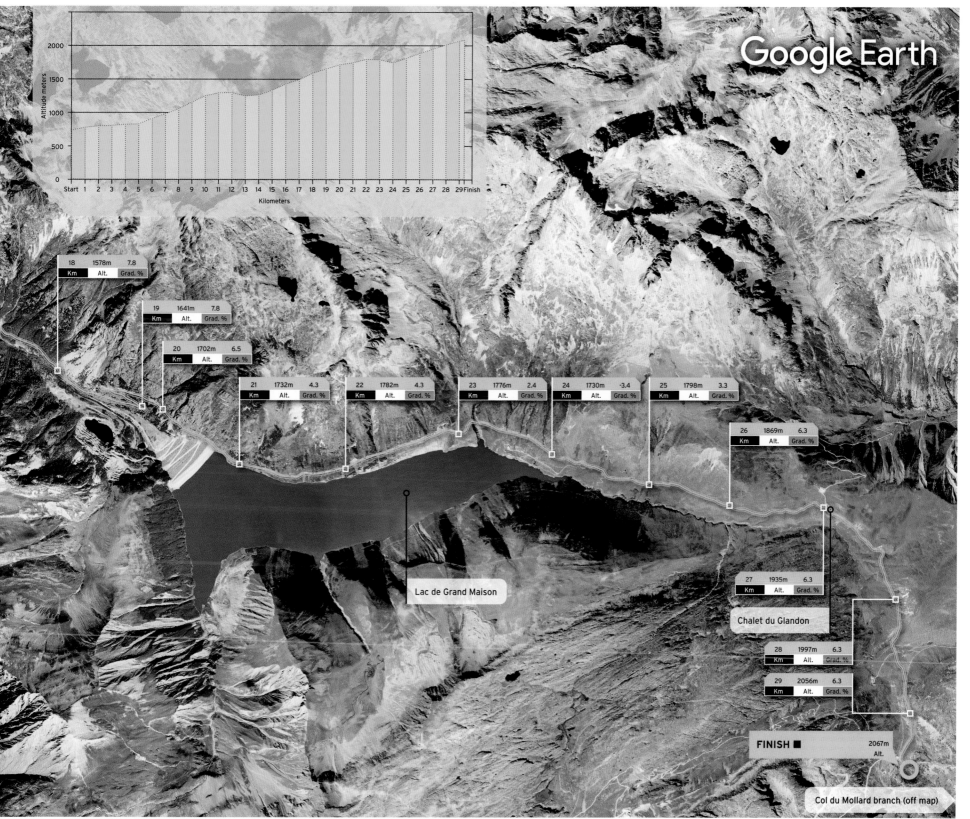

Google Earth

Km	Alt.	Grad. %
18	1578m	7.8
19	1641m	7.8
20	1702m	6.5
21	1732m	4.3
22	1782m	4.3
23	1776m	2.4
24	1730m	-3.4
25	1798m	3.3
26	1869m	6.3
27	1935m	6.3
28	1997m	6.3
29	2056m	6.3

Lac de Grand Maison

Chalet du Glandon

FINISH ■ 2067m
Alt.

Col du Mollard branch (off map)

Route to the Summit

Winding its way up a valley carved by the alpine streams of the Eau d'Olle and the Arvan, the southern ascent of the Col de la Croix de Fer rises and falls past heavy industry, sublime beauty, and everything in between. It's a true alpine archetype.

BARRAGE DU VERNEY

◄ Barrage du Verney

Finished in 1984 to provide hydroelectricity to the Alps and the nearby city of Grenoble, a dozen kilometres west as the crow flies over the Belledonne chain of mountains, the Verney dam holds back the waters descending from the Col de la Croix de Fer and marks the start of the climb to the col. It's a gentle climb to begin with alongside the calm waters of the lake, though the scenery is more industrial than idyllic. However, leaving the reservoir behind sees pylons give way to trees and riders begin the first section of the climb that has the typical staccato rhythm of the mountain. It's a difficult section for riders to pace; they can see little more than a few hundred metres ahead as the thick tree cover obscures the line of sight. At this point over 20 kilometres of effort – around an hour for even the fastest of the Tour's climbers – remain in store. It's no easy warm-up, either. A small section of 10.3% gradient comes after just six kilometres.

Left: Barrage du Verney, where the scenery is more industrial than idyllic.

Défilé de Maupas descent

At the point where the Sept Laux waterfall cascades down, the road drops down four big hairpins into a dark, dank, green microenvironment, the Défilé de Maupas – "Maupas passageway". Sheltered from the sun and watered by spray and meltwater, it's a cold shock to the system for riders, but worse is to come. The road resumes its march upwards with a one-kilometre section of 11% – a very cruel reintroduction to climbing. This stretch is tricky on the way down too; not even the best climbers appreciate a short sharp trip into oxygen debt in the middle of a long descent.

Opposite: Riders descend the geometric hairpin bends at the Barrage du Verney. Above left: The iron cross from which the pass takes its name watches over the highest point of the col. Above right: A small crowd gathers to see Édouard Kablinski and Fermo Camellini lead over the Col de la Croix de Fer in 1947.

◀ Chalet du Glandon

The Col du Glandon has been described as a ladder leading up to the Col de la Croix de Fer. Starting at La Chambre in the Arc valley to the north, the climb passes over the Glandon at 1,924m before descending for 200m and linking up with the southwest route to the Croix de Fer at the Chalet du Glandon. At this point a left turn after the Glandon takes riders on to the final 2.5km of the Croix de Fer, while a right leads down to the Romanche valley. It's a confusing configuration not helped by the proximity of the roads that, on some maps, makes the Glandon appear to be a constituent climb of the Croix de Fer. Situated at this crossroads is the Chalet du Glandon, a bar/restaurant typical of the high Alps offering a sheltered, south-facing terrace cut into the slope. It might be an isolated, weather-beaten outpost but this has got to be one of the best vantage points to watch the Tour de France. The gentle high-altitude slopes can start filling up with tents and motorhomes days in advance of the arrival of the world's biggest annual sporting event

Left: Chalet du Glandon: The ladder to the Col de la Croix de Fer.

Col du Mollard branch

The Col du Mollard (5.7km at 6.8%) seldom receives higher than category two ranking when attacked from a northerly direction, but approaching it from the Croix de Fer brings the challenge of restarting tired legs that have already climbed to 2,000m and switched off on the fast descent. The road swings off to the right 14km down from the Croix de Fer, passes a little bridge and begins climbing again in earnest. Over the top of the Mollard, the road winds down a set of hairpins and returns to the descent from the Croix de Fer just outside Saint Jean de Maurienne.

Allemond

In 1944 Air Vice Marshal Sir Trafford Leigh Mallory, commander in chief of the Allied Expeditionary Air Force and younger brother of Mount Everest pioneer George Mallory, died, with others, in a plane crash in the Alps. The bodies were only found on the southern slopes of the Col de la Croix de Fer the following year. A little museum is now located at Allemond, 27km from the pass, dedicated to the incident. The town is overlooked by the vast peak of Le Rissiou, whose sharp ridge runs directly down to the Lac du Verney where it is perfectly reflected in the calm waters.

Lac de Grand Maison

Close to the pass sits a gorgeous lake, one that's glacial blue with mountain minerals and the sky's reflection. The Lac de Grand Maison sits at just under 1,700m and, surrounded by wide-open vistas, riders see the Aiguilles de l'Argentière on the left and the Cîmes de la Clochette to the right. The road climbs gently along the western shore, although the mountain flanks descend abruptly into this man-made reservoir. After they pass the lake they cross the Rieu Claret stream and prepare for the final 6.3km push to the top, which includes two small sections of over 10%.

The Mountain Kings

The Col de la Croix de Fer has never hosted a summit finish and usually takes its place as a precursor to a mountain showdown. That affords it a unique position as the bike racing connoisseur's climb, a stunning place where tactical manoeuvres begin to take shape and the protagonists of the Tour de France move into position.

Opposite left: Dutch climbing specialist Gert-Jan Theunisse races his gleaming Concorde bike alone on the Croix de Fer in 1989.

Opposite top right: Yellow jersey Greg LeMond gives teammate Bernard Hinault a helping hand on the descent of the Col de la Croix de Fer in 1986.

Opposite bottom right: Vincenzo Nibali soloes over the top of the climb on his way to a stage win in the 2015 Tour at the summit finish of La Toussuire.

1986 — Bernard **HINAULT** and Greg **LEMOND**

1986 is known as one of the greatest Tours of all time and for good reason. It was a dingdong battle between young American Greg LeMond and his team-mate, the five-time French Tour winner Bernard Hinault who had promised to help LeMond after team tactics had shepherded him to his fifth victory in 1985 at the expense of the stronger American. In '86 the pair again comprised the strongest men on the strongest team, La Vie Claire, and on the 18th stage they simple rode away from the rest of the field on the Croix de Fer with 70km remaining. It looked as if Hinault was fully prepared to betray his team-mate in order to bolster his own chances. The Frenchman had lost three minutes on LeMond, now the yellow jersey, on the previous day and it looked to observers as if his chances of winning the Tour were over. Yet he attacked again and again on the first climb of the Col du Galibier in a style that suggested either he didn't think so, or if he did he would go down fighting. Yet for all his pride, Hinault wasn't able to shake LeMond and the pair crossed the finish line hand in hand. Hinault's efforts had won him the stage and cemented his second place overall, but it was LeMond who would win the Tour.

1989 — Gert-Jan **THEUNISSE**

Gert-Jan Theunisse is probably one of the most striking riders to have raced the Tour. With a long brown mullet that would be seen as criminally offensive to modern tastes, the lean, lanky Dutchman flew up the *hors catégorie* climbs of the Tour in the 1980s with his piercing dark eyes focused on the road in front. So wide were the whites of his eyes that it almost seemed as if the white on his jersey and his pristine bar tape had been chosen to colour code with them. In 1989, with the battle between Laurent Fignon and Greg LeMond raging behind him, Theunisse led a small group over the Col du Galibier, broke solo on the Croix de Fer and remained clear all the way up the summit finish on Alpe d'Huez to take a memorable win. Robert Millar, the Scot whose bulky legs, long hair and beaked nose made him equally striking in appearance, futilely pursued Theunisse up the Croix de Fer from Saint Jean de Maurienne but made no inroads into the gap and was absorbed back into the bunch on the Alpe. The Dutchman's PDM team enjoyed a dominant Tour; Sean Kelly won the points classification's green jersey, Steven Rooks the combatitivity prize, and Theunisse clinched the polka dot jersey of King of the Mountains and fourth overall.

1999 — Thierry **BOURGIGNON** and Stéphane **HEULOT**

There's nothing like Bastille Day on the Tour de France. Invariably held in the high mountains, 14 July marks a national holiday for the public and a day for French riders to try their luck in a breakaway. Even if the move is doomed to fail, they will not be denied their slice of airtime, which is guaranteed to bolster their personal profile and bag valuable coverage for their team sponsors. On Bastille Day in 1999 the delightfully named Thierry Bourgignon and Stéphane Heulot tried their luck and launched a two-up move for the greatest of all Tour de France victories: a stage win on Bastille Day atop Alpe d'Huez. The open slopes near the Croix de Fer were bedecked with campervans and happy French fans celebrating *liberté*, *égalité* and *fraternité* as the duo led over the summit to raucous cheers and a corridor of applause. It continued along the Romanche valley and up the next climb but unfortunately they were caught a few kilometres from the finish and an Italian, Guiseppe Guerini, won the stage. But for Thierry and Stéphane it was worth it to lead the Tour over the Croix de Fer on their national holiday; their place in the history of the Tour de France – and no doubt a hero's welcome when they returned home that August – had been assured.

2015 — Vincenzo **NIBALI**

There's an unwritten code in cycling that dictates riders do not attack their rivals when they fall foul of an untimely piece of bad luck, but honour can easily give way to opportunism in the heat of battle when the scent of victory hangs in the air. On the last 2.5km to the top of the Croix de Fer after cresting the Glandon, race leader Chris Froome pulled over to the side of the road to quickly unclip and remove what he later described as a stone or a piece of molten tarmac that had been pulled up by his rear wheel and into his back brake. At exactly that moment defending champion Vincenzo Nibali, whose hopes of overhauling the Brit before Paris were all but over, took off on his own, summiting the Croix de Fer before swooping down to the foot of La Toussuire and riding alone up the final climb to victory. Froome had already been to see Nibali after stage six of that year's race after the Italian laid the blame for a crash at his doorstep, and the yellow jersey paid him another visit after the stage while TV replays clearly showed Nibali taking a good look back to assess Froome's predicament before shifting up a gear and making his move. For Nibali's part, he maintained his innocence and insisted the move was entirely coincidental.

Col du Glandon

1924m

Length: 21.3km
Start: 445m
Ascent: 1479m

The Col du Glandon has seen some of the greatest superpowers in the history of the Tour de France battle for supremacy. Steeper and more mentally challenging, the Glandon is more than equal to its alpine sibling the Croix de Fer.

> 66 I had one of the hardest moments in my career on the Col du Glandon in 1977. I was at the end of my career, and what I had was gone by then. 99
>
> *Eddy Merckx*

It can sometimes be difficult to separate the Col du Glandon from the Col de la Croix de Fer; the conjoined twins of the Dauphiné Alps sit just three kilometres apart, share a common approach from the southwest, and in the Tour de France the Glandon is often incorporated into one *hors catégorie* climb of the Croix de Fer.

Such conglomeration might make the Glandon seem like an inferior half of the partnership, yet while the route from La Chambre that heads due southwest is the shortest and most regular of the three approaches to the two passes, it is undeniably the steepest and most mentally challenging of the lot.

Completed in 1898, 14 years before the Croix de Fer, the Glandon was first crossed in 1947. It was the first Tour after the Second World War but came a full 36 years after the race first visited the gigantic Col du Galibier, which lies 20km as the eagle flies to the east.

Climbing to 1,924m in altitude, the 21.8km route gains 1,474m at an average of 6.75%. Yet the nature of that gain is a mountainous crescendo, with the road slowly getting steeper and steeper up the wide, green valley until the final two kilometres leading to the pass reach 10% and stay there until the top. A Pole and an Italian, Edouard Klabinski and Fermo Camellini, were the very first

over the top in 1947 and the experience of those post-war pioneers can't be too much different to that of riders in the modern era. For racers and amateurs alike, it's like putting your legs in a vice and slowly twisting the screw over the long and painful course of an hour or more. For climbers, it means pushing through the pain barrier and using this perfect springboard to launch an attack and hold on to any advantage down the other side. If even Eddy Merckx has a hard time getting to the top, as he did in 1977, you know the climb presents quite a challenge.

"I liked the Glandon, and every time during my career that the Tour climbed it from the north I led over the top," said Belgian climber Lucien Van Impe, six-time winner of the Tour's King of the Mountains classification between 1971 and 1983 and winner overall in 1976. "The top was a very good place for me to attack because it's difficult to follow a climber there."

The most renowned ascent of the Glandon in recent times came in 2001 on a now infamous stage culminating in a summit finish at Alpe d'Huez. Defending champion Lance Armstrong was yet to assert himself on the race in his usual brash style, and early on the 10th stage his US Postal team was conspicuously inconspicuous. In short, it was a real turn-up for the books.

Smelling blood, the Telekom team of his rival Jan Ullrich drove a furious tempo on the Glandon in an effort to shed the Texan. It was the ideal terrain to do so; on an almost dead straight road from La Chambre, the Glandon is a climb where mental capitulation can precede physical collapse. While hairpin bends occasionally kink into the mountainside, the Glandon offers expansive vistas up the road. This is great for a tourist, but horrible for the Tour rider clinging on for grim death while every neuron and fibre in his mind and body is telling him to stop.

Armstrong, it turned out, was bluffing. After he crossed the Glandon and down the southwest side of the Croix de Fer at the back of a lead group which had been blown to smithereens, he moved up to the front of the pack on Alpe d'Huez, turned around to give Ullrich "the look", and took off up the road.

It was a thrilling moment in Tour history, and one which serves as a brilliant example of the complex psychological and physical war games played out by riders and teams as the Tour de France traverses the great *hors catégorie* passes.

Opposite: **Richie Porte leads his team leader and yellow jersey Chris Froome towards the top of the Col du Glandon, accompanied by a select group of overall favourites during the 2015 Tour de France.**

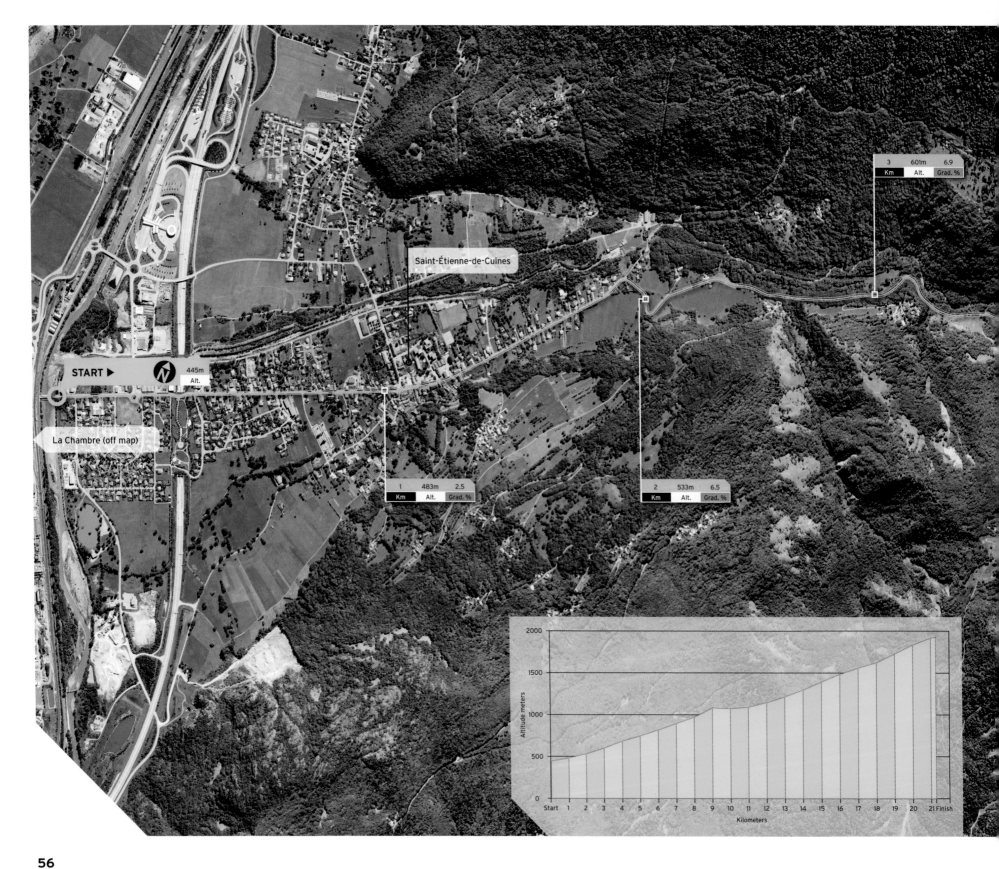

START ▶ 445m Alt.

La Chambre (off map)

Saint-Étienne-de-Cuines

1	483m	2.5
Km	Alt.	Grad. %

2	533m	6.5
Km	Alt.	Grad. %

3	601m	6.9
Km	Alt.	Grad. %

4	685m	6.8
Km	Alt.	Grad. %

5	747m	6.7
Km	Alt.	Grad. %

7	895m	7.5
Km	Alt.	Grad. %

8	969m	7.3
Km	Alt.	Grad. %

6	816m	8.0
Km	Alt.	Grad. %

9	1083m	7.5
Km	Alt.	Grad. %

Google Earth

Le Perrière

Le Villard Martinan

11	1091m	0.8
Km	Alt.	Grad. %

12	1146m	2.9
Km	Alt.	Grad. %

14	1297m	6.9
Km	Alt.	Grad. %

10	1075m	6.8
Km	Alt.	Grad. %

13	1214m	7.0
Km	Alt.	Grad. %

FINISH ■ 1924m
Alt.

Flamme Rouge

20	1832m	11.0
Km	Alt.	Grad. %

16	1484m	9.2
Km	Alt.	Grad. %

21	1915m	10.0
Km	Alt.	Grad. %

15	1392m	9.3
Km	Alt.	Grad. %

17	1558m	8.6
Km	Alt.	Grad. %

18	1621m	6.1
Km	Alt.	Grad .%

19	1725m	7.7
Km	Alt.	Grad. %

Google Earth

Route to the Summit

Featuring long straights and a consistently difficult gradient, the Col du Glandon is no lesser a test than the nearby Col de la Croix de Fer or Col de la Madeleine. Yet riders with previous experience on its slopes can exploit the subtle changes in terrain to their advantage.

◀ La Chambre

To most travellers in this part of France the village of La Chambre is little more than a name on a signpost on the motorway connecting Lyon and Geneva with the Valfréjus tunnel and a route into Italy. However, for bike racing fans of the Tour de France, La Chambre sits at the foot of two of the most famous climbs in the sport: the Col de la Madeleine and the Col du Glandon. It most often takes on a brief role as a linkage between the two as the race finishes off one giant climb and makes a start on the other. In 2015, though, the Tour came to town three times on stages 18, 19 and 20. It came at the culmination of a new climb, the 1,533m Col du Chaussy, on stage 19. Just down the road sits the visually spectacular Lacets de Montvernier, a miniature alpine climb featuring 18 hairpins in a little over three kilometres that also made its Tour debut in 2015.

Left: La Chambre: much more than a name on a signpost on the motorway.

Villard-Martinan

The small hamlet marks a point just over halfway up the route to the Col du Glandon. It offers a small, piecemeal reward to riders in the form of a couple of kilometres that average around 2%. Looking around, riders see bare strips of grass through the forests that denote winter ski slopes, but for those on the Tour, riding flat out, this brief respite will be over in an instant. The road then swings left then right to cross the Glandon stream and resume its typical gradient, pressing on into the tighter valley between the Tête de Bellard and the Cime du Sambuis.

Opposite: **A fractured peloton is dwarfed by the mountains surrounding the Col du Glandon.** Above left: **Eddy Merckx battles on alone after being dropped on the Glandon during the 17th stage of the 1977 Tour de France.** Above right: **Chris Froome wrestles his way through a corridor of fans to rejoin the lead group in the 2015 Tour.**

Left: **The col du Glandon: the finish is marked by a memorial to the Maquis.**

◀ Finish

Sports journalists sometimes make comparisons between cycle racing and warfare, but in reality none can be made. The travails and suffering of sport are incomparable to those of conflict. At the highest point of the Col du Glandon is situated a car park and a small memorial which pays tribute to the Maquis, the men and women who fought in the alpine arm of the French Resistance during the Second World War, in and around the same mountains made famous by the Tour de France today. Compared to some climbs it's an inauspicious pass; the road rises, flattens and swiftly starts descending, with none of the chalets, bars or razzmatazz that often cluster around passes. That said, just down the other side sit the sun umbrellas and plastic tables and chairs of the Chalet du Glandon, a little stone building housing a bar/restaurant and marking the point where the road links up with that leading to the Col de la Croix de Fer.

Flamme rouge

The Col du Glandon saves its best until last, at least as far as climbers are concerned. As if one kilometre at 10.7% wasn't enough, the preceding thousand metres is at 10.4% and includes one small section where the road hits 15%. Even the very best find these gradients tough, but spare a thought for the sprinters in the *gruppetto* who will be searching for that extra sprocket and digging deep into their reserves of willpower. For spectators, however, the vista of the road surrounded by jagged peaks is the visual highlight as well.

La Perrière

More a roadside accumulation of chalets than a proper village, La Perrière comes with a 13% kick adjacent to a summertime campsite just before the crucial section that makes the climb hard. Measurements vary slightly although the three kilometres between 14km and 17km all sit at around 9%. The surroundings are typical of this altitude; green meadows sprinkled with yellow and purple wild flowers, small copses and the occasional allotment tucked away in between. In the distance the snowy peaks begin to creep closer into view.

St Étienne de Cuines

The clock on the Col du Glandon starts ticking at La Chambre but it doesn't get going until the adjacent town of St Étienne de Cuines. Like a pastis with plenty of water before a bottle of full-bodied red, here the very gentle *apéritif* opening kilometres make way for something a little stronger: a section of 8km with a gradient between 6% and 8%. It's where the speeds drop, the intensity ratchets up, and the battle up the Glandon begins. The quiet village is the last settlement of any size until over 50km later over the other side and down towards Allemond.

The Mountain Kings

The Col du Glandon has seen some iconic moments of the Tour de France. From displays of physical strength to opportunist moves and downright dirty tactics, the events here have shown that the Glandon is capable of bringing out the very best – and most unpredictable – bits of bike racing.

1947 Edouard KABLINSKI and Fermo CAMELLINI

The 1947 Tour was the first to take place in the aftermath of the Second World War when a forward-looking France took its first tentative steps on the road to recovery. The Tour de France sought out new destinations and new climbs designed to bring the happy heroics of the race back to Europe. Teams were mustered, including four regional squads from across France, but it was the ragtag band of various nationalities that held sway on stage eight. Riding for a squad that had been cobbled together with riders from Italy, the Netherlands, Belgium and Poland (all countries too small or unable to field a full team) the Pole Edouard Kablinski and the Italian Fermo Camellini broke clear on the Col du Glandon on the stage from Grenoble to Briançon with Kablinski leading over the Glandon and Camellini over the Croix de Fer three kilometres later. Their wheels came off their move after descending to Saint Jean de Maurienne – quite literally as Kablinski suffered a puncture – but the two had already made their mark on the Tour de France and on the history of this great climb.

1981 Lucien VAN IMPE

The Belgian Lucien Van Impe was one of the best pure climbers the Tour has ever known. He was built to climb - and climb quickly - being small, slim and equipped with a tiny torso and a metronomic, fluid and fast natural pedalling style. Yet being poor at time trialling and uncomfortable rubbing elbows with a fast and furious peloton in the flat stages, Van Impe's climbing talent netted him just one overall victory in the race, in 1976. Of course he was also unfortunate enough to come up against the eras of two great Tour riders, Eddy Merckx and Bernard Hinault, who between then would win nine of the 15 Tours that Van Impe started. Unusually for a man hailing from Flanders, Van Impe was at home in the high mountains of the Alps and Pyrenees and he led over the Col du Glandon three times in succession – in 1977, 1981 and 1983 – each time deep into the final week of the Tour and each time leading to a summit finish on Alpe d'Huez. However, he never managed to win a stage on the Tour's most famous mountain; the best he could manage was a third place finish in 1981 on his way to second overall behind Bernard Hinault.

2001 Lance ARMSTRONG

Did Lance Armstrong bluff on the Col du Glandon during stage 10 of the 2001 Tour? Did his rival Jan Ullrich and his team boss Rudy Pevenage get wind of Armstrong's ruse with a sneaky bit of radio tapping? The debate still rages, but as Armstrong and his US Postal team appeared weak over the preceding Col de la Madeleine, Ullrich and Telekom saw an opportunity to stick the knife in and give it a good twist. Their pace up the Col du Glandon was ferocious almost to the point of stupidity: Ullrich's team-mate Alexandre Vinokourov had to ditch bottles he'd just picked up from the team car and sprint to make it back to the lead group. Armstrong meanwhile clung on to the lead group over the Glandon and to the foot of Alpe d'Huez. A few kilometres later he rode up to the front of the bunch and took a long look back at Ullrich. The TV cameras captured the look of surprise and then of realization on the German's steely face as Armstrong looked ahead, got out of the saddle, kicked the pedals and rode off. The stage – and subsequently the Tour – were his.

2015 Romain BARDET

Romain Bardet finished sixth in the 2014 Tour de France but saw his overall hopes in the 2015 race disappear on the first summit finish in the Pyrenees. His redemption came in the form of a fine solo win, forged on the slopes of the Glandon on stage 18. Bardet, a stick-thin climber with a reputation as an intellectual with real tactical nous, attacked a strong breakaway with two kilometres to the col on the southwest side and rode alone over the pass. However, it was the descent of the Glandon that cemented Bardet's stage win. Just behind him fellow young French climber Thibaut Pinot attempted to shadow the move but Bardet's mastery of the fast and technical downhill to La Chambre saw him extend his lead to a comfortable margin while Pinot, notoriously mercurial when it came to going downhill, crashed on a tight left hand bend in pursuit of his countryman, lost time, lost his nerve, and lost any chance of stage victory. Bardet then soloed the stunning 18 hairpins of the Lacets de Montvernier climb in the Arc valley before diving down to St Jean de Maurienne and his first Tour stage win.

Col de la Madeleine

2000m
Length: 19.0km
Start: 471m
Ascent: 1522m

Featuring tranquil surroundings that deceive riders of its seemingly never-ending slopes, the Col de la Madeleine is an alpine classic that has featured in the Tour de France for as long as the road has existed.

> ❝ It's such a long climb that no matter how good you're feeling, you know that you're going to be spending a long time working your way up its slopes. ❞
>
> *David Millar*

It's not the longest climb in the Tour de France, nor is it the highest, but there's something about the way that the Col de la Madeleine feels to ride that makes it one of the most fearsome in the race's history.

On certain maps the pass appears to run in a dead straight line across the Vanoise Alps, one of just two roads (including the Col de l'Iseran) to do so. However, closer inspection reveals that the link between the Tarentaise valley in the north and the Maurienne valley in the south is actually a restless jumble of twists and turns; there are more than 40 bends on the 19 kilometres that make up the southern ascent.

Such is its strategic importance, connecting communities of the Alps, that work was begun on the instruction of local authorities in 1949; and such was the scale of the project that it took 20 years for the road to be completed. It was opened in July 1969 and inaugurated by the passage of the Tour de France just a few days later.

As well as providing riders with a stern physical test – 19 kilometres at 8% on the southern side and 24.5km at 6.3% from the north (with a very tricky, variable gradient) – it performs a practical role. It can be climbed from either direction and remains an essential way for the Tour to navigate its way across the Alps in search of new places and new towns willing to stump up

the cash to host the race. From the northern gateway at La Léchère the race can head on to Albertville and the northern Alps of the Haute Savoie; from the south at La Chambre the race can pick and choose from the Col de la Croix de Fer, Col du Grand Cucheron, Col du Galibier and La Toussuire for a summit finish.

Yet the Madeleine is far from being merely a functional pass. Once out of La Chambre and Le Mollard, and its series of seven straights interspersed with hairpin bends, the road gracefully follows the natural contours of the land, the sort of climb that features bends within bends. It continues to slither its way through soft farmland and little woods, protected and corralled by the ranges of the Lauzière and Échaillon before emerging out of the ski station town of Saint François Longchamp into wide open pastures and a broad bowl of fresh air and sky. It reaches what purports to be a perfect 2,000m in height, although the Tour preferred to say 1,993m until 2012 (when it decided to agree with the road sign at the pass).

The Madeleine can still be a capricious mistress, an alpine siren luring in riders of the Tour with the sweet songs of its tranquil surroundings. It is a deceptively hard climb, particularly on the southern side, and throws up a fast and challenging descent.

And there's no ducking out; given that on each of the 25 occasions it has featured in the Tour the stage has finished elsewhere, it is a climb that has to be conquered in its entirety.

"The descent of the Madeleine is steep and technical, ideal for a lone rider," wrote David Millar in his autobiography. Indeed the now retired Brit, who served a two-year doping ban and returned to the sport in 2007, recalled his time on the Madeleine particularly vividly. He rode it in the 2010 Tour where, injured from a crash in the first week and riding at the very back of the race on stage nine, he followed a police motorbike outrider down the descent in order to save himself from the time cut and the ignominy of having to abandon.

Millar had previous experience of this climb; in 2001 it was where, on stage 10, he unpinned his number and waved goodbye to the Tour. It was that night, he wrote, that he gave in to his demons and allowed himself to be persuaded to dope; nine years later, back at the Madeleine, his refusal to give up helped in part to exorcise them at last.

Opposite: The Tour de France peloton winds its way through the lush green landscape of the upper slopes of the Col de la Madeleine.

START ▶ 471m Alt.

Le Mollard

Col du Chaussy

1	561m	6.6
Km	Alt.	Grad. %

2	626m	6.5
Km	Alt.	Grad. %

3	714m	8.8
Km	Alt.	Grad. %

4	808m	9.4
Km	Alt.	Grad. %

Altitude meters

2000
1500
1000
500
0

Start 1 2 3 4 5 6 7 8 9 10 11 12 13 14 15 16 17 18 Finish

Kilometers

| 7 | 1043m | 7.3 |
| Km | Alt. | Grad. % |

| 9 | 1217m | 8.3 |
| Km | Alt. | Grad. % |

| 8 | 1134m | 9.1 |
| Km | Alt. | Grad. % |

| 5 | 895m | 8.7 |
| Km | Alt. | Grad. % |

| 6 | 970m | 7.5 |
| Km | Alt. | Grad. % |

Google Earth

L'Epalud

12	1438m	5.7
Km	Alt.	Grad. %

10	1287m	7.8
Km	Alt.	Grad. %

11	1381m	9.4
Km	Alt.	Grad. %

Saint Francois-Longchamp

15	1678m	7.8
Km	Alt.	Grad. %

18	1889m	7.1
Km	Alt.	Grad. %

17	1818m	6.9
Km	Alt.	Grad. %

FINISH ■	2000m
	Alt.

13	1518m	8.0
Km	Alt.	Grad. %

14	1600m	8.2
Km	Alt.	Grad. %

16	1749m	7.1
Km	Alt.	Grad. %

Grand Pic de la Lauzière and Cheval Noir

Google Earth

Route to the Summit

While regularly crossing the pass from both sides, the Tour de France has more often than not climbed the Col de la Madeleine from the south, ascending via the many twists and turns and through the village of Saint François Longchamp.

◀ L'Epalud

The gradient on the Col de le Madeleine is classically alpine in nature: unrelentingly steep and consistent for the duration of the climb. However, there is one exception to the profile at the hamlet of L'Epalud, 10.5 kilometres into the climb from La Chambre and a little over halfway to the pass. Deviating from its 8% approximate average gradient, there are two kilometres at 6% with a 500m section at over 12% sandwiched between them which leads up out of the Ruisseau d'Outrier and through the hamlet itself. It's not really enough to trouble most riders, but to those who like to keep a steady rhythm while climbing it will come as an unwelcome interruption. At this altitude the landscape is classic low alpine farmland, with a mixture of small fields, coppices and tiny allotment plots sprinkled between chalets and farm buildings. However, the view of the Massif Lauzière to the north, which appears and disappears through the trees, hints at the altitude metres yet to be climbed.

Left: The steepest part of the Col de la Madeleine comes at L'Epalud.

Saint François Longchamp

Situated at 1,650m altitude, the small ski resort of Saint François Longchamp on the southern slope is a welcome change of scenery for riders on the Col de la Madeleine. The road goes right through the centre of town and marks the point where over two-thirds – or 14 kilometres – of the climb has been completed. It's a pleasant feeling for riders to climb through the town, up above the rectangular chalets and on to the final push to the summit.

Opposite: Towering peaks overlook the climb to the Col de la Madeleine from a distance. Above left: Daniel Becke overshoots a corner on the Madeleine during the 2004 Tour. Above right: BMC's Marcus Burghardt hits top speed descending the broad, straight roads on the Madeleine.

FINISH

◀ Finish

The pass is marked by a large sign indicating 2,000m altitude, a little higher than the 1,993m previously recorded by the Tour de France, and covered in stickers left by amateur riders and tourists who have visited the top. Unlike many of the summits of high alpine passes in the vicinity, there is actually quite a lot going on at the summit of the Col de la Madeleine. A wide, flat saddleback between two peaks, the pass offers plenty of space for buildings and several hiking trails meander off into the adjacent meadows. There are several chalets too, plus a large and rugged restaurant offering local cheesy dishes to tourists, most of whom have driven up and parked in the large car parking space adjacent to the main road. If any should desire to take some local produce home with them, there are several buildings selling the stuff – local Beaufortain cheese or *brebis* made from sheep's milk. They might want to pause before getting back in their cars and setting off for the descent; the views south to the Aiguilles d'Arves are bettered only by those to the north, of the Massif du Beaufortain and Mont Blanc, on a clear day.

Left: There are hot cheesy dinners aplenty at the top of the Col de la Madeleine.

Le Mollard

Riders don't have to wait long to get their alpine hairpin kicks on the Col de la Madeleine. Climbing through Le Mollard, after just 1.8 kilometres of riding from La Chambre, the road switches back on itself eight times in less than three kilometres. This part also marks a starting point for the climb, since the opening mile or so out of La Chambre is a relatively gentle 6%. Here, for the duration of these initial hairpin bends, the average rises to approximately 9%.

Col du Chaussy

4.8km up from the starting town of La Chambre, the route to the Col de la Madeleine runs past a right hand turning which leads to the Col du Chaussy. A charming road to a pass at 1,533m, the Tour de France tackled it for the first time in the 2014 Tour, cycling down the last part of the Madeleine and south onto the Col du Glandon. Just up the road from the turning is a landmark of a chocolatey flavour: the Chocolaterie de la Madeleine.

Grand Pic de la Lauzière and Cheval Noir

The Col de la Madeleine marks the lowest point between two significant peaks in the Vanoise Massif, the Grand Pic de la Lauzière (2,829m) to the north and the Cheval Noir (2,832m), or Black Horse, to the east. The road follows the gulley carved out between their two flanks and the twin peaks, which are popular with hikers, are roughly equidistant from the col; their ensuing ridges guide the road to the pass in a relatively straight line from northeast to southwest.

The Mountain Kings

Rather than soaring success stories of stage wins and summit finishes, the history of the Col de la Madeleine exemplifies the particular trials and tribulations of the riders of the Tour de France when they hit the high mountains. Its slopes demand the very deepest sacrifice and suffering.

Near right: Pierre Rolland tries hard to hide his disappointment after his solo move on the Col de la Madeleine came to naught.

Far top right: Richard Virenque (r) and Gilberto Simoni scrap for mountain points over the Madeleine.

Far bottom right: Yellow jersey Cadel Evans soldiers on while hiding a broken elbow during the 2010 Tour de France.

1981 Phil ANDERSON

The Col de la Madeleine was where the Tour de France dream unravelled for Australian debutant Phil Anderson, who had unexpectedly clung onto race favourite Bernard Hinault from the Pla d'Adet summit finish on stage five through to stage 15 (despite being schooled by the Frenchman in the time trials). The cracks had begun to appear on stage 16 over four tough climbs in the northern Alps but as the race began to climb La Madeleine from the north on stage 17, Anderson dropped off the back altogether as Hinault and Lucien Van Impe raised the pace. It was a mammoth mountain stage, crossing the Madeleine, Col du Glandon and ending with a summit finish at Alpe d'Huez, and over the Glandon Anderson blew up spectacularly. He lost 17 minutes by the finish, dropping out of the top ten. Hinault and Van Impe comprised the top two overall at the end of the stage, however the Frenchman had extended such a vast lead on the mountain goat in the preceding two weeks' flat stages and time trials that the Tour was all but sewn up. Van Impe, however, who led over the Madeleine, would take his fifth of six mountains classifications.

2004 Richard VIRENQUE

Richard Virenque was the French Tour de France hero of the 1990s, winning the polka dot jersey of the King of the Mountains for three years in succession between 1995 and 1997, leading over the Col de la Madeleine and taking the maximum points on the *hors catégorie* climb on each occasion. His long-distance attacks and boyish manner endeared him to his public. However, his tearful downfall came in the Festina Affair of 1998 when the team carer was found with a boot full of performance enhancing drugs ahead of that year's Tour. Virenque returned to the Tour five more times to take three more mountains classifications, but the magic and charm were somewhat lost. The next time he crossed the Col de la Madeleine – on his final Tour in 2004 – he was once again at the head of the race, but lost out to the Italian Gilberto Simoni as the pair strained at every fibre in their bodies to cross the line across the road first. It was a perfect of example of the many battles that take place on the mountains of the Tour. Not only do riders fight for stage wins or the overall victory but for minor classifications, the prestige of leading over a famous climb, or simply for pride.

2010 Cadel EVANS

The ninth stage of the 2010 Tour de France was a rare chance for the Col de la Madeleine to shine. So often a penultimate climb, or even an antepenultimate climb, the Madeleine is rarely the scene of much race defining action. On one notable occasion when it was in 2010, when the stage rolled down the climb to La Chambre and a finish in Saint Jean de Maurienne less than 20km later, the story of the day was not of an heroic attack but a rider's collapse to injury. Cadel Evans had crashed on stage eight of the race but had continued to the finish, remarkably taking over the race lead. However, the injury from the crash proved to be much worse than initially suspected. Evans had fractured his elbow, although didn't tell anyone other than his doctor to avoid the loss of team morale. The raised handlebars and strapping on Evans' elbow gave the game away, though, as did his struggles on the Madeleine. Accompanied by just a few fellow stragglers, Evans suffered the indignity of riding alone with the yellow jersey at the back of the race, losing over eight minutes and waving goodbye to his chance of winning the Tour.

2013 Pierre ROLLAND

Pierre Rolland initially missed the move of the day on stage 19 of the 2013 Tour de France as the solo breakaway rider Ryder Hesjedal moved away early on the stage approaching the foot of the Col de la Madeleine. However, Rolland soon got his act together as the road began to turn uphill and he attacked the chase bunch, riding up to Hesjedal and making the catch on the slopes of the col, which featured with three climbs still to cross before the finish. The pair worked well and pulled out over 12 minutes on the peloton. As the torrential rain began to fall, Rolland's pace on the next climb, the Col de Tamie, was too much for Hesjedal and the Canadian dropped back to the chase group. As the stormy darkness descended, Rolland ground his way over the Col d'Epine. With 20km to go until the finish it looked like his 120km solo move might just work, but on the slopes of the final climb of the Col de la Croix Fry he was cruelly caught by a flying Rui Costa, who went on to win the stage. The Frenchman cut a dejected figure as he finished 16th but was at least awarded the day's combativity prize. It was clearly scant consolation for the man dreaming of his third stage win in three years.

Col d'Izoard

2360m

Length: 19.0km
Start: 1239m
Ascent: 1121m

A formidable climb in the heartland of the Alps, the Col d'Izoard has inspired generations of great champions with its stories and imagery. This climb has come to represent the very essence of the Tour de France in the mountains.

> ❝ The Izoard, this terrible feat, which draws the line between the difficult and the downright terrifying. ❞
>
> *Jacques Goddet*

There's a small portion of gravel, dust and earth taken from the upper slopes of the Col d'Izoard that is now lying in the ground in Castellania, Italy, buried with one of the greatest cyclists of all time: Fausto Coppi. Although the Italian, who died in 1960 after contracting malaria, won plenty of races away from the Tour de France, it was this climb, the Col d'Izoard, which set him apart from the sport's other champions and put him into a league of his own.

The Col d'Izoard is a formidable environment. At 2,360m in altitude it sits alongside the alpine giants in terms of sheer scale, comprising 31.1 kilometres of ascent from Guillestre in the south and 19km from Briançon in the north.

Its history in the Tour doesn't stretch back quite as far as the nearby Col du Galibier – the road was first crossed in 1922, 11 years after the first alpine stage over the Galibier in 1911 – but it is a climb that is no less deserving of its *hors catégorie* status.

Rising from soft valleys through larch and pine forests, the road lulls riders into a false sense of security before metamorphosing into an endless succession of bends. By the time riders pass the towering totem at the summit and the Refuge Napoléon a few hundred metres to the north even the best are exhausted.

The landscape at the summit is what defines the Col d'Izoard. Extra-terrestrial in appearance, the barren rocky slopes reflect the bright sunlight and the wind whistles around unhindered by any trees. It has echoes of Mont Ventoux, yet in reality the place known as the "Casse Déserte" (meaning roughly "broken desert") is something quite unique. Smaller in scale and overshadowed by the Pic de Rochebrune, it is especially dramatic because of the great spires of rock that pierce the vast scree slopes and tower over the road. They say that true winners of the Tour are ones who have led the race through this landscape and over the Col d'Izoard, as Fausto Coppi did in 1949.

"The Tour is won in Briançon before it is won in Paris," according to racer and legendary team director Raphaël Géminiani, referring to the way the mountain stage has frequently finished with the climb of the Izoard from Guillestre and a descent into Briançon.

Géminiani was talking about tactics and strategy – Briançon always marked the conclusion of a decisive mountain stage. But the Col d'Izoard is a climb which also =epitomizes the heroics of the riders and the ideals of the Tour. Riders would soldier on alone while the spires and peaks gave the surroundings a cathedral-like, semi-spiritual quality. Here were gods of the road performing miracles in a sublime environment that might as well have been outer space. The newspaper-buying audience of the early Tours lapped it up. The Col d'Izoard helped create superstars.

"Years ago, [former Tour champion] Louison Bobet told me that leading alone through the Casse Déserte in the yellow jersey was the mark of a true Tour champion, and when I did it in 1975 it was the greatest day of my life," said Bernard Thévenet, recalling the time he prized open the chink in the armour of Eddy Merckx on the Izoard.

It is an adage that perhaps rings less true in more modern times, although it was in the Casse Déserte that Andy Schleck launched his solo move with 60 kilometres remaining of stage 18 in the 2011 Tour, taking a summit victory on the Col du Galibier with a move that echoed the days of old.

Often it is the stars of cycling and their exploits that make mountain climbs famous. Take Alpe d'Huez and its hairpins numbered one to 21, with the names of the winners on its slopes. Yet in an almost unique way the Col d'Izoard has created stars of the Tour de France. It's not surprising that Fausto Coppi wanted to take a little bit of it with him to the afterlife.

Opposite: **Towering spires of rock and barren scree slopes characterize the unique environment of the Col d'Izoard's Casse Déserte.**

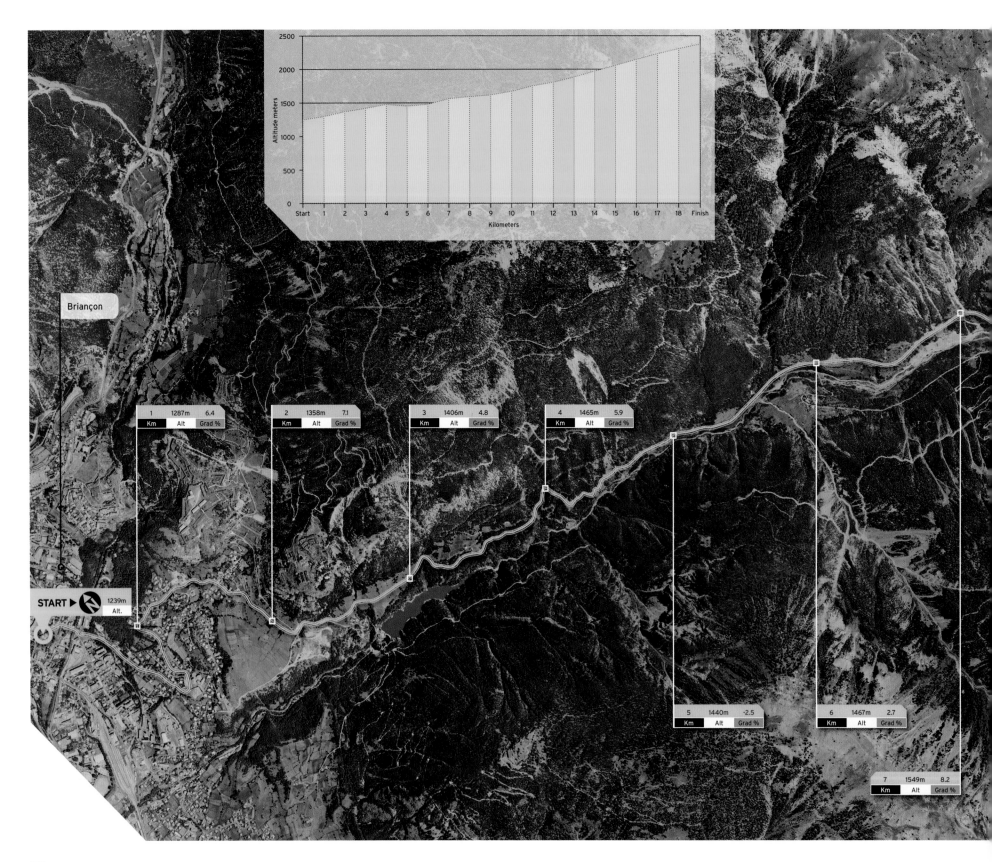

Briançon

START ▶ 1239m
Alt.

1	1287m	6.4
Km	Alt	Grad %

2	1358m	7.1
Km	Alt	Grad %

3	1406m	4.8
Km	Alt	Grad %

4	1465m	5.9
Km	Alt	Grad %

5	1440m	-2.5
Km	Alt	Grad %

6	1467m	2.7
Km	Alt	Grad %

7	1549m	8.2
Km	Alt	Grad %

Google Earth

9	1605m	2.5
Km	Alt	Grad %

10	1658m	5.3
Km	Alt	Grad %

11	1738m	8.0
Km	Alt	Grad %

12	1792m	5.4
Km	Alt	Grad %

13	1868m	7.8
Km	Alt	Grad %

Ravin du Col d'Izoard

15	2041m	8.5
Km	Alt	Grad %

17	2216m	8.7
Km	Alt	Grad %

Refuge Napoléon

Casse Déserte

Tour de France museum

8	1580m	3.1
Km	Alt	Grad %

14	1957m	8.9
Km	Alt	Grad %

16	2129m	8.7
Km	Alt	Grad %

FINISH ■   2360m Alt.

18	2292m	7.6
Km	Alt	Grad %

Bobet and Coppi Memorials (off map)

Image © Landsat © Google 2014

77

Route to the Summit

"Endless" was the word chosen by Tour founder Henri Desgrange to describe the Col d'Izoard. "It spins you along, makes you believe that you have got the better of it, and just as you let out a sigh of relief it hits you with the sort of kick that would startle a mule."

◀ Casse Déserte

The spectacular, otherworldly environment of the Casse Déserte is one of the visual highlights of the Tour de France. The slopes of the Col d'Izoard are made from the fossilized remains of sea creatures that died in the Tethys Ocean between 250 and 140 million years ago, whose compressed shells turned to rock and were pushed up to the surface by the formation of the Alps. The result is the spectacular lunar landscape on the southern slopes of the mountains above 2,000m in altitude where pinnacles of rock emerge from vast scree slopes, their colours shifting and dancing with the passage of shadows from the clouds. Grasses and small pine trees have taken hold in some of the more sheltered spots, but by and large the upper slopes are a barren landscape. It's a hostile place to ride a bike; the bright sun reflects off the rocks, the thin air swirls around, and the road is edged on one side by steep slopes and on the other by an enormous drop towards the Torrent de l'Izoard.

Left: The Casse Déserte is the hallmark of the Izoard.

Refuge Napoléon

On his return from his first exile in Elba, Napoleon ordered the construction of six mountain refuges to thank the region for the warm welcome he received there as he made his way back to Paris. They were only finished by the end of the 19th century. Today the refuge at the Col d'Izoard is run by Monique Guion and sits just north of the pass. At the col itself stands a large stone column, erected in 1934 to remember Baron Berge, who had the modern-day road constructed.

Opposite: Vincenzo Nibali improvises a new way to hold his bottle as he needs two hands on the bars to negotiate the descent of the Col d'Izoard Above left: The simple memorial to Fausto Coppi and Louison Bobet near the pass of the Izoard. Above right: At 2,360m, the highest point of the Col d'Izoard is up in the clouds.

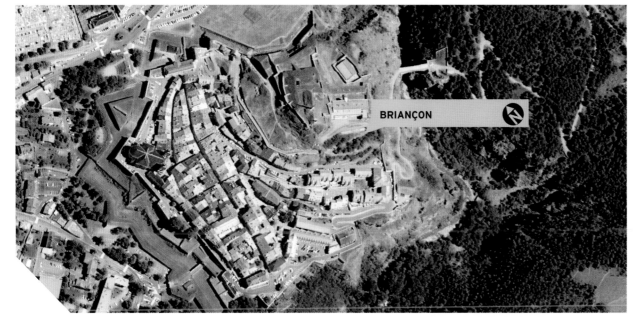

BRIANÇON

◀ Briançon

The bustling alpine town of Briançon sits at a crossroads in the mountains, with roads heading off in four directions. The Col d'Izoard begins immediately to the southeast of the town, with the town acting as a gateway northwest to the Col du Lautaret and northeast to the Col du Montgenèvre, although the latter has only featured in the Tour de France 10 times due to its position on the Italian border. Briançon itself has hosted a stage start or finish 33 times in the history of the Tour, regularly appearing from the 1920s through to the 1960s. However, the modern trend for summit finishes has seen the town demoted to a passing point on routes across the mountains, and the last time it hosted a finish was in 2007. It's a marked contrast in scale to Guillestre, the small town that marks the beginning of the Col d'Izoard from the southern side, although this too leads onwards to further key climbs. The ski station of Risoul overlooks the town and has hosted one summit finish, while the enormous Col de Vars and Col Agnel, both over 2,000m, also begin in the town.

Left: Briançon: an alpine crossroads at the heart of the Tour.

Ravin du Col d'Izoard

After a gentle start from Briançon, at the small village of Cervières the northern ascent of the Col d'Izoard turns due south, heads into the pine and larch forests, and gets steeper. Rising to around 8.5% for the remaining 10 kilometres, it's a particularly hot and stifling climb as the route twists and turns its way up the Ravin du Col d'Izoard. Only in the final few kilometres do the trees begin to thin and the cold mountain air to sting the riders' damp jerseys.

Bobet and Coppi memorials

Tucked away on a small outcrop dangling precariously on the steep slope just south of the pass amid the Casse Déserte are memorials to the two riders who left the biggest marks on the history of the Col d'Izoard: Fausto Coppi and Louison Bobet. Erected by the Tour organizers, the simple silhouettes of black stone are mounted on white marble and face towards the modern-day riders of the Tour, away from the elements and the hot summer sun.

Tour de France museum

At the summit stands a little museum dedicated to the Col d'Izoard in the Tour de France. Since 2003, however, it has been closed to the public and the simple concrete building is beginning to fall into decay. Opened in 1989, it was the initiative of a local mayor and the former owner of the Refuge Napoléon. Once it was home to loaned photographs, old bikes and two of Louison Bobet's yellow jerseys, but the items have now been returned to their original owners.

The Mountain Kings

Of all the sport's grand settings, this is one of the most potent king-makers in cycling history. From Philippe Thijs in 1922 to Andy Schleck in 2011, the Col d'Izoard has been a place for riders to prove their credentials as heroes of the Tour de France for almost 100 years.

Previous pages: Louison Bobet, the first man to win three Tours, climbs alone on the Col d'Izoard in 1953.

Opposite top: Fausto Coppi (l) and Gino Bartali are given roadside encouragement as they annihilate the field of the 1949 Tour on the slopes of the Col d'Izoard.

Opposite bottom left: Bernard Thévenet crowns his 1975 Tour win with a solo move on the Izoard.

Opposite bottom right: The Pélissier brothers Henri (r) and Francis share a light moment. Henri would win the 1923 Tour with help from Francis.

1923 Henri **PÉLISSIER**

Before the Second World War, the Col d'Izoard regularly featured in a stage from the French Riviera to Briançon, a format of around 275 kilometres and including three passes in succession over 2,000m: the Col d'Allos, the Col de Vars and finally the Col d'Izoard. So it was in 1923, when stage 10 travelled from Nice and deep into the Alps. It was a day for Henri Pélissier. His team-mate Ottavio Bottecchia, whose French at the start of the Tour extended only to the phrases "no bananas", "lots of coffee" and "thank you", was in the race lead. But the talented young Italian was about to fall victim to that potent combination at the Tour: bad luck, bad form and dastardly tactics from a rival team-mate. Pélissier attacked Bottecchia as he changed gear on the Col d'Allos, which meant taking out the rear wheel and swapping it round. The Frenchman was 29 minutes and 52 seconds in arrears to Bottecchia at the start of the day, but so catastrophic was Bottecchia's capitulation, and so potent was Pélissier's final solo ascent of the Col d'Izoard, that on arrival in Briançon the Italian was third overall, 13 minutes down.

1949 Fausto **COPPI**

By stage four of the 1949 Tour de France, Fausto Coppi, competing in his first edition after winning that year's Giro d'Italia, had incredibly already lost more than 36 minutes in the general classification. Riding on an Italian team packed full of stars, including defending champion Gino Bartali, Coppi set himself to the task of recouping his arrears. Stage 16 saw the Tour tackle a mammoth 275km stage from the Mediterranean at Cannes to Briançon. On the final climb of the Col d'Izoard, Coppi and Bartali, clearly the two best men in the race, rode off alone. Bartali flatted and Coppi waited, an act that would be almost unimaginable in the modern race. Coppi allowed his team-mate the stage win (it was Bartali's 35th birthday) and, as a result of their work, to don the yellow jersey. The pair had finished over five minutes clear of Jean Robic in third place, and only three other men could remain within 12 minutes of them. Bartali led Coppi in the general classification by 82 seconds at the end of the stage and when Bartali crashed the following day, Coppi's overall Tour victory was all but assured.

1953 Louison **BOBET**

In the absence of 1952 victor Fausto Coppi, the 1953 race represented a changing of the guard in the Tour de France. There to capitalize on it was Louison Bobet, who set up his first Tour win with a tactical masterclass displayed on the slopes of the Col d'Izoard. His team-mate Adolphe Deledda went up the road on the first climb of the Col de Vars on stage 18 with two other riders, and later Bobet followed a move by the Spanish rider Jesus Lorono, before dropping him on the descent. Deledda was informed of his team leader's move and, after waiting for Bobet, did the donkey work for him on the flat 20km approach to the Izoard. Bobet then took flight, biting out great chunks of time from his rivals. None other than Coppi himself, who had ascended to greatness on the Izoard four years before, was there to watch Bobet pass the summit, standing with his camera and his lover Giulia Locatelli – their affair had scandalized Italy. "Thanks for coming!" Bobet shouted between gasps for air. Despite a flat tyre, Bobet still won in Briançon by five minutes and 23 seconds on the runner-up, catapulting himself into the race lead by more than eight minutes.

1975 Bernard **THÉVENET**

Just as Fausto Coppi did for Louison Bobet's day in the spotlight on the Col d'Izoard, so Bobet paid a visit to Bernard Thévenet, the new yellow jersey wearer in the 1975 Tour, on the eve of the stage over the same climb. Thévenet had finally wrested the jersey away from Eddy Merckx in the famous stage to Pra-Loup the previous day, and Bobet's advice was to attack. Holding just 58 seconds' lead over Merckx, Thévenet knew he needed more time if he was to withstand a wounded and angry Merckx. Bobet's words obviously struck a chord; Thévenet dropped the entire field on the Col d'Izoard, riding alone over the Casse Déserte to a convincing win in Briançon. Unlike the stages where he took time from Merckx on the Puy de Dôme and Pra-Loup, where the Belgian was suffering from the immediate effects of a punch to the abdomen, this was the definitive stage win that Thévenet needed – he was two minutes and 22 seconds ahead of Merckx at the finish. Although Merckx would win the following mountain stage by two seconds after crashing and breaking his jaw, it was an act to salvage his pride rather than victory in the race.

Col de Joux Plane

1691m

Length: 11.7km
Start: 710m
Ascent: 981m

The Col de Joux Plane plays mischievously with the riders of the Tour de France. Hiding its challenges behind the façade of an alpine utopia, it is a devilish climb with an even more diabolical descent. Its difficulties can take riders by surprise, especially as it features in the Tour only occasionally.

> **❝** I always knew that my best chance of getting rid of Delgado would come going down the Joux Plane rather than up it. **❞**
>
> *Stephen Roche*

The Col de Joux Plane is one of the hardest climbs in the Alps. But you wouldn't know it from looking at it. Just 1,700m at its highest point, the road to the pass is a bucolic nirvana of green meadows, lush woods and alpine flowers tucked up in a little pocket of the northern French Alps sandwiched between Switzerland and Lake Geneva.

For the 2016 race the Joux Plane was given the distinction, like its loftier, more famous cousins Mont Ventoux and Alpe d'Huez, of being the final climb on the penultimate stage of the Tour de France. Even the Tour's boss Christian Prudhomme acknowledged that it might not fulfil everyone's expectations of a grand finale.

"The paradox is that around Mont Blanc, the highest mountain in Europe, the passes aren't actually very high," he said almost apologetically. Indeed for riders that like their climbs big, expansive and intimidating, the Joux Plane can be more than a touch disappointing. Even its name, which means "flat forest", is hardly in the same league as the windy Mont Ventoux or the terrifying Tourmalet, is it?

If the visual surroundings are at first disappointing, the sheer effort that goes into getting up the climb is a revelation, because riding this nirvana is like descending into Dante's seven circles of hell. It was first climbed by the Tour in 1978, making it relatively modern by the standards of the Tour's most famous climbs. Its heyday was in the late 1970s and 1980s, since when the Tour has returned approximately twice a decade, most recently in 2016. It is thus not the sort of climb that riders get a lot of practice on.

Nor does it require the sort of constant, high-intensity effort they expect from the Alps and practise in training. The climb's average statistics – 11.6 kilometres at 8.5% from the south in Samoëns, the only side ever climbed by the Tour – say nothing of the sections of 12% that spring out of nowhere. The Joux Plane is an irregular and unpredictable climb.

Nor do the statistics say anything of the oppressive heat, a result of it being both south facing and lower in altitude than most other *hors catégorie* mountain climbs. They make no mention of the tantalizing glimpses of the ice-cold glaciers around Mont Blanc that offer torturous reminders of cool, refreshing water while riders wallow in a sweaty mess; nor the fact that cruelly even those little gaps in the trees or tight switchbacks never reveal the difficult bits that are just around the corner.

"The Joux Plane was the hardest climb of the Tour," said Australian rider Mick Rogers, with a hint of surprise, after the Tour climbed it in 2006. "It wasn't the right day for me on that climb!"

Another aspect of the Joux Plane deception is that one of its most difficult sections is the descent. Each time that the Tour has ridden over the climb it has finished in the town of Morzine at the foot of the northern slope, which involves a potent mix of irregular and unpredictable curves and high speeds. It has never had to play precursor to other climbs, but it isn't a famous summit finish either; the Joux Plane has to be considered as an obstacle that must be both ascended and descended if it is to be conquered.

"The Joux Plane is not only a very fast descent but it's quite treacherous as well," said 1987 Tour winner Stephen Roche.

For all Roche's understatement, a small mistake on the descent of the Joux Plane can have serious ramifications. Carlo Tonon crashed in 1984, suffering head injuries that left him in a coma and later with a permanent disability. The same year Pedro Delgado broke his collarbone when he came off on a section of gravel.

It might not be one of cycling's most famous climbs but, as riders of the Tour de France soon find out, the Col de Joux Plane is a climb more than worthy of their utmost respect.

Opposite: The loneliness of the long distance cyclist: Floyd Landis scales the Col de Joux Plane alone during his miraculous stage win during the 2006 Tour de France.

Altitude meters

2000

1500

1000

500

0

Start 1 2 3 4 5 6 7 8 9 10 11 Finish

Kilometers

4	1026m	5.6
Km	Alt..	Grad. %

5	1098m	7.2
Km	Alt.	Grad. %

Les Turches

START ▶	710m
	Alt.

1	795m	8.5
Km	Alt.	Grad. %

2	866m	7.1
Km	Alt.	Grad. %

3	970m	9.6
Km	Alt.	Grad. %

6	1170m	7.2
Km	Alt.	Grad. %

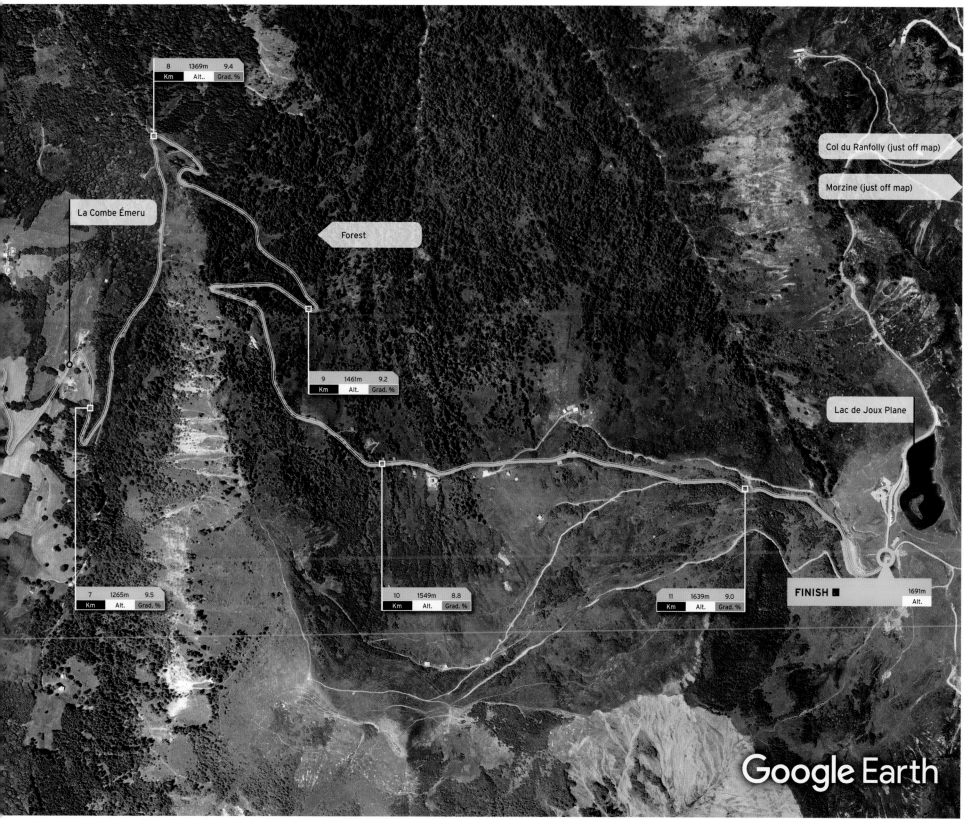

La Combe Émeru

Forest

Col du Ranfolly (just off map)

Morzine (just off map)

Lac de Joux Plane

8	1369m	9.4
Km	Alt..	Grad. %

9	1461m	9.2
Km	Alt.	Grad. %

7	1265m	9.5
Km	Alt.	Grad. %

10	1549m	8.8
Km	Alt.	Grad. %

11	1639m	9.0
Km	Alt.	Grad. %

FINISH ■	1691m
	Alt.

Google Earth

Route to the Summit

Although it lasts less than 12 kilometres and stops 300m short of the 2,000m mark, the Joux Plane makes up for its lack of size by cruelly cramming all the difficulty of an alpine giant into a miniature package.

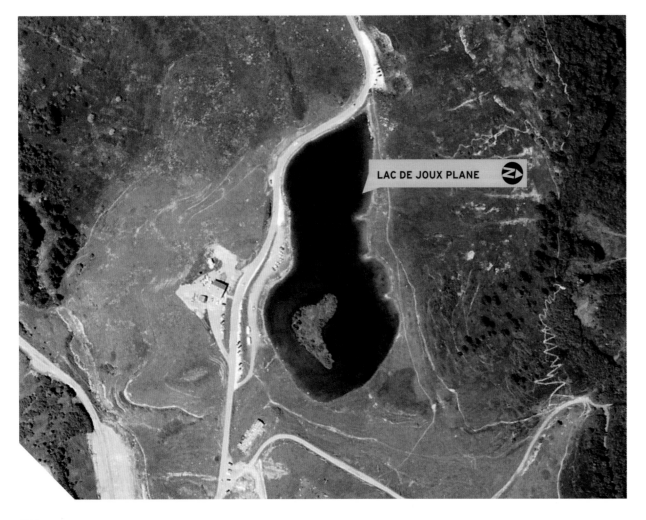

LAC DE JOUX PLANE

◀ Lac de Joux Plane

The very top of the Col de Joux Plane opens out into a wide bowl around which the road curves slowly. From here, riders can look to their left and back down along the final few hundred metres of the climb. In summer the landscape is like a tourist brochure for holidays in the Alps; it is bright, sunny, and home to a small herd of cattle whose cowbells pierce the silent air with their dissonant chimes. It's a relatively sheltered col too, topping out at just 1,691m altitude and benefiting from the natural protection offered by the surrounding hillsides. It's a place where the weather tends to remain mild and gentle, although stifling heat can be problematic to riders in July. The round depression is a natural place for a lake to form, even if the Lac de Joux Plane is little more than a pond in alpine terms. Despite the difficulty of its ascent and its proximity to the highest mountain in the Alps, Mont Blanc, the Joux Plane lacks the grandiose surroundings and soaring adjacent peaks of its alpine cousins to the south.

Left: The Lac de Joux Plane sits at the top of the pass.

Forest

Given that "joux" means wood, it's hardly surprising that a good proportion of the climb of the Col de Joux Plane ascends through forest. Beginning 8.5 kilometres after the start in Samoëns, the thick, green trees on the south-facing slopes turn the road into a labyrinth of irregular straights, corners and gradients. It leaves riders feeling disoriented, and even the best can find it difficult to settle into a rhythm as they twist and turn, dip and duck through the foliage.

Opposite: Carlos Sastre rides in pursuit on the Joux Plane in 2006. Above left: The borders of the Lac de Joux Plane offer spectacular views east towards the highest mountain in the Alps: Mont Blanc. Above right: Sean Kelly once clocked 124kmh on the northern descent of the Col de Joux Plane.

◄ Morzine

A busy ski town in the winter and full of cyclo-tourists and mountain bikers in the summer, Morzine is a cycling town through and through. The Col de Joux Plane enters Morzine on a small road from the south; on a normal day the road is a quiet route out of the town ignored by the majority of traffic taking the main road south via Les Gets and Taninges. Like the southern ascent, the road is a little the worse for wear in places and seems never to settle on a consistent gradient, often throwing up more severe gradients around sharp corners. The result is a road that makes a fast and technical descent even more difficult. Although stages over the Joux Plane have always ended in town, the Tour often zooms through Morzine from other directions as it continues immediately onto the final approach to a summit finish at Avoriaz, a ski station overlooking the town and conjoined by a fast, flowing climb of 11.4km at 6.8%. Aggressive riders aim to stretch out the peloton through the town and hit the slopes to Avoriaz with as much momentum as possible.

Left: Morzine sits at the foot of a white-knuckle descent off the Col de Joux Plane.

Les Turches

One small moment of respite on what is otherwise an unrelentingly steep climb comes four kilometres out of Samoëns, just after the hamlet of Les Turches. It is just 600m of road at an average of 3%, sandwiched by kilometre sections at 9.1% and 9.4%. This false flat isn't going to offer much help to the riders of the Tour. With 6km to go, if they're struggling by this point then they haven't got much chance of surviving to the top.

La Combe Émeru

One kilometre after the flattest section of road comes perhaps the steepest of the entire climb, a ramp of 400m at an average of 11.2% just before the farmstead at La Combe Émeru. For a climb with a fickle, oscillating gradient, this severe test marks the halfway point of the ascent in typical style. And it's here, at 1,200m, that riders are able to catch their first glimpses of the snowy peak of Mont Blanc on the southeast horizon.

Col du Ranfolly

The main route up and down the Col de Joux Plane on the D354 is littered with offshoots and turnings leading to remote chalets, farm huts and hiking trails. One such turning sits at the Col du Ranfolly, a small pass at 1,655m situated 3km from the Joux Plane in the Morzine direction. It means that riders have to climb back up 30 vertical metres during the fast descent from the Joux Plane, although the road quickly drops away with some eye-watering steep drops.

The Mountain Kings

A relative newcomer in Tour de France terms, the Joux Plane has made regular appearances in the race since the late 1970s. Riders have a complex relationship with it, and it could perhaps be called a "Marmite" climb: they tend to either love it or hate it.

Opposite left: Local boy Jacques Michaud digs deep on the Col de Joux Plane on his way to a stage win in 1983.

Opposite top right: Lance Armstrong is pursued by Didi The Devil on his infamous bad day on the Joux Plane in 2000.

Opposite bottom right: Floyd "The Praying Landis" Landis claimed an incredible stage win into Morzine in 2006 that was later stripped from him.

1983 Jacques MICHAUD

Jacques Michaud is one of hundreds of riders for whom a stage win in the Tour de France was the pinnacle of their professional careers. For a Frenchman like Michaud, the term *vainqueur d'une étape du Tour de France* is a badge of honour for life, one which ensures a small piece of sporting immortality. Born in the Genevan French suburb of Saint Julien en Genevois, Michaud grew up riding the climbs of the Haute-Savoie Alps around Morzine, and the Col de Joux Plane was one he knew well. On stage 18 from Alpe d'Huez to Morzine, perhaps the hardest stage of the 1983 race, Michaud benefited from the battle going on behind him between the overall favourites. Laurent Fignon, riding a revelatory Tour and in the yellow jersey for the first time in his career, clung on to the wheels of Dutch mountain man Peter Winnen and Australian powerhouse Phil Anderson. The trio, drenched in sweat and bottled water, appeared to be riding through treacle and pedalling almost in slow motion on the steep slopes. Meanwhile the lithe Michaud powered on ahead, alone, and swooped down to Morzine to realize a dream shared by every little French boy across the country and take his beautiful solo Tour de France stage win.

1984 Sean KELLY

Sean Kelly certainly wasn't a mountain climbing specialist. In his heart, the farmer's boy from Ireland was a man for the tough, cold and grimy conditions of the one-day classics of northern Europe. But, boy, could Kelly descend. Perhaps the best example of his prowess was the 1992 Milan–San Remo one-day classic, where he pulled off a daredevil descent of the final small climb to catch Moreno Argentin and win the race. However, it was on stage 19 of the 1984 Tour de France, a mammoth alpine stage including five mountain passes, that "King Kelly" reportedly clocked his highest ever speed going downhill: 124kmh, or 77mph. Kelly made the claim during one his recent TV commentary stints, although how he registered his speed in the days before cycle computers, he didn't say. The descent off the Joux Plane in that Tour was particularly treacherous and tragic. Spanish star Pedro Delgado crashed out of the race with a broken collarbone, and his compatriot Carlo Tonon collided with a spectator at speed going down the hill and suffered a fractured skull. In a coma for two months, he emerged permanently disabled. Tragically Tonon took his own life 12 years later at the age of 41.

2000 Lance ARMSTRONG

It was on the slopes of the Col de Joux Plane that Lance Armstrong endured what he described as "without a doubt my worst day on the bike". Having missed a bag of food from his team at the preceding feed zone – a crucial error in the final week of the Tour de France when riders' energy reserves are near rock bottom – the American claimed to have suffered a hunger knock (better known to British riders as a "bonk") as the tough slopes began. His rivals Jan Ullrich and Richard Virenque couldn't believe their luck; watching him rock his shoulders and labour on the pedals – the tell-tale signs of a rider on the brink of collapse – the duo sped away to the pass and down the other side to the finish in Morzine. Virenque won the stage solo and Ullrich gained 90 seconds on the yellow jersey. Luckily for Armstrong he could limit his losses and keep the race lead, but he later admitted: "I could have lost the Tour." The Joux Plane was a bit of a bogey climb for Lance, though he clearly loved getting the better of it in the end. "I was thinking of the Joux Plane all week," he said after exorcising some of his demons with a stage win in Morzine in the 2002 Critérium du Dauphiné, a traditional warm-up race for the Tour which takes place each June.

2006 Floyd LANDIS

Whether you think it was fabulous or farcical, the 17th stage of the 2006 Tour de France, finishing over the Col de Joux Plane and into Morzine, is one of the most jaw-dropping Tour stages in living memory. The American Floyd Landis had cracked spectacularly the previous day, going from race leader to 11th, but put himself back in contention with a 120km solo move to win in Morzine by almost six minutes. Attacking early on the warm-up climb of the Col des Saisies, Landis benefited from hesitation in the bunch to extend his lead to such vast proportions. Adopting his trademark "Praying Landis" position during the descents – which saw him put his forearms close together, dip his elbows and scrunch up his upper body to make him look a bit like the insect named the praying mantis – he flew down the Joux Plane to defend his advantage from some panicked chasing behind him. Landis went on to win the Tour overall on the penultimate stage time trial, but it later transpired that Lazarus Landis's miraculous powers of recovery were down to synthetic testosterone: he tested positive for it after stage 17 and following a long and protracted legal battle (and final confession) eventually had his Tour awarded to Oscar Pereiro.

Col de l'Iseran

2770m

Length: **48.0km**
Start: **815m**
Ascent: **1955m**

The longest and, for many years, the highest climb in the Tour de France, the Col de l'Iseran is almost too big for the Tour. Used sparingly due to its potential to conjure up extreme weather conditions even in the summer, it never fails to make an impact in the race.

> **❝** The Iseran rules over majestic surroundings of torrents and snowfields, where tunnels that could accommodate underground trains grow beneath the snow. **❞**
>
> *Antoine Blondin*

The second time the Tour de France crossed the mighty Col de l'Iseran was a time trial, comprising 64.5 kilometres from Bonneval sur Arc up the southern ascent, over the top and down to Bourg Saint Maurice in 1939.

To put it in perspective, that single climb contained more time trialling than in the entire 2016 Tour de France and only slightly less than the distance against the clock in the 2014 and 2015 editions combined. That start town of Bonneval sits at 1,835m altitude already. The Col de l'Iseran is big.

So big is it that until the Cime de la Bonette was tackled in 1962 the Iseran was, at 2,770m high (local maps claim 2,764m), the highest point the Tour de France had ever reached. Accounting for the nature of the Bonette, the Iseran technically remains the highest mountain *pass* in Tour history. It is certainly still the longest climb in the Tour, totalling 48 kilometres from the town of Bourg Saint Maurice to the pass.

"The microscopic towns, whose slate roofs merge with the rock, give the valley such dizzying proportions as to dissolve human scale ... the snow is so white below, so calm, in an azure blue as spicy and refreshing as a *vin de pays*," wrote legendary French journalist Antoine Blondin while waxing lyrical about the climb. Although Blondin was notorious for his florid prose (and had probably picked up a glass or two of *vin de pays* before his pen) it's true that the Iseran is on a scale experienced nowhere else on the route of the Tour.

It maintains a wonderful sense of isolation and, to a certain extent, desolation. The open rocky slopes around the 3,237m Signal de l'Iseran peak and the Crête des Lessières is a barren, inorganic environment. While the two valleys that it links are rich in woods and meadows they are, besides the odd ski resort, devoid of any large towns. That said, the climb is so big that even if there were any, they would be far below.

In fact there is a certain contrivance to the climb. It is not, as many alpine passes are, an ancient and well-worn byway. It was made for the Route des Grandes Alpes, a long-distance touring route between Geneva and Nice which passes the 2,000m mark eight times, including over the Col du Galibier and the Col d'Izoard. Opened in 1937, the Col de l'Iseran was the austere jewel in the crown of the route and Europe's highest tarmac road pass.

As is often the way, though, bigger doesn't necessarily mean better. The Iseran is so long and features such gentle average gradients – 4.2% from the south and 4.1% from the north – that it offers little for the most dynamic climbers in the Tour. Equally that length can put off any riders from making daring moves for fear that the distance will take its toll and leave them vulnerable to counter-attacks. It's not exactly a popular climb, and that's before taking into account the unlit tunnels on the northern side alongside the Lac du Chevril which make for a disorienting (and somewhat terrifying) cycling experience.

The Tour itself is reluctant to utilize the climb, having done so just six times since its first visit in 1938. In part this is due to the effect it has on the racers, but it is principally down to the unpredictability of the conditions at such a high altitude. Even in July, when the Tour takes place, the weather conditions can conspire to undermine the world's biggest bike race, as was the case when storms and gales rattled the race in 1996 and forced riders and teams to cross by car, an ironic turn of events given then road's initial *raison d'être*.

Potentially the Col de l'Iseran could host a summit finish in a future Tour, but whether anyone would want it to is a different question altogether. Nevertheless, it remains the Tour de France's highest true pass, and a climb that is more than worthy of respect.

Opposite: **The 2007 Tour de France peloton finds safety in numbers as it scales the longest climb ever to feature in the Tour, the mighty 48km Col de l'Iseran.**

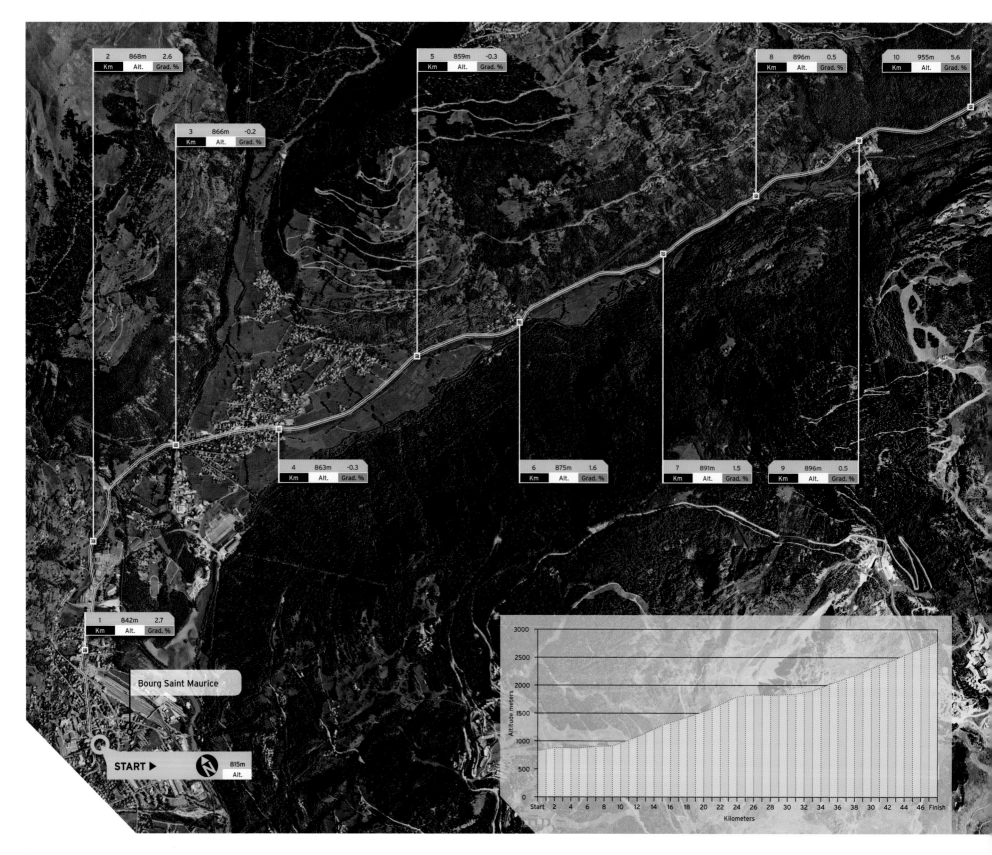

2	868m	2.6
Km	Alt.	Grad. %

3	866m	-0.2
Km	Alt.	Grad. %

5	859m	-0.3
Km	Alt.	Grad. %

8	896m	0.5
Km	Alt.	Grad. %

10	955m	5.6
Km	Alt.	Grad. %

4	863m	-0.3
Km	Alt.	Grad. %

6	875m	1.6
Km	Alt.	Grad. %

7	891m	1.5
Km	Alt.	Grad. %

9	896m	0.5
Km	Alt.	Grad. %

1	842m	2.7
Km	Alt.	Grad. %

Bourg Saint Maurice

START ▶	815m
	Alt.

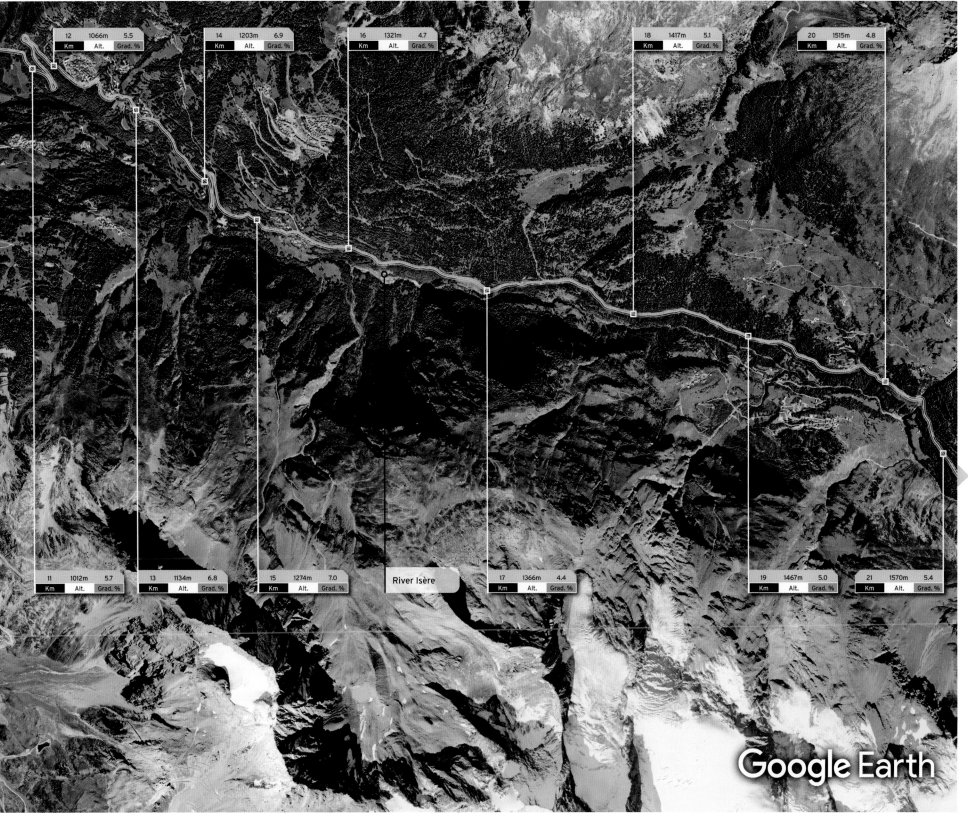

12	1066m	5.5
Km	Alt.	Grad. %

14	1203m	6.9
Km	Alt.	Grad. %

16	1321m	4.7
Km	Alt.	Grad. %

18	1417m	5.1
Km	Alt.	Grad. %

20	1515m	4.8
Km	Alt.	Grad. %

11	1012m	5.7
Km	Alt.	Grad. %

13	1134m	6.8
Km	Alt.	Grad. %

15	1274m	7.0
Km	Alt.	Grad. %

River Isère

17	1366m	4.4
Km	Alt.	Grad. %

19	1467m	5.0
Km	Alt.	Grad. %

21	1570m	5.4
Km	Alt.	Grad. %

Google Earth

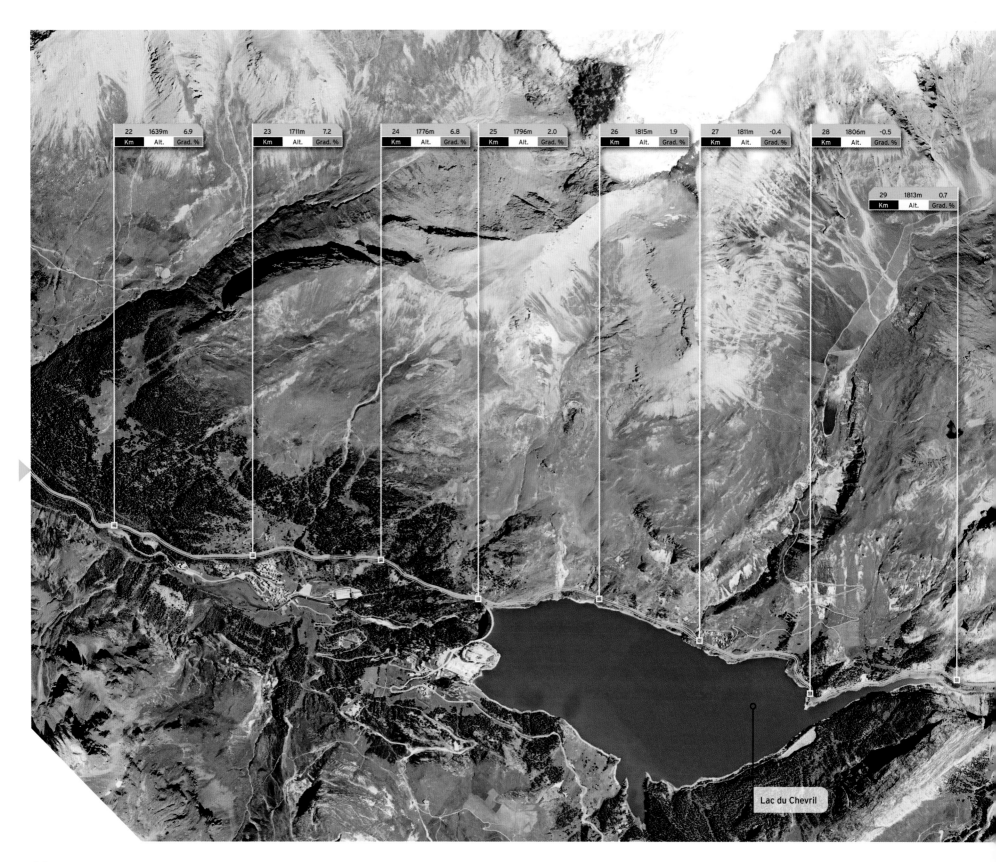

22	1639m	6.9
Km	Alt.	Grad. %

23	1711m	7.2
Km	Alt.	Grad. %

24	1776m	6.8
Km	Alt.	Grad. %

25	1796m	2.0
Km	Alt.	Grad. %

26	1815m	1.9
Km	Alt.	Grad. %

27	1811m	-0.4
Km	Alt.	Grad. %

28	1806m	-0.5
Km	Alt.	Grad. %

29	1813m	0.7
Km	Alt.	Grad. %

Lac du Chevril

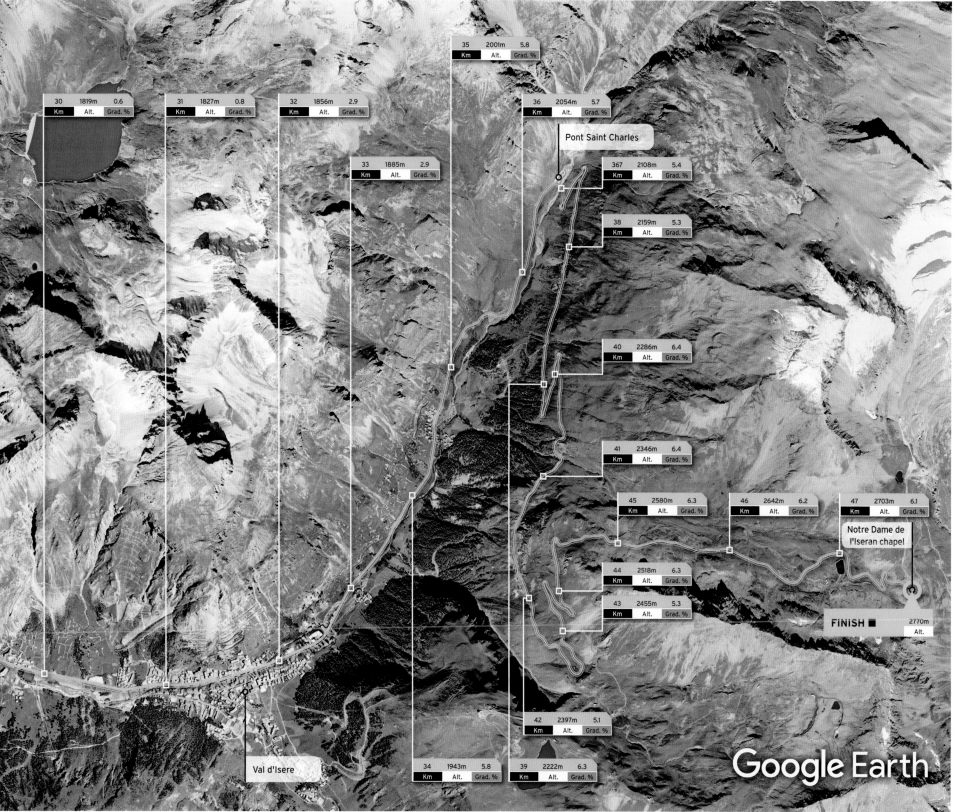

30	1819m	0.6
Km	Alt.	Grad. %

31	1827m	0.8
Km	Alt.	Grad. %

32	1856m	2.9
Km	Alt.	Grad. %

35	2001m	5.8
Km	Alt.	Grad. %

36	2054m	5.7
Km	Alt.	Grad. %

Pont Saint Charles

33	1885m	2.9
Km	Alt.	Grad. %

367	2108m	5.4
Km	Alt.	Grad. %

38	2159m	5.3
Km	Alt.	Grad. %

40	2286m	6.4
Km	Alt.	Grad. %

41	2346m	6.4
Km	Alt.	Grad. %

45	2580m	6.3
Km	Alt.	Grad. %

46	2642m	6.2
Km	Alt.	Grad. %

47	2703m	6.1
Km	Alt.	Grad. %

Notre Dame de l'Iseran chapel

44	2518m	6.3
Km	Alt.	Grad. %

43	2455m	5.3
Km	Alt.	Grad. %

FINISH ■	2770m
	Alt.

Val d'Isere

42	2397m	5.1
Km	Alt.	Grad. %

34	1943m	5.8
Km	Alt.	Grad. %

39	2222m	6.3
Km	Alt.	Grad. %

Google Earth

Image © Landsat © Google 2014

Route to the Summit

Measuring 48 kilometres from start to finish, the Col de l'Iseran is a long, drawn out climb that slowly works its way up along the River Isère. Gradually the air becomes cooler and the landscape more beautiful as it leaves the busy ski resorts behind.

◀ Pont Saint Charles

Fifteen kilometres from the pass of the Col de l'Iseran the road swings abruptly right in a broad hairpin bend, crossing the Isère River on the Pont Saint Charles. This final section of the climb – the most challenging and the most beautiful – would be long enough and tough enough to form a separate climb in its own right. But here the road is already at more than 2,000m of altitude, and riders have ridden for more than 30 kilometres to get there. The bridge marks the end of the busy main road that serves the ski resorts in the Isère valley and the road begins to climb more steeply at an average of 6%. Regular hairpins offer some respite from the exhausting effort of climbing at this altitude and after close to two hours on the bike. As the road tracks west, the landscape opens up to the right-hand side and the valley, which has hitherto been directly behind riders, becomes visible at last. The road slowly turns south, skirting around the Crête des Lessières before one last push to the pass.

Left: The Pont Saint Charles heralds the beginning of the end.

Notre Dame de l'Iseran chapel

On what was for a time the highest road pass in France there sits, somewhat incongruously, what is still the country's highest chapel: Notre Dame de l'Iseran. Designed by notable French architect Maurice Novarina and finished in 1939, it sits low on the skyline with its distinctive blend of 1930s architecture and rugged stone construction. The chapel is also known as Notre Dame de Toute Prudence: worthy advice for the riders and travellers attempting to pass it.

Opposite: Nothing else in the Tour de France matches the Col de l'Iseran for sheer scale. Above left: Snow is a regular feature of the pass of the Iseran, even in the height of summer. Above righ: The ice cold glacial melt water cascades down the Isère River.

RIVER ISÈRE

◀ River Isère

Snow that falls on the upper slopes of the Col de l'Iseran and trickles past the road during the summer melt will eventually make its way to the Mediterranean Sea thanks to the Isère. The river passes from the col, which marks the watershed, right down in a large arc to the city of Grenoble and onwards to the Rhône. The northern road to the pass follows the course of the river almost right up towards its source. As riders start climbing out of Bourg Saint Maurice the gradient is gentle and easy going for the opening nine kilometres until the village of Viclaire, where it steepens for the first time. It does so again at Saint Foy Tarantaise, rising to around 6.5% where it remains for the next 12 kilometres, staying close to the river. The Isère then broadens out into the glacial Lac du Chevril with the road sticking to its eastern shore before the town of Val d'Isère, where both swing left to head due east. Both then run close together right up to the Pont Saint Charles, where the stream continues east towards the Italian border and the road turns west.

Left: The River Isère flows down the length of the Col de l'Iseran.

Lac du Chevril

The middle, flattest section of the climb from Bourg Saint Maurice is where the road skirts the shores of the Lac du Chevril high up in the wide Isère valley. It's a rather unpleasant experience for amateur riders due to the regular interruptions of long tunnels. The water from here feeds the hydroelectric power station at the Tignes dam, holding the waters back from the valley and helping power the ski stations dotted along the valley, including Tignes and Val d'Isère.

Val d'Isère

The final settlement on the northern ascent from Bourg Saint Maurice, the ski town of Val d'Isere – 16.5km from the pass – is a sort of base camp for the climb. In fact, the whole valley is a winter sports mecca, with the resorts of Tignes and Les Arcs both within striking distance. The town itself, with the broad main road running through the centre of it, has hosted the Tour three times with stage finishes in 1963 and 1996 and a stage start in 2007.

Bourg Saint Maurice

The small town at the very foot of the climb is a confluence for three alpine giants of road cycling and the Tour de France: the Col de l'Iseran, the Cormet de Roselend and the Col du Petit Saint Bernard, which crosses into Italy. It is also a short hop from the summit finish of La Plagne. At around 850m in altitude, the town is a high water mark of sorts; it is here that the railway line from down the valley finishes and the main road splits into smaller distributaries.

The Mountain Kings

07

The sheer scale of the Col de l'Iseran has often proved too much for the Tour de France. In its 78-year history it has conspired to halt riders trying to break away, slow those trying to chase them, and hinder the progress of the race altogether.

1959 Louison **BOBET**

Seldom do riders get to go out with such bathos and romance as Louison Bobet during the 18th stage of the 1959 Tour de France. The triple Tour winner of the 1950s had been dropped early on the mammoth mountain stage that would eventually decide the outcome of that year's Tour. It was on the Col du Galibier, the first climb of the day, that Bobet lost touch, but he soldiered on for 100km to the following climb of the Col de l'Iseran, finally getting off his bike at the highest point of the Tour. The image of Bobet being helped off his bike is one which sticks in the memory; the great champion who in his prime was a paragon of youth and exuberance had been broken by the race, turned into a wizened, shrunken figure shivering in the cold mountain air. The stunned faces of those around him are clear to see as they gently wrap their great champion in a blanket and bundle him into a team car, while the man himself can almost scarcely believe what is happening. Ahead of Bobet the future generation rode on to contest the stage and ultimately the Tour, with complex politics of the peloton helping Federico Bahamontes defend his lead from the regional French team rider Henri Anglade.

1963 Federico **BAHAMONTES**

The 16th stage of the 1963 Tour de France was a day remembered less for the action over the climbs of the Col de la Croix de Fer and finally the Col de l'Iseran than for the remarkable conditions on the high point of the race, the Iseran. Even in July, thick banks of compacted snow remained on the upper sections of the pass. Faced with a potentially enormous detour around Albertville and Bourg Saint Maurice to reach the scheduled finish on the northern flanks of the climb in Val d'Isère, the organizers simply tunnelled through the ice to open up the road to the Tour. It was fortunate for the race that health and safety was less of a consideration to Tour organizers than it is today, and fortunate for the riders that the ice didn't collapse on top of them as they and their support vehicles thundered through the narrow tunnel. The undisputed King of the Mountains of the time, Federico Bahamontes, won the stage but the dogged Jacques Anquetil, who in 1963 was climbing better than ever, finished just three seconds later. With a 54.5km time trial to come two days before the finish in Paris, this wasn't enough for Bahamontes to put together an overall victory and Anquetil comfortably won a record-breaking fourth Tour.

1992 Claudio **CHIAPUCCI**

Miguel Indurain was the chalk of the 1992 Tour de France; an almost robotic, risk averse winning machine, he had the largest lungs, the biggest heart and the strongest legs of the bunch and a permanent glazed look that gave nothing away. Claudio Chiapucci was the cheese; a hot-headed little Italian with a cheeky grin and a penchant for daft, long-range attacks that usually came to nothing, or ended up backfiring and losing him huge chunks of time. Very occasionally however they paid off, and when they did they were something truly special to behold. The first true alpine test of the 1992 Tour took riders over the climbs of the Col des Saisies, the Cormet de Roselend, the Col de l'Iseran, the Col du Mont Cenis and the summit finish at Sestrières. Chiapucci attacked on climb number one; by the time he reached the Iseran he was alone. So utterly suicidal did his move appear that the peloton chose not to chase until late in the day, reasoning that the exhausting climbing would tire Chiapucci enough to do the job for them. Yet he survived, willed on by the Italian fans that had nipped across the border, to take a memorable solo stage win on a rare day where Chiapucci gambled and won.

1996 Bjarne **RIIS**

The peloton did cross the Col de l'Iseran during the 1996 Tour de France but not under its own steam and on four wheels rather than two. As the Tour awoke on the morning of 8 July, it drew open its curtains to wild weather, and winds of over 100kmh had brought fresh snowdrifts on the high passes of the Iseran and the Col du Galibier. Organizers shortened the stage to just 46 kilometres, and riders climbed and descended the mountains in the warm, dry conditions of their team cars. The stage started on the lowest slopes of the Col du Galibier descent in Monêtier les Bains, following its original route. Bjarne Riis leapt out of the gates like a greyhound chasing a rabbit; he pummelled his rivals with attack after attack, and when he finally had them on the ropes on the climb of the Col du Montgenèvre he delivered the sucker punch. It was a stage made for Riis's strengths, albeit ones that were chemically enhanced; in a little over an hour he blasted his way to a solo win and as the dust settled he had shown himself to be the strongest rider in the race. He would go on to win the race, but in 2007 those storms on the Iseran would be echoed metaphorically for Riis when he confessed to having achieved it by doping.

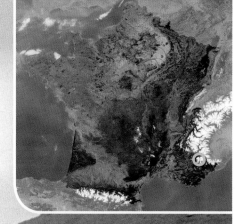

Col de la Bonette

The Col de la Bonette, or more specifically its loop road the Cime de la Bonette, is the highest point the Tour de France has ever reached. Almost three kilometres above sea level, the road to the barren peak is a fearsome and awe-inspiring place.

❝Climbing over 2,700m above sea level like this gave me a host of reasons to appreciate everything I had lived through on the bike. I pressed gently on the pedals, admiring distant views, weighing each second as if it were a tiny shard of time that had taken flight ...❞

Laurent Fignon

The Col de le Bonette speaks of the human fascination with climbing new heights. The col itself sits at 2,715m. However, in the mid-twentieth century the residents of the nearby towns at the foot of the pass realized that by adding on a loop around the Cime de la Bonette, the barren peak adjacent to the pass, they could make it even higher.

So they did. The result was the Cime de la Bonette: 2,802m above sea level. The Tour de France climbed it for the first time just after the last stretch of tarmac was laid in 1962.

It might be the highest point that the Tour has ever reached but the Col de la Bonette is not, as is claimed on signs at the foot of the climb, the highest paved road in Europe. For starters, the 2,802m Cime de la Bonette is technically not part of the col in the sense that it is not the lowest point between two peaks. It is a loop road around the Bonette peak which joins up with the col a few metres shy of the pass in either direction to form a figure of eight shape.

What's more, at 2,715m, the Bonette itself is pipped by the Iseran (2,770m), Agnel (2,744m) and Italy's Stelvio (2,757m) passes when it comes to sheer altitude. Finally, there are far higher tarmac roads in Europe, the highest being the 3,392m Pico de Veleta dead end road in Spain's Sierra Nevada.

To complicate matters even further there is a third col, the Restefond, which leads down a side track from the main route over the pass on the northern side. Even the Tour gets confused by it all. When in 2008 it last passed over what is technically the Cime de la Bonette, it called it erroneously the climb of the "Col de la Bonette-Restefond".

The dubious claims have somewhat undermined what the locals came together to create, but they shouldn't undermine the place. Highest road or not, the climb to the Bonette is a sumptuous journey through the rugged beauty of the Mercantour national park where the dark rocks create more of a moonscape than the bleached limestone of Mont Ventoux. *"Ils ont roulé sur la Lune,"* wrote celebrated Tour journalist Philippe Bouvet in 1993.

On one of the southernmost of the high alpine passes, the proximity of Provence is palpable. Here the landscape is rich in colour and warmth like the swirling brushstrokes of Van Gogh's sunflowers. The col generally opens in the first or second week of May, between a fortnight and a month earlier than the likes of the Col du Galibier to the north.

It's a climb with a distinct human history, too. Besides the battles of the Tour de France it has hosted great military movements, beginning with the megalomaniacal campaigns of Napoleon I and continuing

through to the Second World War with the completion of the huge barracks by the Col de Restefond. These weren't an early attempt at military altitude training; rather they were crucial installations for the Battle of the Alps in 1940.

Of course the huge slopes and daunting task of riding a bike up them has spiced up the Tour de France every time it has visited. The climb is 26km from Saint Etienne de Tinée in the south, with an average gradient of 6.4%, and 24.0km from Jausiers in the north, giving an average of 6.6%. Both contain ramps of over 10%, with the most severe ramps of 15% coming just before the high point of the Cime in a frantic, altitude grabbing frenzy.

The Tour has visited just four times. There is something deeply alluring about these heights and, as Laurent Fignon discovered on his solo valedictory ride in 1993, something particularly poetic and poignant about travelling through them on a bicycle. And, regardless of it not being the highest road in Europe, the Cime de la Bonette is still the highest the Tour has ever been. For that alone it is worth its place among the greatest climbs of the Tour de France.

Opposite: **July 1989 and the bright primary colours of Robert Millar's TVM team kit stand out like a jewel in the austere green-grey environment of the Col de la Bonette.**

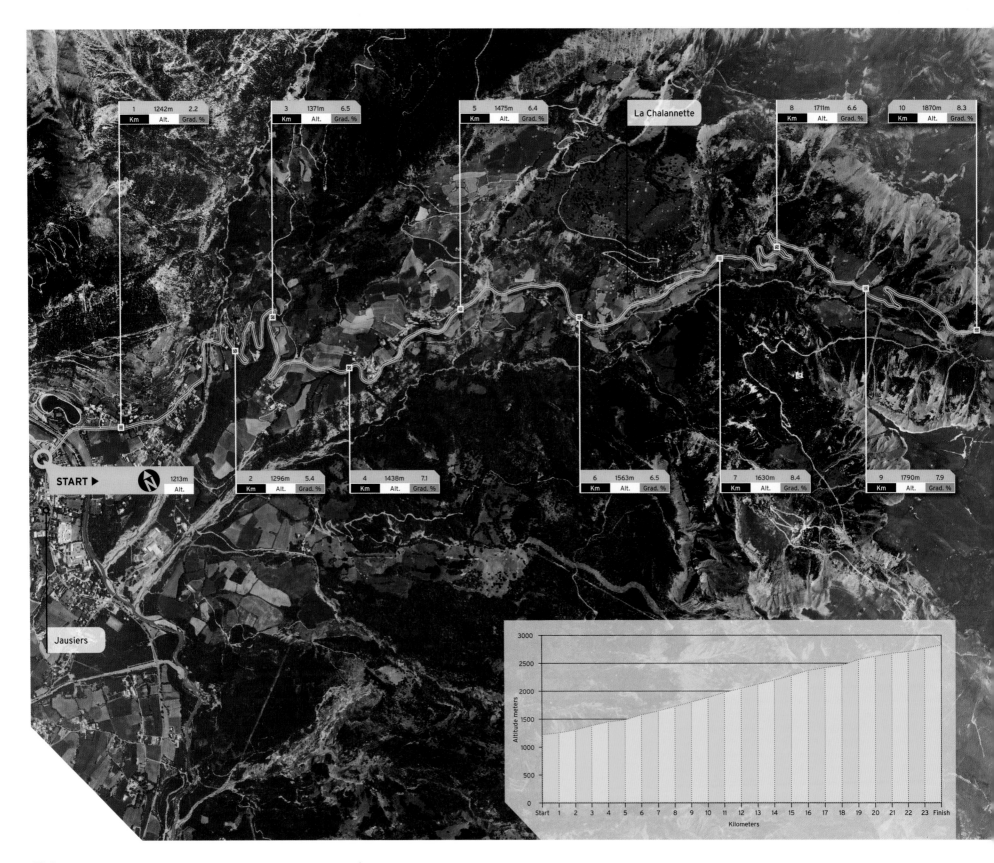

1	1242m	2.2
Km	Alt.	Grad. %

3	1371m	6.5
Km	Alt.	Grad. %

5	1475m	6.4
Km	Alt.	Grad. %

La Chalannette

8	1711m	6.6
Km	Alt.	Grad. %

10	1870m	8.3
Km	Alt.	Grad. %

START ▶ | 1213m | Alt.

2	1296m	5.4
Km	Alt.	Grad. %

4	1438m	7.1
Km	Alt.	Grad. %

6	1563m	6.5
Km	Alt.	Grad. %

7	1630m	8.4
Km	Alt.	Grad. %

9	1790m	7.9
Km	Alt.	Grad. %

Jausiers

Altitude meters

3000
2500
2000
1500
1000
500
0

Start 1 2 3 4 5 6 7 8 9 10 11 12 13 14 15 16 17 18 19 20 21 22 23 Finish

Kilometers

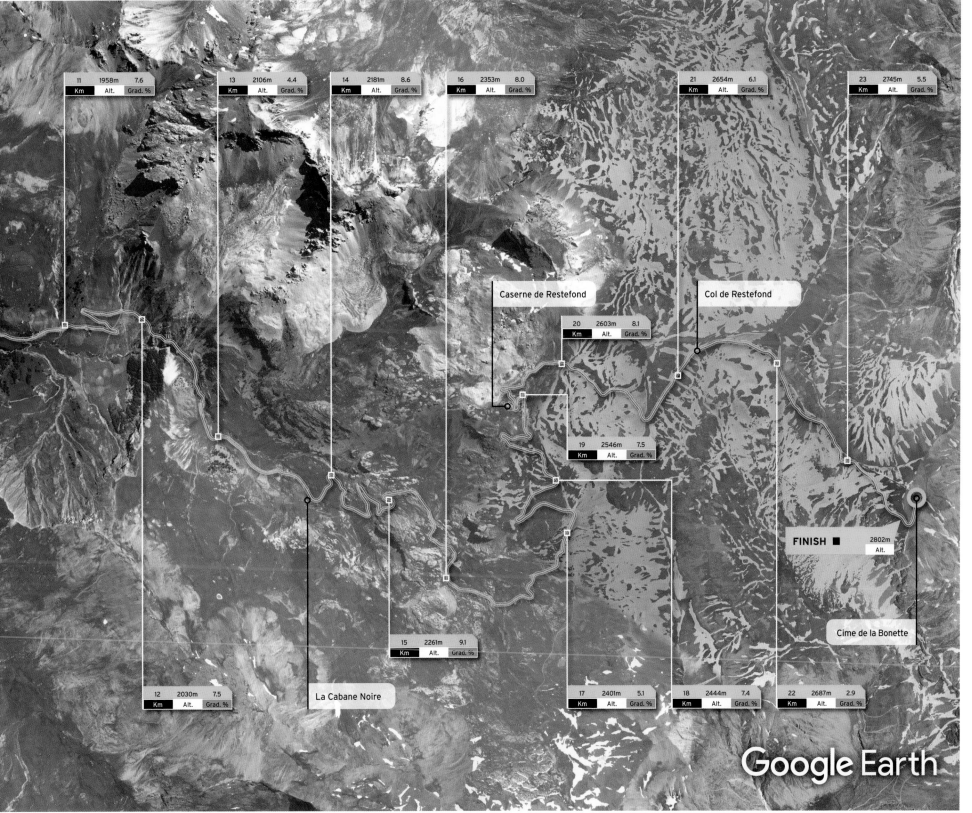

11	1958m	7.6
Km	Alt.	Grad. %

13	2106m	4.4
Km	Alt.	Grad. %

14	2181m	8.6
Km	Alt.	Grad. %

16	2353m	8.0
Km	Alt.	Grad. %

21	2654m	6.1
Km	Alt.	Grad. %

23	2745m	5.5
Km	Alt.	Grad. %

Caserne de Restefond

Col de Restefond

20	2603m	8.1
Km	Alt.	Grad. %

19	2546m	7.5
Km	Alt.	Grad. %

FINISH ■	2802m
	Alt.

Cime de la Bonette

15	2261m	9.1
Km	Alt.	Grad. %

12	2030m	7.5
Km	Alt.	Grad. %

La Cabane Noire

17	2401m	5.1
Km	Alt.	Grad. %

18	2444m	7.4
Km	Alt.	Grad. %

22	2687m	2.9
Km	Alt.	Grad. %

Google Earth

Route to the Summit

The Col de la Bonette has been climbed from the north and south sides twice each by the Tour de France. It is the northern ascent from Jausiers, however, that has made the climb famous in the Tour. It also tells the story of the mountain's history as a strategically important defensive position, for the road is littered with evidence of its military past.

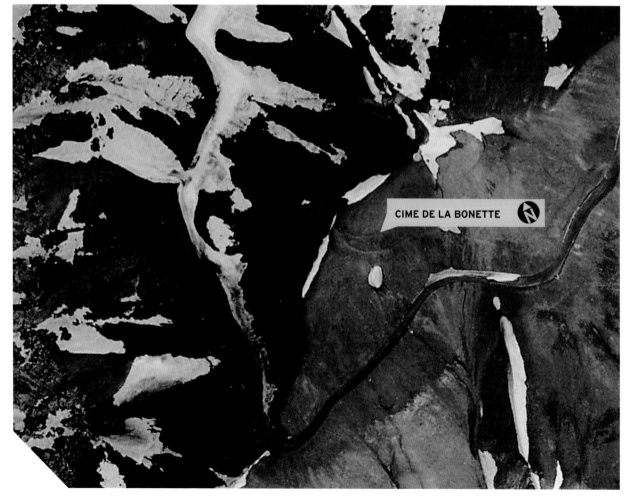

◄ Cime de la Bonette

The Cime de la Bonette is the 2,860m peak of barren black rock that lends its name to the pass. In the 1960s it was lassoed by a loop of tarmac extending from either side of the col, taking the tarmac to a maximum altitude of 2,802m and taking the civic pride of the local communes to the stratosphere. As we have learned, however, their new road is not, as claimed, the highest road in Europe. The Pico de Veleta (Spain) and the Ötztal Glacier Road (Austria) are the highest points that tarmac has reached, while there are many dozens of gravel and dirt roads that climb higher. Still, this doesn't make the Cime de la Bonette any less worthy or any less impressive. It offers stunning, almost 360-degree views over the barren but beautiful peaks of the Mercantour national park, and the final push to the highest point reaches gradients approaching 15%, as if squeezing out every last possible altitude metre. At the top there's a plaque on a monolith nobly marking the significance of the road.

Left: The Cime de la Bonette, the highest point the Tour has ever reached.

Caserne de Restefond

Around two kilometres below the Col de Restefond is a remarkable set of buildings that make up the Caserne de Restefond, or the Restefond barracks. Strategically close to the Italian border, the square of buildings shaped like a roman villa were begun at the turn of the twentieth century and enlarged during the Second World War as part of the Maginot Line of fortifications that ran along France's eastern border from the Mediterranean to the North Sea.

Opposite: The derelict military barracks of the Caserne de Restefond.   Above left: "They rode on the moon": the Tour skirts the lunar landscape of the Cime de la Bonette.   Above right: A select group of favourites rides a high tempo on the Col de la Bonette in the 2008 Tour.

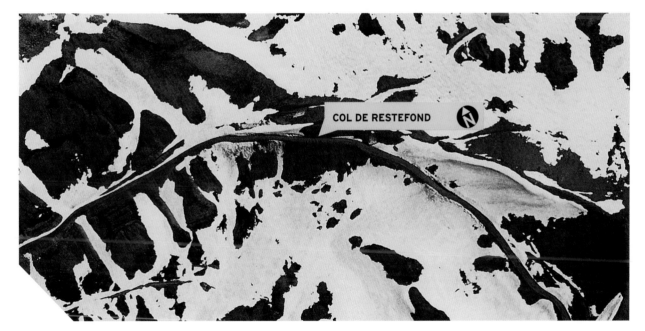

◄ Col de Restefond

Just 1.2 kilometres north of the Col de la Bonette is another col, the Col de Restefond, which offers another route south via a dirt road accessible to mountain bikers during the summer months. At 2,680m it is nevertheless a real col, marking the low point between the Restefond summit and the Cime des Trois Serrières and linking the catchments for the Restefond and Granges Communes streams. However, a few hundred metres downhill and north lies the Faux Col de Restefond – the "fake col". This imposter is not a real col; actually it is nothing more than a gravel track heading off to the right and leading down along the Restefond ravine to the southwest. This sprinkling of cols, real and fake, gives the Tour de France a slight identity crisis whenever it passes the climb. To take them all into account, it officially names the climb Col de la Bonette-Restefond or Cime de la Bonette-Restefond. Neither is strictly correct – the loop road is not a col, nor does the Cime de la Bonette road have anything to do with the Restefond. Regardless of that, the lengthy title does at least bring the gravitas that the place deserves.

Left: The Col de Restefond sits just below the Col de la Bonette.

Jausiers

A pretty village that sits at the foot of the Col de la Bonette in the Ubaye valley, Jausiers is full of lively buildings including the hilltop belltower of the Clocher de Jausiers and the whitewashed Château des Magnans. From Jausiers the Tour can head to any number of high passes, including the Col de Vars, Col d'Allos and the Col de Larche, which sits on the Italian border. The rugged 2,780m Col du Parpaillon, never used by the Tour, overlooks the village.

La Cabane Noire

Another building with a military history, the "black cabin" acted as a wooden barracks on the supply line to the Restefond barracks higher up. The casements and military hardware scattered all around the climb betrays the fact that the various installations were not completed when hostilities opened in the Battle of the Alps in June 1940. At 2,150m high, this point 10 kilometres from the summit has an average gradient of 9%, making it the hardest section of the climb.

La Chalannette

A tiny hamlet nestled in the lower slopes of the Bonette, La Chalannette is a steady 6km climb out of Jausiers and marks the start of the tougher sections of the ascent. Beginning at 6.5%, the road rises to around 8% for the following 14km, only flattening out in a handful of places. Besides a few hairpin bends immediately out of Jausiers, this also marks where the road starts to twist and turn its way up the valley with a series of switchbacks as it marches south.

The Mountain Kings

04

Whether it's losing their heads and missing a high speed turn or floating up in a peaceful state of transcendence, climbing to over 2,800m altitude on the Col de la Bonette and Cime de la Bonette can do strange things to the riders of the Tour de France.

1962 Federico **BAHAMONTES**

The Tour de France tackled the Cime de la Bonette as soon as it could, and less than two years after it was finished and the final piece of tarmac had dried, the 1962 Tour rode over it on stage 18. A variation on the theme of the classic French Riviera to Briançon mountain stage, riders left the small resort of Juan les Pins on the Mediterranean coastline and hit the Bonette as the first climb and replacement for the Col d'Allos. First over the top, appropriately, was the greatest climber of his era, and arguably of all time, Federico Bahamontes. However, one thing Bahamontes was not was a great descender, and with the climbs of the Col de Vars and Col d'Izoard remaining, his lead over the Bonette wasn't enough on which to built a stage victory. In fact a combination of hesitation, defensive tactics and some untimely flat tyres meant that the climbers failed to wrestle any time from Jacques Anquetil on the day and remarkably it was a sprinter, the big and burly Emile Daems, who won the stage. No matter for Bahamontes: the "Eagle of Toledo" won the King of the Mountains classification by the time he reached Paris, his fourth of six titles in his career.

1993 Robert **MILLAR**

While one ponytailed rider – Laurent Fignon – was dropping back, another was breaking clear at the front. In this instance it was the little Scot Robert Millar, whose eagle-beak nose, dark sunglasses and flowing brown ponytail made him look like he was riding away from the stage at a Status Quo concert. He was in fact riding away from Pedro Delgado, who he dropped early on the climb in order to continue on alone into the empty landscape, unmistakable in the primary colours of his TVM team kit. He bobbed his way up the final steep ramp to the Cime de la Bonette surrounded by fans but in his own personal purgatory, out of the saddle and grimacing as he stomped on his pedals. As he crossed the summit he slapped a cotton cap over his head, zipped up his jersey and flew down the other side of the climb and into Saint Etienne de Tinée. He held out for most of the final climb to Isola 2000 too, but was eventually swamped by the breathless pace of the peloton led by Miguel Indurain. Having left all his energy on the Bonette, Millar couldn't stick with them and finished seventh, one minute down on stage winner Tony Rominger.

1993 Laurent **FIGNON**

The double Tour de France winner Laurent Fignon remembered well his time riding up the Col de la Bonette on stage 11 of the 1993 Tour de France, but not because he was in with a shout of winning. Riding what would be his last Tour, and one of his last races as a professional, he suddenly drifted back from the lead group of riders. He had decided that enough was enough. "I can remember it very clearly," he recalled in his autobiography. "I rode up the whole climb in last place. Because I wanted to. I put my hands on the top of the bars and savoured it all to the full. I was breathing deeply as I lived through my last seconds in bike racing, which I had thought would never end for me. This col was all mine and I didn't want anyone to intrude." Fignon's disillusion with the sport, which was then entering its darkest period of drug abuse, is cited as his reason for abandoning on the day's final climb to Isola 2000. It was a beautiful yet sad way for him to say goodbye to the Tour and, finding he was no longer able to contend for the overall classification as he had done in his prime, Fignon quit racing for good that August. He died in 2010 from metastatic lung cancer aged just 50.

2008 John Lee **AUGUSTYN**

The little South African climber John Lee Augustyn can probably be said to have a complex relationship with the Col de la Bonette. Flying down the first part of the descent from the Cime de la Bonette loop road in the breakaway at the front of the race, he looked back behind him at precisely the wrong moment and overshot a right-hand bend. He then flew again, quite literally, over the edge of the climb and slid down the scree slope. "Coming over the top, at that altitude, my heart was pumping, the adrenaline was rushing," he recalled. "All you're thinking is 'I could win a Tour de France stage!'" Pausing to check himself over, the then 22-year-old was helped back up to the road by a nearby fan before realizing that his bike was still down the mountain side. Despite waiting for a replacement he continued on to finish the stage at the foot of the climb in Jausiers in 35th position, quite a remarkable achievement considering how close to death his little detour had taken him. These exploits would later enable Augustyn to pursue a second career. He retired from cycling for a second time in 2014 due to a persistent hip injury, and now sells cycle clothing branded "Col de la Bonette".

Cormet de Roselend

1967m

Length: 20.3km
Start: 740m
Ascent: 1227m

With a character as distinctive as its unusual name, the Cormet de Roselend pass is accessed via a narrow gorge and a steep ledge that takes riders up to another world altogether. The blue waters of the defining Lac de Roselend make it undoubtedly one of the most beautiful of the great alpine climbs.

> **❝** I flew past that and off the edge of the cliff, and I hung in the air, feeling motionless, weightless, stopped in time, a hundred feet above the trees. **❞**
>
> *Johan Bruyneel*

The Cormet de Roselend has only been passed by the Tour de France 10 times. It's a travesty that it hasn't happened more often. Perhaps this climb is hindered by its remote location; the pass dissects a very remote part of the Alps, deep into the mountain range, and at its highest point is a very long way from anywhere else. Nor is it the sort of pass that the Tour can easily combine with other climbs; the nearest passes to the east are the gargantuan Col de l'Iseran and the Col du Petit-Saint-Bernard, which passes into Italy. To the west lies the Col de la Madeleine, another 2,000m giant. All of these options involve a lot of riding, a lot of climbing and a lot of commitment.

Perhaps it is because it doesn't quite reach the magical 2,000m mark itself – coming in just 32m short at 1,968m. Indeed its critics would point out that the Cormet de Roselend falls between two stools; it isn't quite long or high enough to offer a real *hors catégorie* challenge, and at the same time it's not short enough, or conveniently located, to offer a dynamite summit finish.

Yet this pass deserves its place as one of the Tour's legendary climbs. Cormet means col in the local dialect and, right down to its name, this place offers something a bit quirky and a bit different to its alpine neighbours. It's a hipster alp, one that would grow a beard, wear a checked shirt and drink craft beer.

The dominant characteristic of the climb is the Lac de Roselend, an unfathomably pure blue sapphire set in the Massif du Beaufortain. It's hard to imagine that before the 1960s this lake – or reservoir, to be accurate – didn't exist. It appears so natural. But underneath the waters and the layers of silt lie the original road to the pass and the remains of the village of Roselend, which gives the climb its name. Both were inundated in the 1960s following the construction of the Roselend dam.

The lake now acts as a moat protecting a lost world, standing guard on the western side of the pass between the narrow Défilé d'Entreroches gorge out of Beaufort and the upper plateau that is traversed by the final few kilometres of the climb.

That western ascent narrowly outranks the east in terms of popularity in the Tour – six ascents to four since the first in 1979 – although the two are very similar in nature: approximately 20 kilometres in length and starting off hard before beginning to ease towards the pass. The roads owe that unusual dome shape to the mountain plateau that makes up the surroundings of the Cormet de Roselend. Peculiarly the pass is flanked by tufts, hillocks and marshes which lie in a depression between the high peaks on the same Beaufortain ridge that continues to Mont Blanc to the northeast. And yet, when you are standing there, those mountains feel a long way off. The final few kilometres of the road are

relatively flat, offering an exhilarating finale to the climb as riders fly through the crisp, thin air.

The Cormet de Roselend has always featured relatively early on in the Tour's mountain stages; it has seldom had a decisive role to play but instead opens itself up to the more quirky and memorable alpine exploits. Indeed it isn't about stage winners and yellow jerseys on this pass.

This is where burly sprinter Thor Hushovd gobbled up the intermediate sprint points on a lone attack in 2009. It is also a place where crashes have taken their toll. It's where Johan Bruyneel flew into a ditch in 1996 before dusting himself off and continuing. Even his recollections of the event point to the alpine majesty of the climb – his feeling of hanging in the air, stopped in time. A crash in 2007 brought down David Arroyo and Michael Rogers; the former hit a relatively soft patch of vegetation and could carry on, but the latter hit a crash barrier and retired with a broken collarbone.

The Cormet de Roselend might not conform to the stereotype of its neighbouring alpine climbs but it is refreshingly charming, well loved and well respected just the way it is.

Opposite: **The Tour de France peloton stretches out as the gradients of the Cormet de Roselend begin to take their toll on some riders.**

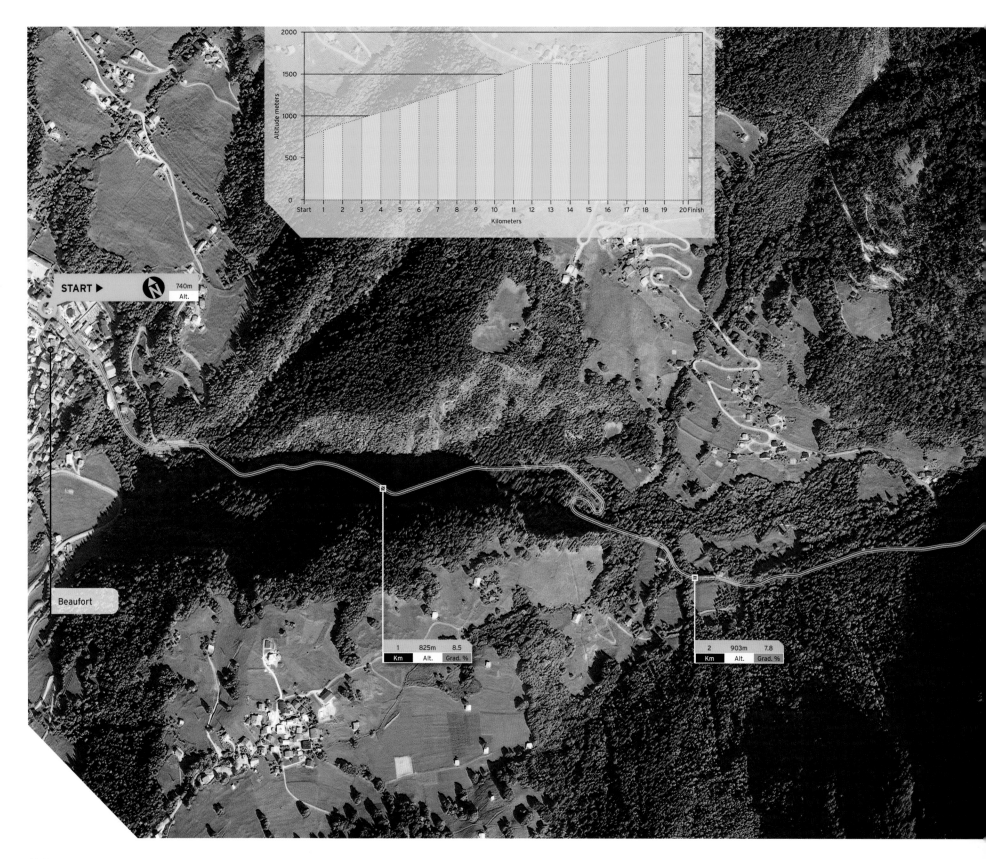

START ▶ 740m Alt.

Beaufort

Km	Alt.	Grad. %
1	825m	8.5

Km	Alt.	Grad. %
2	903m	7.8

4	1042m	7.0
Km	Alt.	Grad. %

5	1099m	5.7
Km	Alt.	Grad. %

9	1384m	6.6
Km	Alt.	Grad. %

11	1541m	7.7
Km	Alt.	Grad. %

10	1464m	8.0
Km	Alt.	Grad. %

3	972m	6.9
Km	Alt.	Grad. %

6	1180m	8.1
Km	Alt.	Grad. %

7	1248m	6.8
Km	Alt.	Grad. %

8	1318m	7.0
Km	Alt.	Grad. %

Google Earth

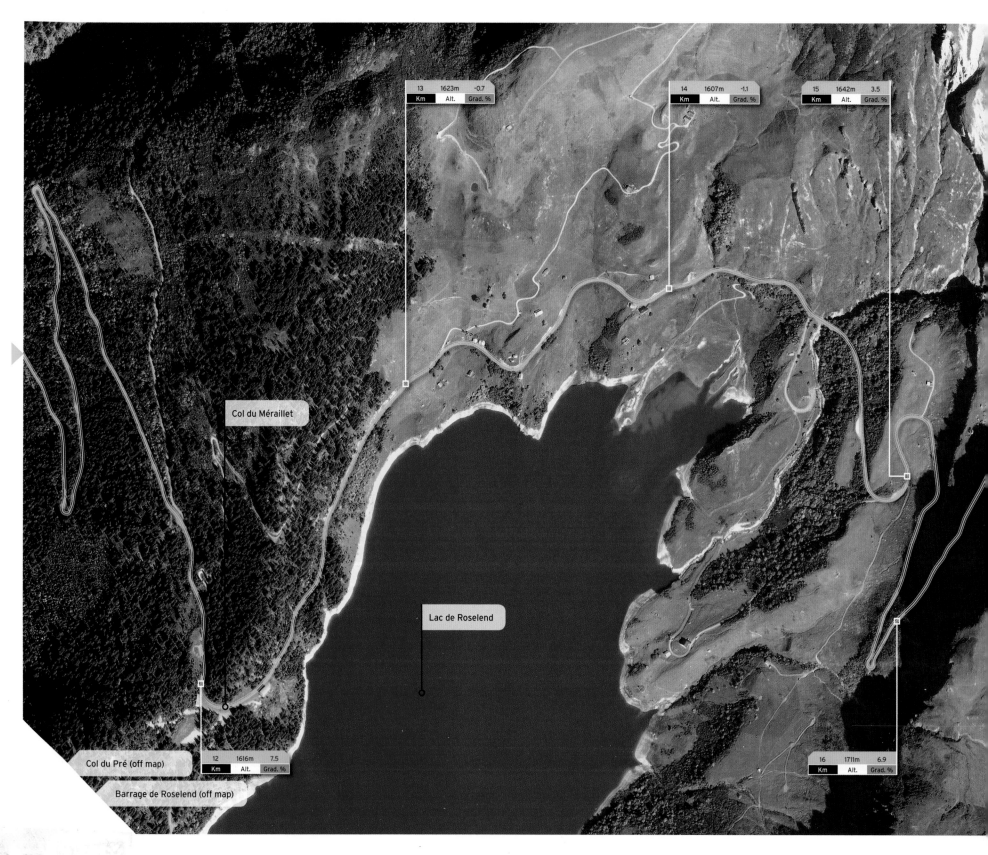

13	1623m	-0.7
Km	Alt.	Grad. %

14	1607m	-1.1
Km	Alt.	Grad. %

15	1642m	3.5
Km	Alt.	Grad. %

Col du Méraillet

Lac de Roselend

Col du Pré (off map)

Barrage de Roselend (off map)

12	1616m	7.5
Km	Alt.	Grad. %

16	1711m	6.9
Km	Alt.	Grad. %

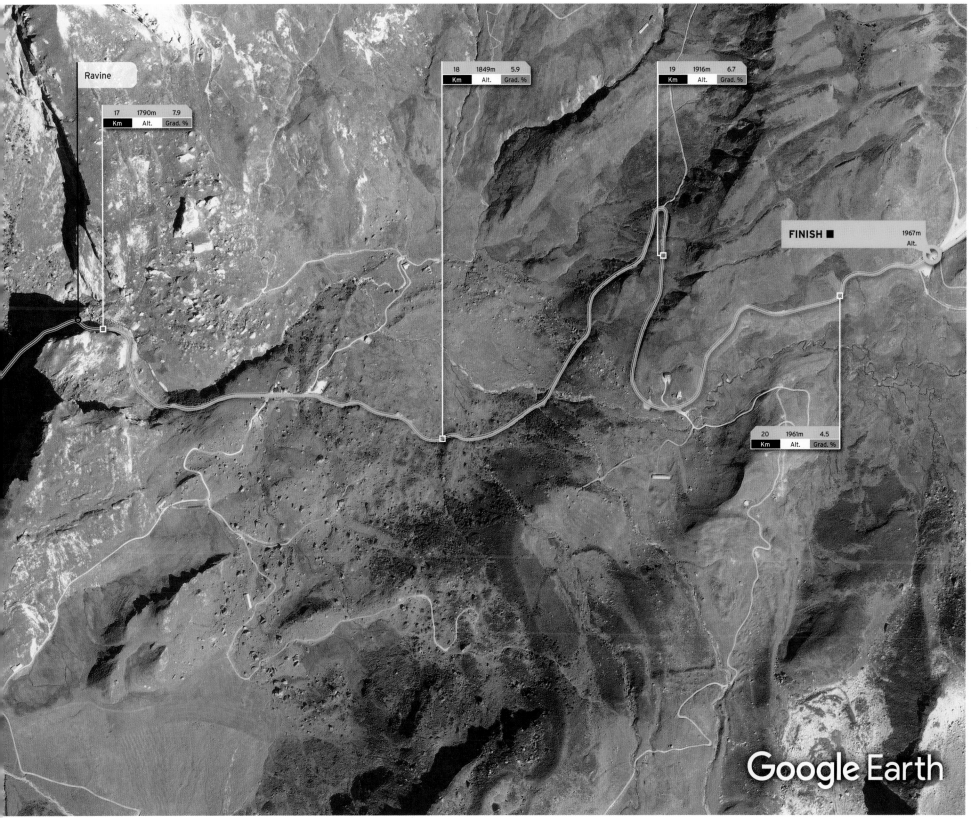

Ravine

17	1790m	7.9
Km	Alt.	Grad. %

18	1849m	5.9
Km	Alt.	Grad. %

19	1916m	6.7
Km	Alt.	Grad. %

FINISH ■	1967m
	Alt.

20	1961m	4.5
Km	Alt.	Grad. %

Google Earth

Route to the Summit

With chalets, gorges, detours and the most arrestingly beautiful alpine lake, the Cormet de Roselend is a cyclo-tourist's dream. It might not feature very often, but when it does that spectacular beauty certainly isn't lost on the Tour de France.

LAC DE ROSELAND

◄ Lac de Roselend

The crowning glory of the Cormet de Roselend is the majestic Roselend lake, a man-made mirror of tranquil alpine waters that reflect the azure blue sky when the sun is shining and glow pastel blue when it isn't. Alongside the lake is a 2.5km section where riders float downhill and then along the northern shores before climbing up again and resuming the march east to the pass. All the while the lake dominates the landscape, framed by the peaks of the Pointe de Presset, the Roches Merles and the Crête des Gittes. It hasn't always been this way; the lake didn't exist before 1960, but it began to fill following the construction of the hydroelectric Roselend Dam. In doing so it drowned the alpine village of Roselend, which gives the climb its name, and the waters now rest at 1,557m, depending on the season. Very occasionally the lake is drained to allow inspection of the dam, although silt has covered the remains of the village. In 1962 a new chapel was built on the shores of the lake to replace like-for-like the one in the village, over whose submerged remains the little stone building now gazes.

Left: The Lac de Roselend dominates the climb to the Cormet de Roselend.

Barrage de Roselend

A right turn at the Col de Méraillet drops riders down a 20% ramp to the road along the Barrage de Roselend, the vast concrete dam holding back the waters of the man-made lake. It makes for a worthwhile detour: look north and you are faced with a vertiginous drop straight down; look south and you see the cerulean still waters of the lake. Although the Tour has yet to tackle this part of the Cormet de Roselend, it would make for a stunning and stern test.

Opposite: **The Cormet de Roselend sits just below 2,000m in altitude.** Above left: **Riders climb up and away from the Barrage de Roselend in 2006.** Above right: **The chapel overlooking the Lac de Roselend enjoys one of the finest views in the French Alps.**

◀ Beaufort

It might not be visually obvious where the climb of the Cormet de Roselend begins; the sign marking the start of the ascent can be overlooked in the jumble of street furniture and shop fronts in the busy little town of Beaufort. But riders certainly know it from the smell. Climbing gradually up the Doron valley from the west, they enter town past the Coopérative Laitière de Beaufort, the local cheese cooperative where milk from the cows grazing the nearby mountain pastures is turned into the famous Beaufort cheese. All along the climb are reminders of this thriving local agriculture; when it's not the actual presence of cows in tiny patches of grass alongside the road, it is the clusters of metal milk churns awaiting collection by the co-op's delivery van or the distant chiming of cowbells in the air. Beaufort itself is a happening little place, nourished by the milk trade along with the winter and summer tourist industry. However, riders quickly leave civilization behind as they depart through the claustrophobic Défilé de Entreroches gorge, speeding along with fresh legs at a relatively gentle gradient of 6.5%.

Left: Beaufort, famous for its cheese, is where the climb starts.

Col du Pré

Forming a back road from Beaufort to the dam wall along the Lac de Roselend, the Col du Pré sits at 1,703m above the lake. Twelve kilometres long, it is almost equal in length to the principal road up the Cormet de Roselend via the Col de Méraillet, but the final seven of those sit between 9 and 11% gradient. It is not a nice climb and it makes for a fast, technical descent. To date the Tour has never passed over it, but it can surely only be a matter of time before it does.

Ravine

Climbing up and away from the Lac de Roselend, the road to the col passes through a breathtakingly rugged ravine where the water and ice of the Nant des Lautarets have carved their way through the mountain to leave a narrow passageway through exposed rock. Coming 4km from the highest point of the pass, the feature is a gateway to the final section of the climb and welcoming riders at the other side are boggy fields and the Refuge du Plan de la Laie.

Col de Méraillet

The biggest chunk of climbing that riders will work through on their way up to the Cormet de Roselend comes between 5 and 12 kilometres from the top, where a series of regular hairpins step steadily up the mountain from the campsite at Les Fontanus to the 1,605m Col de Méraillet. This road, northwest facing and sheltered from the sun, is an archetypal Alpine slog, 9% steep and seven kilometres long. Riders are glad to get it out of the way and move on to the next section.

The Mountain Kings

Having featured just 10 times and never as a final climb, the Cormet de Roselend hasn't quite been given the star treatment from the Tour de France's great riders. But its slopes have witnessed exploits just as exciting as those on the race's other big name climbs.

1995 Alex ZÜLLE

Stage nine of the 1995 Tour de France was a relatively short, fast 160km mountain stage over four climbs, passing the Côte de Héry, the Col des Saisies and the Cormet de Roselend and ending in a summit finish on La Plagne. The bespectacled Swiss Alex Zülle was the "best of the rest" against Miguel Indurain, who appeared to be his usual indomitable self in his quest for a fifth Tour win. Zülle probably knew that he stood no chance against the mighty Spaniard in a straight fight to a summit finish and so decided to play his hand early, breaking clear on the Cormet de Roselend with 50 kilometres to go. As Zülle rode away, Indurain decided to sit tight and wait until the bottom of La Plagne to make his move. Zülle's tactics proved to be the right ones, as he remained free to take the stage and progress towards a final overall finish of second, but it was a successful day for Indurain too. Although he finished over two minutes back from his Swiss rival, he kept Zülle at arm's length in the hunt for the yellow jersey while also extending his lead over the rest of the field by over two minutes.

1996 Johan BRUYNEEL

The Belgian rider who would go on to manage Lance Armstrong's US Postal team remembered clearly his eventful day on the Cormet de Roselend in 1996. Riding down the descent at breakneck speeds and in torrential, cold rain on stage seven from Chambéry to Les Arcs, he hit a spot of gravel on a tight turn and rode his front wheel into a large rock on the side of the road next to a small stone wall. "I flew past that and off the edge of the cliff, and I hung in the air, feeling motionless, weightless, stopped in time, a hundred feet above the trees," he recalled in his autobiography *We Might As Well Win*. Bruyneel eventually crash-landed in a small ditch, and fortunately the only thing broken was his fall as he collided with a small tree. With his orange and white Rabobank team jersey covered in mud and with a panic-stricken look on his face, he was dragged back up to the road. The sensible thing to give him would have been medical attention; instead he was given his bike, told straight away to ride on and down the climb to the end of the stage in Les Arcs, where remarkably he finished the stage in 20th place.

2002 Dario FRIGO

The bleach blond-haired Italian's victory at the end of a day-long breakaway forged on the Cormet de Roselend should have been cause for much more celebration than there was. It was a fine win by Dario Frigo, who broke away with three other riders on the first climb of the day, the Cormet de Roselend, and stayed away over the Col des Saisies, the Col des Aravis and the Col de la Colombière. He outsprinted his rivals Guiseppe Guerini and Mario Aerts in Cluses to take the biggest win of his career. However, Frigo had emerged from a less than exemplary period in the career of a professional cyclist. Sacked by his previous team the previous year having been caught by police with a bag full of performance-enhancing drugs, some of which was real and some of which turned out to be nothing more than salt water sold to him for £500 by a bloke in Milan airport, he returned to the Tour with the small and relatively unknown team Tacconi Sport. Unrepentant, Frigo enjoyed his win a lot more than the sporting public. "I don't think of the past; I just want to think of beautiful things and this win is a beautiful thing," he said.

2009 Thor HUSHOVD

Named after the Norse god of thunder, the big, burly Norwegian rider Thor Hushovd made an impressive sight when he led over a mountain climb. Hushovd, wearing the green jersey of points classification leader, decided to put the hammer down on stage 17 over the Cormet de Roselend, Col des Saisies and Côte d'Arâches in order to sweep up intermediate sprint points and extend his lead in the competition ahead of Mark Cavendish. Hushovd perhaps found motivation from criticism he had received after crying foul after Cavendish's sprint three days earlier, which saw the Manxman relegated to last place and drop back in the fight for the green jersey. Looking good to win the competition overall, Hushovd perhaps needed to dismiss the feeling that his jersey might not have been fairly won. He certainly did just that. Breaking clear and climbing the Cormet de Roselend alone, he caught and passed the breakaway group on the descent and stomped on over two more climbs to take first place in two intermediate sprints, earning him a vital 12 points.

3
CLASSIC CLIMBS OF THE PYRENEES

Wild, unpredictable, and with steep and ever-changing gradients, the Pyrenees are the domain of the pure mountain climber. In this range on the Spanish border between the Atlantic Ocean and the Mediterranean Sea, the environment can turn at the drop of a hat from a misty theatre lit by the limelight of following vehicles to a hot cauldron of colour and noise. And what the mountains may lack in sheer altitude they more than make up for in character; they are in many respects the toughest in the Tour de France.

Opposite: The last of the day's lingering Pyrenean mists burn off under the bright afternoon sun as the Tour tackles the Col du Tourmalet.

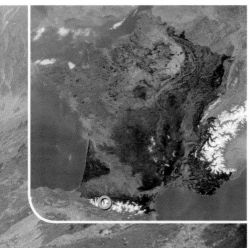

Col du Tourmalet

2115m

Length: 17.2km
Start: 847m
Ascent: 1268m

High enough to touch the clouds, jaw-droppingly beautiful, and the most popular high mountain in the history of the race; the Tour de France seldom leaves the Pyrenees without paying a visit to the incomparable Col du Tourmalet.

" Passé Tourmalet. Très bonne route. Parfaitement praticable. "

Joseph Steinès

If one had to choose a climb to sum up the Tour de France, it would be the Col du Tourmalet. The very name includes the word Tour, and although it derives from a Gascon portmanteau word meaning "the distance mountain", the French name translates roughly as "bad trip": pretty apt considering those first visits the Tour paid to it.

The highest paved pass in the French Pyrenees at 2,115m, the Col du Tourmalet is at times painfully ugly and at others stunningly beautiful. It passes through trees, fields, deep gorges and exposed mountain slopes; at the top the road simply drops off and carries on down the other side.

From the pass you can see for miles in either direction, although the view west down towards Barèges is particularly expansive. Stand here during the Tour and you can watch the riders get smaller and smaller, appearing and disappearing out of view, for a full 20 minutes.

It has been passed by the Tour more times than any other mountain – 80 times up to 2015 – and its frequency has given it the nickname *l'incontournable:* "the unavoidable one".

The climbs from the west and the east are exactly the same average gradient but are two very different beasts. The road from Luz Saint Sauveur through Barèges is marginally longer – 18.8 kilometres – and passes in a neat, straight line through what appears to be a fold in the landscape, gradually emerging from it before a final leg-breaking set of hairpins lead to the pass. From Sainte Marie de Campan the 17.2km road curves around through soft fields and woods, eventually bringing the towering peaks and the monstrosity of La Mongie ski station into view. Passing through this high-rise blemish on the landscape, the tarmac wiggles its way step by step to the top.

The very first ascent saw the Tour dare to achieve what at the time must have seemed almost impossible. If the mud, the cold, the emptiness, the gradient and the terrible equipment weren't enough to bring a rider to a halt, in July 1910 there had even been recent reports of bear attacks in the vicinity. Joseph Steinès, a colleague of Tour founder Henri Desgrange, had reconnoitred the climb earlier in the year and, after almost dying of exposure in a snowstorm near the top, stiffened his upper lip and send the somewhat misleading telegram back to Paris: "Passé Tourmalet. Très bonne route. Parfaitement praticable." Over the Tourmalet. Very good road. Perfectly feasible.

In 1913 Eugène Christophe cemented his place in Tour history when he broke his forks descending the eastern flank of the pass. Even 102 years after Christophe, the Tourmalet remains a symbol of adversity and perseverance. In 2015, the Australian Tour debutant Zak Dempster battled on to the finish line despite painful saddle sores, getting dropped and climbing the Tourmalet alone at the back of the race with over 60 kilometres to go. He was so far behind that fans around him thought the race had ended and had started to pack up and walk back down the mountain.

"On the Tourmalet there were a fair few fans in the way," he said. "But it's not Wimbledon, you're not playing on Centre Court where you can just do your thing. It's the Tour de France, and that's just part of it . . . you've got to fight and I wasn't going to go quietly into the night."

It's rare for a mountain to remain a show-stopper through more than a century of the Tour de France, and while it might no longer be haunted by impassable roads and imminent bear attack, the Col du Tourmalet is as impressive now as it was in 1910.

Symbolized by the metal statue of the cyclist heaving at his handlebars and gasping for breath that sits at the pass during the summer months, the history of the Col du Tourmalet is intimately bound up with that of the Tour de France. The two are a symbiotic pairing, and both are all the better for it.

Opposite: **Fausto Coppi glances behind him to assess his opposition as he ascends out of the mist and onto the upper slopes of the Tourmalet during the 1952 Tour. Behind him, riding in an open-top Jeep, is Tour director Jacques Goddet, whose memorial now stands at the pass.**

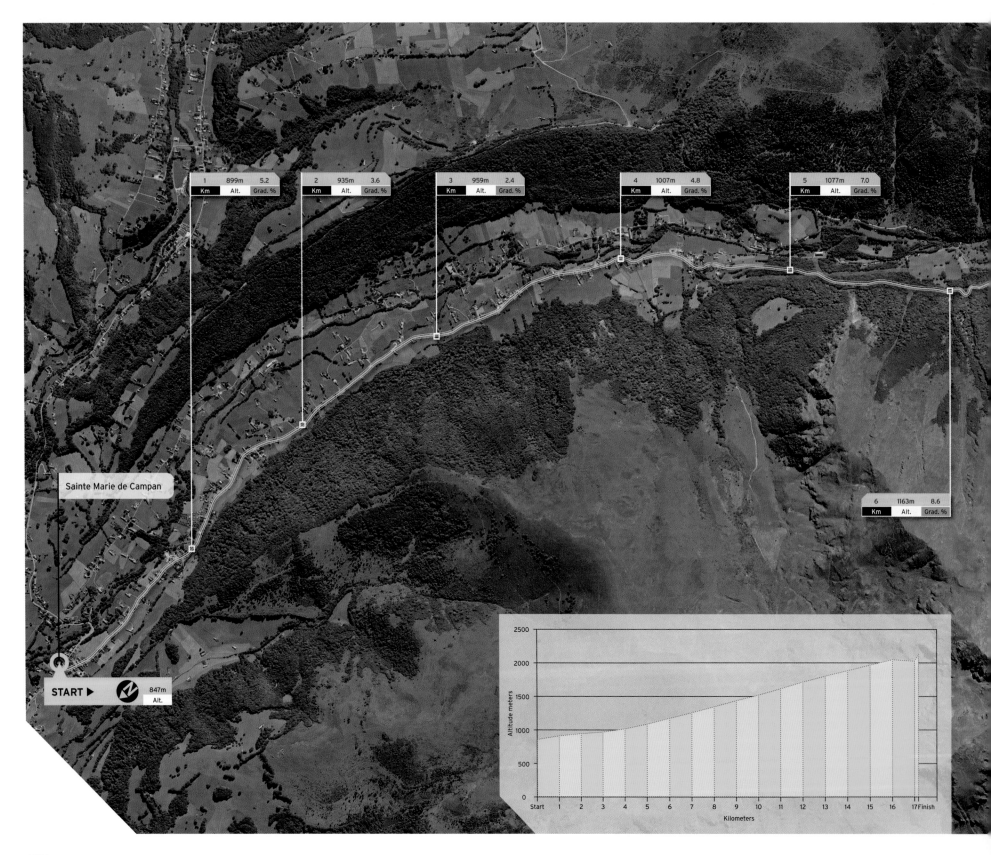

1	899m	5.2
Km	Alt.	Grad. %

2	935m	3.6
Km	Alt.	Grad. %

3	959m	2.4
Km	Alt.	Grad. %

4	1007m	4.8
Km	Alt.	Grad. %

5	1077m	7.0
Km	Alt.	Grad. %

6	1163m	8.6
Km	Alt.	Grad. %

Sainte Marie de Campan

START ▶   847m
          Alt.

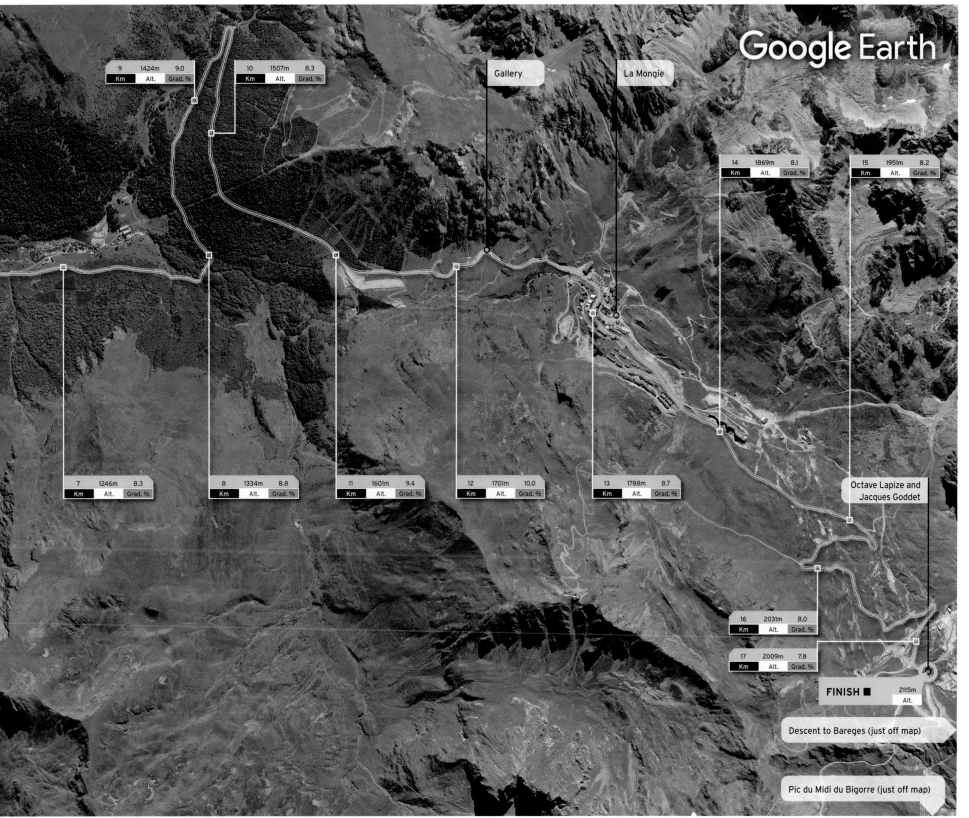

Google Earth

Gallery

La Mongie

9	1424m	9.0
Km	Alt.	Grad. %

10	1507m	8.3
Km	Alt.	Grad. %

14	1869m	8.1
Km	Alt.	Grad. %

15	1951m	8.2
Km	Alt.	Grad. %

7	1246m	8.3
Km	Alt.	Grad. %

8	1334m	8.8
Km	Alt.	Grad. %

11	1601m	9.4
Km	Alt.	Grad. %

12	1701m	10.0
Km	Alt.	Grad. %

13	1788m	8.7
Km	Alt.	Grad. %

Octave Lapize and
Jacques Goddet

16	2031m	8.0
Km	Alt.	Grad. %

17	2009m	7.8
Km	Alt.	Grad. %

FINISH ■	2115m
	Alt.

Descent to Bareges (just off map)

Pic du Midi du Bigorre (just off map)

Route to the Summit

The Col du Tourmalet is landscape of contrasts. On the eastern route to the pass, the road goes from gorges to fields to exposed slopes while passing through quiet, traditional villages as well as noisy, brutish ski stations. And riders always do well to keep an eye open for animals.

LA MONGIE

◄ La Mongie

Amid all the natural beauty of the eastern side of the Col du Tourmalet sits an improbably ugly ski station made up of high-rise buildings and sprawling chairlifts. La Mongie is 12km from Sainte Marie de Campan and 5km from the col itself, surrounded by stunning vistas and the soaring presence of the Pic du Midi du Bigorre, which serve to highlight what an eyesore the settlement is. At least the road climbs up and out of La Mongie quickly; the steepest sections of the eastern ascent come through the wide streets with wooden chalets and shops selling tourist tat, around 3km in all between 9% and 10% gradient, with occasional steeper bits. This is arguably the hardest part of the climb after more than half an hour climbing, and during the Tour the roads are heaving with fans and holidaymakers. La Mongie has hosted three summit finishes in the Tour with stage victories going to Bernard Thévenet (1970), Lance Armstrong (2002) and Ivan Basso (2004).

Left: La Mongie: at least it's over with quickly.

Gallery

Like an extended portico to a spur of mountain half a kilometre downhill of La Mongie, two galleries in quick succession give the climb of the Tourmalet a touch of glamour. Although little more than concrete tunnels open at the northern side, they wouldn't look out of place in a car chase scene from a James Bond film. For cyclists riding uphill they present no additional difficulties, but for cyclists flying downhill on the sweeping bends at speeds approaching 90kmh, the immediate change in lighting presents an exhilarating challenge.

Opposite: The King of the Mountain points at the top of the Tourmalet have always been hotly contested. Above left: Riders will always do well to be wary of roaming animals on the Col du Tourmalet. Above right: Basque climber Haimar Zubeldia rides past his supporters and into the clouds in La Mongie.

PIC DU MIDI DU BIGORRE Ⓝ

◄ Pic du Midi du Bigorre

The 2,877m peak stands due north of the Col du Tourmalet, accessible by a gravel road from the pass, or by gondola from La Mongie. The peak is currently famous for its observatory, clinging to the rocky summit and featuring all manner of equipment, from spectrographs used to analyse the atmospheres of Mars and Venus to telescopes funded by NASA to study the moon in preparation for the Apollo programme. Rumours of a future Tour de France summit finish on the peak have been swirling for several years. If it were pulled off it would be the highest Tour summit finish in history (and potentially a rival to the Cime de la Bonette as the highest road ever used by the race). However, to make this happen the organizers would have to improve the surface considerably. Given the number of cyclo-tourists who ride up and down the Tourmalet and mountain bikers who continue up to the peak, any such work wouldn't go unnoticed.

Left: Will there, one day, be a summit finish at the Pic du Midi du Bigorre?

Descent to Barèges

Like the crest of a wave, the slopes of the Tourmalet get steeper and steeper to their climax at the col. The first part of the descent to Barèges is the most technically demanding section of the climb and the place where the consequences of any mistakes are most serious. There are no barriers and the sinuous road, which features sections at 13% and tight hairpins bends, simply drops off a steep, rocky slope. Get it wrong here and riders risk falling a very long way down. However, the views west are simply stunning.

Sainte Marie de Campan

Sitting at the confluence of the roads leading to the Col du Tourmalet and Col d'Aspin, the small town of Sainte Marie de Campan has a long history of hosting the Tour. Neither a ski station nor a tourist town, it is far enough up the Adour valley to retain plenty of rural charm. It is also famous for its curious tradition of placing effigies around and about the village – these come as a surprise to new visitors, who come across them staring blankly while leaning out of windows or standing guard on balconies.

Jacques Goddet and Octave Lapize

At the col itself stand two memorials. One is a simple brass bust of Jacques Goddet, the second director of the Tour de France between 1936 and 1986. Each year the Tour awards the prize of the "Souvenir Jacques Goddet" to the first rider over the Tourmalet. The other is a vast statue of Octave Lapize, made in bright silver metal; his mouth scoops up the thin mountain air. Goddet remains there all year round but each autumn Lapize is put on the back of a truck and taken down to Bagnères de Bigorre for his winter home, returning again in June.

The Mountain Kings

80

Such epic surroundings as those on the climb of the Col du Tourmalet cannot fail to stir the riders of the Tour de France into epic exploits. From Octave Lapize in 1910 to Alberto Contador and Andy Schleck in 2010, they've been doing so for well over 100 years.

Previous pages: A solo rider tackles the wilderness of the Col du Tourmalet during the 1920 Tour de France.

Opposite top: René Vietto seems unperturbed by a plane crash as he turns the screw on his rivals in the 1947 Tour.

Opposite bottom left: Alberto Contador (l) and Andy Schleck duel it out in the mist on their way to the first summit finish on the Tourmalet in 2010.

Opposite bottom right: Octave Lapize was determined to be the first man to lead the Tour over the Tourmalet, even if it meant getting off and pushing.

1913 Eugène CHRISTOPHE

The Col du Tourmalet is renowned as being the setting for one of the earliest dramas in Tour history. Descending the pass in 1913, Eugène Christophe crashed heavily on the rutted track (this was the era of heavy bikes and wooden wheels) and broke the fork of his bike. He picked himself up off the ground, dusted himself down and walked down the mountain to the nearest forge (in Sainte Marie de Campan) in tears. Christophe began to repair his machine; however, in an incident that serves as a reminder of the harsh rulebook of the early Tours, he was penalized 10 minutes by race organizers. While he hammered away at his own machine he enlisted the help of someone else: the seven-year-old blacksmith boy, pumping the bellows. This contravened the rule which said riders were not allowed to receive outside assistance, although the penalty was scant punishment considering the mishap had already cost him more than three hours. Christophe fixed his bike and continued to finish the stage at Bagnères de Luchon. Christophe never won the Tour during his career, and would suffer the same unfortunate mishap in the Alps in the 1922 edition. However the events of 9 July 1913 would cement his place in the annals of cycling history.

1926 Lucien BUYSSE

Stage 10 of the 1926 Tour de France has gone down in history as about as bad as the Tour ever gets. On a mammoth 326km stage, riders left Bayonne for Bagnères de Luchon in the early hours of the morning in cold rain. Over the climbs of the "Circle of Death" it only got worse – freezing fog and sodden tracks slowed progress and were described afterwards as *dantesque*: hellish. A rider called Gustave Van Slembrouck was in the lead but his Tour was to come unstuck in the mud as the Belgian Lucien Buysse, riding the Tour with his two brothers Jules and Michel, attacked almost from the gun. Still grieving from the news earlier in the race that his daughter had died, Buysse stretched his lead in the sleet over the Col du Tourmalet and rode alone over the Aspin and Peyresourde, arriving in Bagnères de Luchon over 25 minutes clear of his nearest rival and almost two hours ahead of Van Slembrouck, catapulting him into yellow that he would retain until Paris. Buysse's average for his day in hell was just 18.9kmh; riders behind him found shelter in bars and even took lifts in cars just to make it to the finish as search parties were launched in order to account for all the riders.

1947 René VIETTO

In 1947 René Vietto was the standout favourite and the home nation's best chance of victory. He was a popular rider too – he had famously sacrificed his chances in the 1934 race by handing his bike to team leader Antonin Magne, and a photograph of him sitting on a stone wall in tears remains an icon of the Tour. He attacked on stage two of the 1947 race to take an early lead. Vietto was one of the Tour's best ever pure climbers, and through the Alps and then the Pyrenees he stoutly defended his lead, narrowly avoiding a plane crash on the Col du Tourmalet on stage 15. The light aircraft, chartered by French newspaper and then Tour owners *l'Equipe*, was being used as a spotter plane but came down just metres from the road; two reporters were pulled from the wreckage and both survived. The winner on that day was Jean Robic, who wouldn't be a threat overall until the final stage where he infiltrated a break and won the race overall. These days such tactics on the final stage are all but unheard of, with an unwritten rule stopping riders from attacking the yellow jersey. By that point Vietto was out of contention; he had held on to the lead until the penultimate stage, a brutal 139km time trial where he lost 15 minutes and, with it, the Tour.

2010 Alberto CONTADOR

The Tour was treated to a duel in the mist on the second consecutive stage to feature the Col du Tourmalet in 2010, marking 100 years since the first visit to the mountains. On the summit finish at the col from the western ascent via Luz Saint Saveur, having first crossed the Col de Marie Blanque and Col du Solour, Andy Schleck and Alberto Contador went head to head, with the Luxembourgeois Schleck trying in vain time after time to attack and distance the Spaniard, who was in the yellow jersey. Side by side, their breathless ascent in the close, dramatic atmosphere of the Tourmalet with Schleck in pure white and Contador in bright yellow is one of the most memorable moments of modern Tours. Schleck won the stage by a whisker but, with two sprint stages and a time trial remaining, Contador (the stronger time triallist) had all but sealed the Tour. Or so he thought. It later transpired that Contador had returned a positive doping test in Pau the day before the stage to the Tourmalet. The Spaniard protested that the presence of the steroid clenbuterol in his urine sample was due to the consumption of contaminated beef. Regardless, Contador was stripped of the 2010 Tour title in 2012, with the honours passing to Schleck.

Col d'Aubisque

1709m

Length: **30.1km**
Start: **455m**
Ascent: **1254m**

Stunning, endlessly changing and deceptively difficult, the Col d'Aubisque is a climb whose blood courses thick with Pyrenean pedigree. Yet with that physical perfection comes a slightly crazy temperament and a tendency towards engendering the unpredictable. The Col d'Aubisque has borne witness to some of the most dramatic and memorable moments in Tour history.

❝ Vous êtes assassins! ❞
Octave Lapize

Wim Van Est didn't start the 1951 Tour de France with the knowledge that by the end of it his face would be selling watches. But then that's what surviving a 70m drop down a ravine while leading the Tour can do for you.

Despite abandoning that year's race Van Est, the first Dutchman to wear the yellow jersey, became the face of advertisements for Pontiac watches with the slogan "Seventy metres deep I dropped, my heart stood still but my Pontiac never stopped."

Ever since Van Est miraculously survived his fall off the edge while descending the mountain at speed, there has been a tradition of dramatic and even bizarre things taking place when the Tour de France has tackled the Col d'Aubisque.

Whether featuring as the final climb on Eddy Merckx's unparalleled solo ride to Mourenx in 1969, as the place where Bernard Thévenet lost his senses in 1972, or indeed as the final sordid hurrah of the soon to be disgraced Michael Rasmussen in 2007, the Col d'Aubisque has frequently set the scene for some of the more unusual acts in Tour history.

The race has been riding the Aubisque ever since 1910, when the pass was the penultimate climb in the very first Pyrenean stage. It was here that Octave Lapize famously derided his taskmasters as murderers, crying "Vous êtes assassins!" The race has been back regularly ever since,

crossing the Aubisque or the nearby Col du Soulor 92 times since that first visit.

But the Aubisque is very different in nature from its neighbours to the east, the Col du Tourmalet, the Col d'Aspin and the Col de Peyresourde. Rather than being a straightforward east–west passage across the mountains, the Aubisque is a jumbled collection of peaks and valleys that trickle down from the 2,613m Pic de Ger, which dominates the southern skyline.

From the west, the climb begins in Laruns and rises almost 1,200m over 16.6 kilometres, giving a tough average gradient of 7.2%. Following on from a deceptively easy opening few kilometres, the western ascent features the steepest section of the whole climb: a sudden jolt at 13% alongside the Cascade du Valentin as the road climbs out of Eaux Bonnes. From then on the tarmac seldom drops below 8% as it winds its way past the Gourette ski station and onwards to the pass.

From the east, the 19.5km road rises from Argelès Gazost in a series of steps; first it hops out of town to Arrens Marsous before cutting its way back and forth up a mountainside to the Col de Soulor. It then heads downhill for two kilometres shortly before the final rise to the Aubisque itself via the jaw-dropping Cirque du Litor. Even within these large stages, riding the road is like navigating a little trawler through stormy

seas in the Bay of Biscay. Waves of asphalt roll in one after another; just when riders think they've got into some sort of rhythm, they are hit by another barrage of swell and thrown off course.

The road can of course be on the receiving end of those very storms. As the westernmost of the high Pyrenean passes used by the Tour, the Col d'Aubisque is less than 100 kilometres away from the sea and the very worst weather systems of the Atlantic. The higher altitudes are often a damp, misty and dark place to be.

When the fog clears, the landscape at the 1,709m pass reveals itself to be a labyrinth of peaks, valleys and swirling rock strata. Overhead, eagles soar into caverns and beyond cliff edges, while semi-wild horses and cattle graze the idyllic meadows that sit perched alongside the highest point.

Frankly, these sweet green fields are an incongruous ending for such an unpredictable and, at times, hostile climb. The Pyrenees have a reputation as a wild environment, but of all the *hors catégorie* climbs in the range, the Col d'Aubisque must be the wildest of the lot.

Opposite: The swirling peaks of the Western Pyrenees look on as the Tour de France peloton climbs to the Col d'Aubisque in the baking July sunshine.

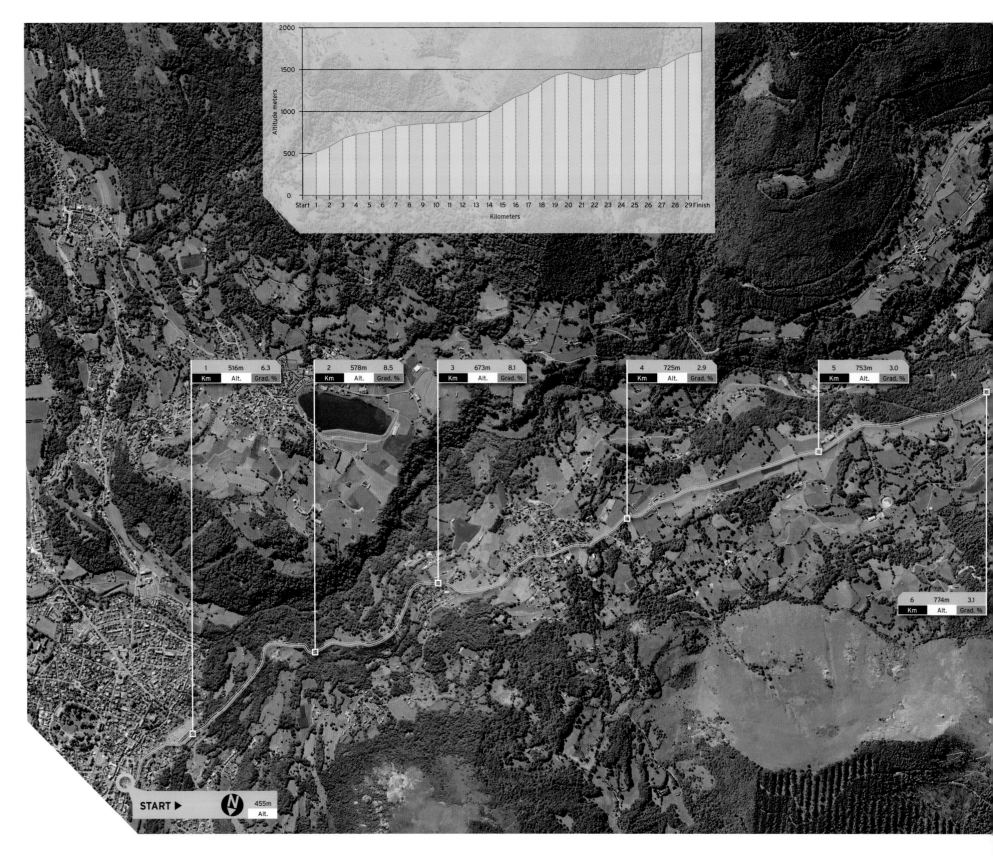

Altitude meters

2000

1500

1000

500

0

Start 1 2 3 4 5 6 7 8 9 10 11 12 13 14 15 16 17 18 19 20 21 22 23 24 25 26 27 28 29 Finish

Kilometers

Km	1	Alt. 516m	Grad. % 6.3

Km	2	Alt. 578m	Grad. % 8.5

Km	3	Alt. 673m	Grad. % 8.1

Km	4	Alt. 725m	Grad. % 2.9

Km	5	Alt. 753m	Grad. % 3.0

Km	6	Alt. 774m	Grad. % 3.1

START ▶

N

455m
Alt.

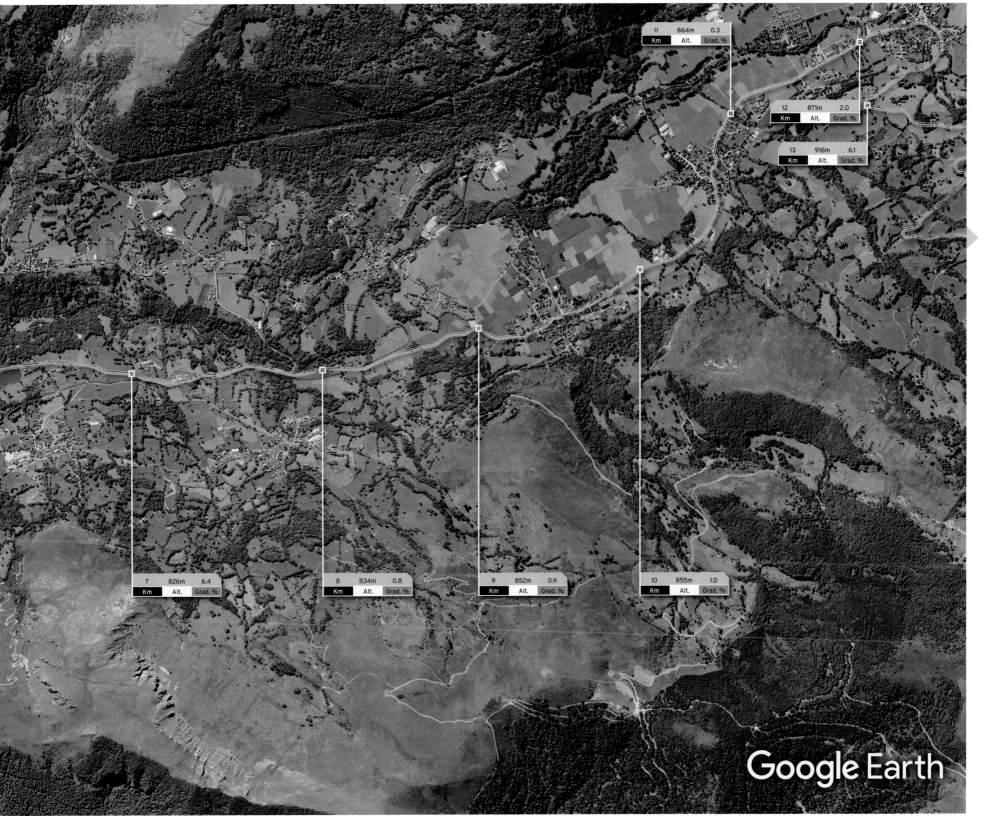

11	864m	0.3
Km	Alt.	Grad. %

12	871m	2.0
Km	Alt.	Grad. %

13	916m	6.1
Km	Alt.	Grad. %

7	826m	6.4
Km	Alt.	Grad. %

8	834m	0.8
Km	Alt.	Grad. %

9	852m	0.9
Km	Alt.	Grad. %

10	855m	1.0
Km	Alt.	Grad. %

Google Earth

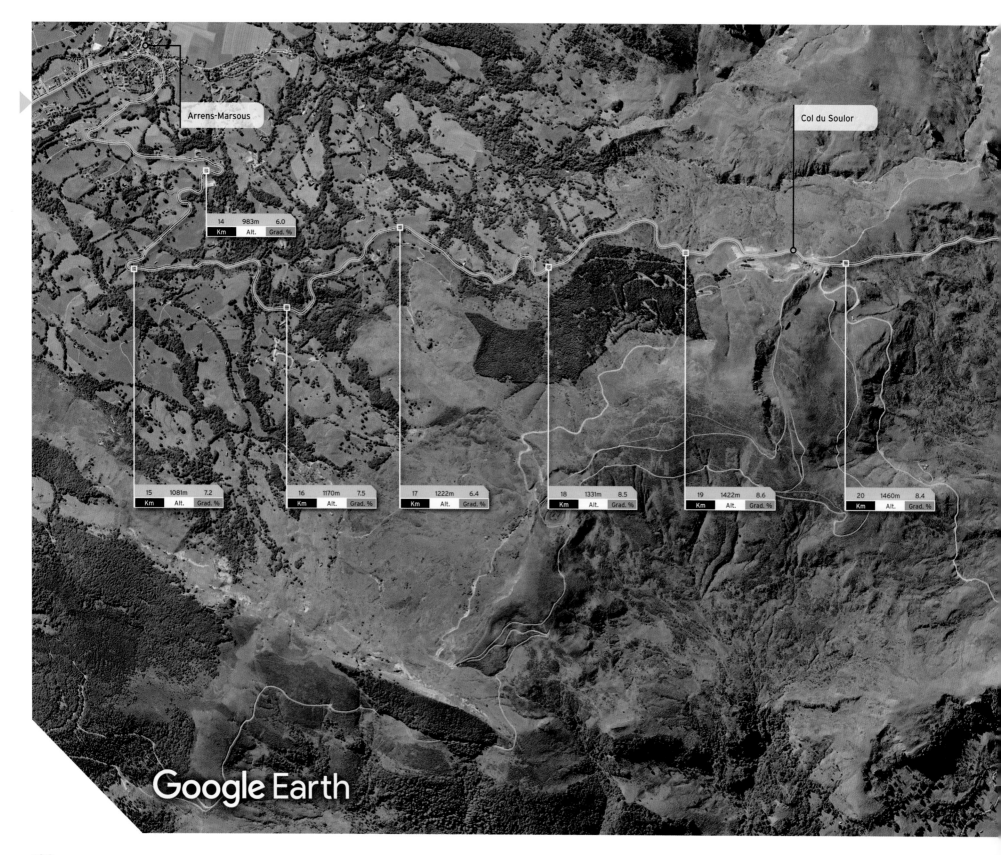

Arrens-Marsous

Col du Soulor

14	983m	6.0
Km	Alt.	Grad. %

15	1081m	7.2
Km	Alt.	Grad. %

16	1170m	7.5
Km	Alt.	Grad. %

17	1222m	6.4
Km	Alt.	Grad. %

18	1331m	8.5
Km	Alt.	Grad. %

19	1422m	8.6
Km	Alt.	Grad. %

20	1460m	8.4
Km	Alt.	Grad. %

Google Earth

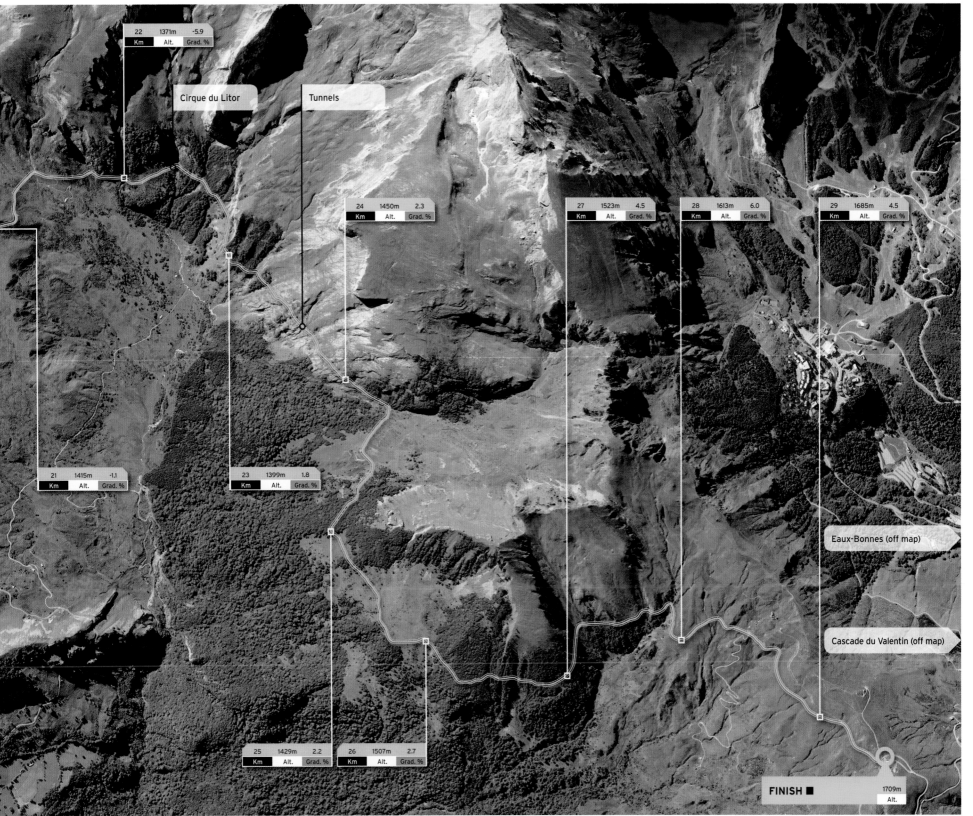

Cirque du Litor

Tunnels

22	1371m	-5.9
Km	Alt.	Grad. %

24	1450m	2.3
Km	Alt.	Grad. %

27	1523m	4.5
Km	Alt.	Grad. %

28	1613m	6.0
Km	Alt.	Grad. %

29	1685m	4.5
Km	Alt.	Grad. %

21	1415m	-1.1
Km	Alt.	Grad. %

23	1399m	1.8
Km	Alt.	Grad. %

Eaux-Bonnes (off map)

Cascade du Valentin (off map)

25	1429m	2.2
Km	Alt.	Grad. %

26	1507m	2.7
Km	Alt.	Grad. %

FINISH ■	1709m
	Alt.

Route to the Summit

The Col d'Aubisque takes riders on a real journey. What starts as a gentle road meandering through a landscape of peaceful agrarian surroundings slowly metamorphoses into a sublime notch of asphalt clinging on to a barren cliff face.

CIRQUE DU LITOR

◀ Cirque du Litor

Perhaps one of the most magnificent sights in the Tour de France is that of the peloton slowly making its way along the Cirque du Litor. Here a narrow vein of road runs like a lode of precious mineral through the vast grey-brown side of a natural bowl gouged out by glaciers millennia ago. The road curves in and out of the little valley formed by the Arriou de l'Escala stream, running northwest from the Col du Soulor towards the Col d'Aubisque. The road was built in the 1860s to link the spa towns of the Pyrenees, and the relatively steady gradients of the current road avoided a steep drop down from the Aubisque. The Cirque du Litor is more commonly home to flocks of mountain sheep, whose milk goes to make the local *brebis* cheese. Around and about, above road level and below it, vultures and eagles circle in the huge cavern of air. The road itself is actually a very easy climb, averaging no more than 3% for the four kilometres out of the nadir between the Aubisque and Soulor.

Left: *Eagles soar over the Cirque du Litor.*

Arrens Marsous

The village of Arrens marks the beginning of the toughest kilometres of the eastern ascent of the Col d'Aubisque; the road turns right out of the Gave d'Azun valley and begins to switch back and forth up the uncomfortably hot south-facing slopes to the Col du Soulor. It also marks a physical transition, where the calm and sheltered agricultural surroundings of fields and farmyards begin to turn into the windswept and barren environment of the high mountains.

Opposite: Three giant bikes stand alongside the Col d'Aubisque.   Above left: The road to the col coils around the contours of the land.   Above right: A series of tunnels lead to the pass from the eastern ascent via the Col du Soulor.

◀ Finish

The summit of the Col d'Aubisque offers, on a good day, some of the finest views in the Pyrenees. Directly south is the Pic de Ger, while southwest lies the swirling rocky mass of the Pic du Midi d'Ossau. North, either side of the Soum de Grum, the landscape drops away towards the plains, the Adour valley and the town of Pau. This pretty town in the shadow of the Pyrenees has welcomed the Tour 67 times in its history, which places it third overall behind Paris and Bordeaux for the hosting of stage starts and finishes. From either direction, the climb of the Aubisque begins to ease off over the pass, which is a rounded-off meadow rather than a sharp crest like the Col du Tourmalet. The final kilometres from west and east both average around 6%, allowing riders a final fast surge to the summit. Perched on the top is a squat chalet, and alongside it sits a battered concrete mile-marker plus a trio of giant steel bikes in yellow, green and polka dot. With the road dropping away out of sight to the west, they make quite a sight and demonstrate the central role cycling has played in the history of this pass.

Left: The top of the pass is a gentle finish to the climb.

Cascade du Valentin

A picture postcard viewpoint on the western slopes from Eaux Bonnes, the Valentin waterfall was a popular beauty spot for early tourists, who came to this part of the Pyrenees in the late nineteenth century to bask in the fresh mountain air and romantic surroundings. These days the waterfall is all but obscured from the road by a curtain of trees, but the sound of falling water still marks the point where the climb gets steepest, with a section at 13%.

Eaux Bonnes

The road as we know it across the Col d'Aubisque was initially constructed (in dirt and gravel) to link the nascent spa towns in the Pyrenees with one another, although shepherds and muleteers had been crossing this chain of mountains on foot and on horseback for many centuries before that. Eaux-Bonnes is one such spa town, albeit a relatively small one, and features the neo-gothic architecture typical across the region. The name means "good waters".

Tunnels

Wet, unlit and several hundred metres long; the tunnels shortly before the Col d'Aubisque on the eastern side are, for the Tour, a brief inconvenience at worst. Perhaps they even offer welcome respite from the bright sun. Going downhill, however, they are something else entirely. Flying off the col at speeds of 80kmh, riders enter the tunnel flat out in a long line and have no time for their eyes to adjust to the light. A false move on the grimy, greasy roads could spell disaster.

The Mountain Kings

From falling into a ravine to forgetting altogether where you are, it seems riders of the Tour de France who have set out to make their way up and over the Col d'Aubisque can scarcely do so without something out of the ordinary taking place.

1951 Wim VAN EST

A track racing star in his native Holland, Wim Van Est was a stocky, powerful rider whose rugged features appeared always to be turned upwards into a smile. Nobody expected this gentle giant to don the leader's yellow jersey in the 1951 Tour., but that's exactly what he did after winning the 12th stage from Agen to Dax. The following day Van Est set about the impossible task of defending his lead over the high Pyrenees. It was his first experience of the mountains, and having already lost several minutes to a lead group by the summit Col d'Aubisque he fell twice on the high-speed descent, the second time tumbling around 70m down a ravine. "When I fell I kicked my bike away and held my hands over my head," he later recalled. Miraculously Van Est survived – riders before and since have been hurt much more after falling much less – and the first people on the scene saw him scrambling up the mountainside, crying in shock and relief. Using their spare tyres, his support team and nearby fans cobbled together a makeshift rope and hauled Van Est back to the roadside. Owing to the extent of his injuries, Van Est didn't continue the Tour. Nor did his Dutch team – the recovery operation had reportedly ruined all their spare tyres.

1972 Bernard THÉVENET

The Frenchman and future double Tour winner crashed heavily with three other riders during the seventh stage of the 1972 Tour while descending the Aubisque via the Col du Soulor. Apparently unhurt save for a few grazes, Thévenet continued onwards to Pau before turning back to his team car and his Peugeot team *directeur sportif* and asking the somewhat odd question of where exactly he was. "In the Tour," came the reply. It later transpired that Thévenet had suffered concussion, no doubt exacerbated by the lack of helmets in the professional peloton during the 1970s. Those that did exist were little more than leather caps stuffed with padding: unthinkably crude and unprotective by today's standards but unthinkably hot and stuffy according to the riders of the time. Thévenet had at least figured out that he was in France and pulled out the stage map from his jersey pocket to remind himself of the remainder of the day's riding. However, the Col d'Aubisque became Thévenet's forgotten climb; he told the race doctor that evening that he would have struggled to finish the stage had the race climbed the Aubisque. Not wanting to upset his patient, the doctor simply nodded and went along with it.

1985 Stephen ROCHE

Twenty-four hours after the famous deception on Luz Ardiden which prevented Greg LeMond from riding to win the Tour, the American recalled physically pushing Bernard Hinault up the Col d'Aubisque. The climb was the summit finish to one of the shortest road stages in the history of the Tour, the 52.5km 18th stage of the 1985 edition from Luz Saint Sauveur to the summit of the Col d'Aubisque. Remarkably that very afternoon the Tour drove down the western ascent to Laruns in order to do it all again, riding 83.5km up and over the Aubisque on its way a finish in the town of Pau. The winner of the summit finish atop the Aubisque was Stephen Roche, an Irishman who would go on to win the Tour outright two years later in 1987 on his way to the rare "triple crown" of cycling: the Giro d'Italia, Tour de France and world championships. Roche was a real threat in 1985 and his stage win helped him finish third overall. A relatively revolutionary piece of technology helped him too: his skinsuit. Roche became one of the first riders to wear a tight-fitting one-piece garment on the 18th stage of that year's race and, unlike short split mountain stages, that is one idea that took off, even if it took nearly 30 years to do so.

2007 Michael RASMUSSEN

In 2007 the Col d'Aubisque finally got its day in the limelight with a summit finish on stage 16, only the second in the history of the climb. However, the attention was wrongly stolen by the villain of the story, Michael Rasmussen, who won the stage but was then chucked off the Tour de France in disgrace. The morning had already seen minor protests following the booting out of Alexandre Vinokourov and his Astana team following a positive test for a homologous blood transfusion. The Dane nicknamed "The Chicken" because of his pale, skinny frame that looked like a scrawny, plucked bird, started the day in the yellow jersey. Winning the stage should have been the crowning glory of his career – a solo stage win that, owing to it being the final mountain stage, would have all but secured the overall Tour title. However, it emerged that evening that Rasmussen had missed several anti-doping tests in the previous year and allegedly lied about his whereabouts to anti-doping testers. The evidence warranted dismissal from his team and the Tour; before the *gendarmerie* managed to make it to his hotel that evening to haul him in for questioning, their bird had already flown, bundled out in a car in the dead of night to ignominy and disgrace.

Col du Soulor

So often overshadowed by the Col d'Aubisque, the bigger half of the set of conjoined twins, the Col du Soulor is a hidden Pyrenean pearl. However, it shouldn't be any other way; this climb's modesty is all part of its charm.

The Col du Soulor is a rare unspoilt remainder of the Pyrenees' rural past. It's the closest that modern-day Tour de France riders can come to going back in time and experiencing the sights, sounds and smells of mountain climbing in the early days of the Tour.

So often the gateway climb to the Col d'Aubisque, the Soulor sits 10.1 kilometres to the east of the Aubisque pass, and if the Tour de France wants to cross the Aubisque, it has to cross the Soulor. Whenever it does so, the Soulor doesn't receive a classification. It is subsumed into the Aubisque, resting in its shadow, which tends to obscure its own distinctiveness and character.

The toughest sections of the entire climb of the Aubisque from the east come just before the Col du Soulor as the road climbs steeply up a south-facing ledge. However, the Tour doesn't have to cross the Aubisque in order to climb the Soulor. The col is a meeting point for a third road from the north, and it's this road that is so unique. The road ascends tranquil, grassy slopes and winds its way up the natural path of least resistance, which makes it such a shame that the Soulor has only featured 20 times as a stand-alone climb in the Tour.

The route begins in the village of Arthez d'Asson and climbs 22 kilometres up the Ouzon valley at an average of 4.9%. However, like a half-pipe in a skate park, the gradient slowly increases as the road approaches the high pass at 1,474m. It increases to 7% in the former mining village of Ferrières after 10 kilometres, and then to 9% in Arbéost 4km later. It's a tricky proposition for any rider, and the climb is awarded either first category or *hors catégorie* status in the Tour when it does warrant its own rank.

That said, its role as a preparatory climb for bigger challenges that lie further down the line of mountain stages means that few exploits of renown have taken place on its slopes. But serving as an appetizer, a crucial warm-up on the toughest days in the mountains, is what gives the Soulor its charm. It's a place that likes to be out of the spotlight and off the beaten track, and that wild feel extends to the weather too. The col marks the border between the regions of the Hautes Pyrénées to the east and the Pyrénées Atlantiques to the west, and frequently the cool, damp conditions of the latter can roll in off the sea and shroud the Aubisque and Soulor in mist.

Despite the relatively busy collection of chalets at the col itself, part of the climb's charm is the complete absence of ski stations and spa towns. Indeed there is no real reason for anyone to ascend the road, other than to reach the col itself or for the sheer pleasure afforded by its sumptuous, sweeping bends.

Pla d'Adet

1680m

Length: 10.7km
Start: 825m
Ascent: 855m

Short, sharp and steep; Pla d'Adet is a long way from being the longest or the highest climb in the Tour de France but there's a good reason why it is one of the hardest.

"Pla d'Adet is the kingdom of Raymond Poulidor where he would accomplish, along those ten breathtaking kilometres, one of his greatest ever achievements."

Christian Laborde, French author

Pla d'Adet is a climb that looks as if it shouldn't be there. The ski station at the summit above the town of Saint Lary Soulan is cut off from the valleys around it by steep rock faces rising up from the valley floor. It acts like a wall that must be scaled before access to the plateau can be gained, but that's exactly what the road does.

Ascending in two almost dead straight lines north and then southwest, the first four kilometres of the road follow a ledge that looks to have been slashed into the bare rock. There are few places in cycling where the forces of gravity are so obviously on display.

It's an intimidating sight, in particular from the cable car that links the town with the summit in a steep straight line and affords the best view over the climb in its entirety. It's clear from such a bird's eye view that although it runs for only 10.7 kilometres, Pla d'Adet is one of the hardest climbs in cycling.

It is steep – with an average gradient of over 8% – and features steeper sections approaching 12% at regular intervals. It is brutally exposed to the wind that whips around the cliffs and valleys. When the road heads up the gulley by the village of Espiaube and out on to the Crête de Coudet, surrounded by a crown of Pyrenean peaks, the mid-afternoon sun turns it into a crucible. According to some, it is the hardest climb in the Pyrenees.

Since 1974 it has hosted nine summit finishes in the Tour, which puts it third on the all-time list, behind Alpe d'Huez and Puy de Dôme. The latter is now closed to bikes, which means it should be only a matter of time before Pla d'Adet moves up to number two. There's no chance of it being anything other than a finish – the dead-end road effectively ends at the cliff edge overlooking Saint Lary. So close is it to the town (and so unusual the climb's name) that the ski station is prosaically known as Saint Lary 1700, while the Tour generally calls the finish Saint Lary-Pla d'Adet.

The Tour uncovered Pla d'Adet during a period where it was looking for exciting, new, modern destinations to spice up the race, and it couldn't have got off to a better start in life. Alongside the spectacular views afforded across the Aure valley, the first summit finish saw a stage victory for French favourite Raymond Poulidor (affectionately known as "Poupou") at the expense of the "unbeatable" Eddy Merckx.

Poulidor, whose tanned, lean face and pointy features were accentuated by pitch-black eyebrows and sideburns (this was the 1970s, remember), attacked at the foot of the climb, put two minutes into the Belgian and took what would be his seventh and final Tour stage at the age of 38. It was a rare moment of excitement for the French public in a Tour

stifled by Merckx and his team, and a moment which still resonates today. In 2013 a plaque marking Poulidor's attack was unveiled in advance of its 40th anniversary. "At this point he launched a decisive attack to a solo victory at Pla d'Adet. At 38 years old he finished second in the Tour de France," it reads.

Never mind that Merckx won his record-equalling fifth Tour by over eight minutes, after limiting his losses on Pla d'Adet when Poulidor really ought to have attacked earlier and genuinely threatened his yellow jersey. The home public love to look back through rose-tinted spectacles at a rare moment where one of their riders could come close to "The Cannibal". As a rider Poulidor was nothing if not defensive, and perhaps it was the thought of the tough climb to Pla d'Adet, then a complete unknown, that stopped him from attacking earlier.

Nevertheless, the fearsome locale has cemented its place in the Tour de France. It was where Poupou won his last stage, and where he cracked the uncrackable Eddy Merckx. Anything capable of doing that is worthy of its place in the pantheon of great Tour climbs.

Opposite: All eyes – at home and on the roadside – are on the yellow jersey of Vincenzo Nibali as he keenly marks his rivals on the steep slopes to Pla d'Adet.

Google Earth

Saint Lary Soulan

Vignec

START ▶ 806m
Alt.

Vielle Aure

1   885m   6.8
Km   Alt.   Grad. %

Cutaway road

2   990m   9.9
Km   Alt.   Grad. %

3   1091m   10.1
Km   Alt.   Grad. %

4   1183m   9.7
Km   Alt.   Grad. %

Pla d'Adet

FINISH ■

	1680m
	Alt.

10	1625m	7.1
Km	Alt.	Grad. %

9	1560	8.0
Km	Alt.	Grad. %

8	1493m	3.4
Km	Alt.	Grad. %

7	1449m	10.9
Km	Alt.	Grad. %

Espiaube

5	1280m	8.7
Km	Alt.	Grad. %

6	1353m	7.8
Km	Alt.	Grad. %

Altitude meters

2000

1500

1000

500

Start 1 2 3 4 5 6 7 8 9 10 Finish

Kilometers

Route to the Summit

Right from the very first kilometre, the road to Pla d'Adet starts off hard and doesn't get easier until the finish line is in sight. Heading north out of Saint Lary Soulan the road begins climbing almost immediately and, with no easy introduction, gaps in the peloton very quickly start to appear.

CUTAWAY ROAD

◄ Cutaway road
Arguably the toughest section of the climb comes in the opening four kilometres where the road is cut into the rock face to escape the Aure valley and ascend towards the ski stations. After a relatively gentle opening kilometre, in the climb's next three kilometres the road ascends 300m at an average of 10%. However, this only tells half the story; more than a kilometre is over 12% and a further 500m are at 11%. What's worse is that besides one big hairpin offering a slight visual respite, the road is dead straight and rears up in front of riders, offering nowhere to hide. The south-facing rock reflects the hot sun on to them, and being so close to the bottom of the climb at a relatively low 800m, riders don't benefit from the refreshing coolness that comes with altitude. It's only after four kilometres that the road doubles back on itself twice over two hairpins, turning its back on the steepest ramps and curving ever so slightly west.

Left: The toughest part of the climb comes early on.

Saint Lary Soulan
Sitting on La Neste d'Aure river, in winter Saint Lary Soulan is one of the bigger skiing resorts in the Pyrenees. It doesn't quite possess the same traditional charm as Bagnères de Luchon to the east and sits on one of the few roads to cross over the Pyrenees and into Spain. This valley road is notorious for turning into one enormous car park whenever the Tour comes to visit as the fans, holiday-makers and everyone involved in the Tour all attempt to travel back down the valley.

Opposite: Raymond Poulidor drops Eddy Merckx to win on the Tour's first visit to Pla d'Adet in 1974. Above left: The 2005 Tour peloton squeezes past the campervans and fans towards the top of Pla d'Adet. Above right: Lance Armstrong battles to hold the wheel of Ivan Basso, also in 2005.

PLA D'ADET TOP

◄ Pla d'Adet top

The summit of Pla d'Adet is actually less than a kilometre as the crow flies from the town at the foot of the climb, Saint Lary Soulan. However, it is 861m higher up, located artificially (and slightly perilously) on the edge of a cliff. It's a typical small ski station: a busy collection of chalets, hotels and bars clustered around the limited flat space at the summit. In fact the locale is so small that it has a hard time hosting the Tour de France these days; the accoutrements of the finish line are crammed into the narrow street, the enormous publicity caravan has to perch itself on a series of angled gravel tracks around the finish area, while the cavalcade of press and VIP vehicles has to park at the base in Saint Lary Soulan, which means taking the cable car up. The road becomes fairly flat as it reaches this brief plateau, and apart from a small ramp of 9% for a few hundred metres, the final four kilometres of the climb begin to level out with an average of approximately 5%.

Left: The ski station at the top of Pla d'Ade can barely cope with the Tour de Franace's entourage.

Espiaube

Up the rock ledge and through the village of Soulan, the climb skirts the right bank of the Ruisseau de Saint Jacques stream. At Espiaube the road bends 180 degrees left to cross the stream and head south to Pla d'Adet. However, a right-hand turn off the main road heads west to the Col du Portet, a high mountain road reaching 2,215m but too narrow to ever have featured in the Tour. After a series of tight switchbacks this road loops back around to Lac de l'Oule, making for a popular circuit for cyclo-tourists.

Vignec

The official start of the climb, Vignec is not a particularly remarkable or picturesque village. It sits just outside Saint Lary Soulan and from this point, as riders pass the campsites, chalets, refurbished old buildings and closed ski rental shops, the first part of the climb is almost entirely visible. If riders had forgotten just how hard Pla d'Adet is, there can be no mistaking it now. Behind them, riders would be able to sense the very summit leaning over them, although a glance would only show it silhouetted in the sun.

Vielle Aure

Located beside the bright, bleached grey stone at the very foot of the imposing rocky face of the Coume de Trauassere, residents in the hamlet of Vielle Aure used to make a living mining slate and manganese from the tunnels dug into the mountainside. Nowadays the mines are closed, but there's a little museum preserving the tunnels and objects of interest, located just off the road to the summit of Pla d'Adet a kilometre or so out of Vignec. The road rises rapidly along the rock face, making this certainly no easy introduction to the climb.

The Mountain Kings

Whether it is the last hurrah of a Tour de France icon, the crowning achievement of a climbing great or the emergence of a new Tour hero, a short and sharp summit finish on Pla d'Adet has seldom failed to produce legendary performances.

1974 Daniel **MANGEAS**

One man who remembers well the first time the Tour de France visited Pla d'Adet is Daniel Mangeas, not a rider but the speaker of the Tour for 40 years beginning on 15 July 1974. That day the car belonging to the Tour's existing announcer overheated and broke down in the broiling Pyrenean sun, while Mangeas made it to the finish with the publicity caravan. "Albert Bouvet [the Tour organizer] found me on Pla d'Adet at the finish and said there is nobody available to be commentator, you have to commentate," Mangeas recalled. He saw Raymond Poulidor, the "eternal second", finally take advantage of a rare weakness in Eddy Merckx to win the stage and reclaim time overall. As was often the case in his career, Poulidor left it too late to make any meaningful inroads on Merckx's lead and the Belgian went on to win his fifth Tour. Mangeas never missed a Tour stage from that day onwards, until finally hanging up his Tour microphone at the end of the 2014 race. However, his distinctive commentary at stage starts and finishes has become an aural hallmark of the modern-day Tour.

1976 Lucien **VAN IMPE**

Stage 14 of the 1976 edition won the Tour de France for Lucien Van Impe, his first and last overall victory in the race. Potent rider (and former winner) Luis Ocaña had attacked early on the stage and was soon joined by Van Impe, although only after the Belgian was threatened with being run down by his team manager Cyrille Guimard, sat behind him at the wheel of the team car, if he didn't do so. The pair worked well over the Col de Peyresourde and on the flat approach to Pla d'Adet, while behind them Joop Zoetemelk, the closest threat overall, played a dangerously defensive game. Van Impe blew Ocaña away on the final summit finish, taking the stage and the yellow jersey. It was one of the Belgian's greatest rides, and proof that on his day there was nobody in the world who could climb as well as he could. Despite a breathless chase it was too little too late for Zoetemelk; his reluctance had cost him over three minutes and all but handed the Tour to his Belgian rival. He came second in Paris, the third of six times that he would do so in his career.

1981 Phil **ANDERSON**

A newspaper in Phil Anderson's hometown of Melbourne described his feat on Pla d'Adet in 1981 as "like a 19-year-old cricketer from Rome taking 10 wickets at Lord's". Those words give an indication of the surprise caused when the 23-year-old Anderson clung on to Bernard Hinault's wheel on the agonizing climb to become the first Australian – indeed the first man from outside Europe – to pull on the yellow jersey of leader of the Tour. Riding his first edition, Anderson was supposed to be looking after his team leader Jean-René Bernaudeau but accidentally found himself in the lead group, minutes ahead of him. His team boss gave the Australian the green light to ride for himself and, pumped up with youthful energy, he set about doing so, hanging on to the Frenchman. He only fully realized the scale of his achievement a good while afterwards. Anderson lost the jersey to Hinault – a man who certainly enjoyed putting riders back in their rightful place – after the following day's time trial but rode to tenth overall that year; and went on to take two fifth places later in his career.

2014 Rafal **MAJKA**

Rafal Majka only found out he would be riding the 2014 Tour a few days before the race began; and despite it being his first Tour start, he wasn't best pleased about it. The Pole, then 24, had ridden to sixth in the Giro d'Italia and feared the impact of the fatigue on his health and future career. However, he was handed a free rein to look after himself in the opening fortnight of the race. Fortunately it meant he could sidestep the constant battling that marked out the opening week; the result was a rider with still relatively fresh legs as the race hit the Pyrenees, allowing him to make dangerous breakaway moves. That was how he won stage 17, even managing a cheeky wink to the cameras as he knew the victory was in the bag with a kilometre to go. The man who called him over the line was none other than Daniel Mangeas, returning at the end of his Tour commentary career to the place where it began. The points on offer at the summit set Majka on his way to becoming Poland's first King of the Mountains later that week in Paris. Not bad for a late call-up.

Luz Ardiden

1715m

Length: 14.7km
Start: 710m
Ascent: 1005m

The most perfect sequence of hairpins set amid the most perfect mountain landscape, the upper slopes of Luz Ardiden are a photographer's paradise. But the dramas that have unfolded prove that this Pyrenean pin-up is much more than just a pretty face.

> **"** Winning races takes patience and tactics, and to attack you have to have a certain amount of gas in the tank ... I knew it would come to the Tourmalet and Luz Ardiden. **"**
> *Greg LeMond*

Luz Ardiden is one of the most aesthetically pleasing climbs in the Tour de France. Looking down from the summit, the slither of tarmac takes the form of a spectacular series of hairpin bends appearing out of nowhere, often rising out of the mist.

The irregular bends that swirl around the contours of the Pic d'Ardiden are almost too good to be true. It's as if an image of a climb has been digitally enhanced to make an idealized, visually perfect piece of road. And it almost has been, in the sense that it was contrived. The road was only finished in 1975 to bring winter sports enthusiasts from the town of Luz Saint Sauveur to the ski station that gives the climb its name. This isn't a time-honoured pass between two valleys, born out of necessity and shaped by practical use; it is a road designed and built primarily with recreation in mind.

The image of the final few kilometres is the sort of vista that imprints itself on to the memory of Tour fans, offering a snapshot of the Pyrenees. In addition to the Tour the climb has twice hosted a finish of the Vuelta a España, the three-week Tour of Spain. If an alien landed on Earth and asked you to show it an example of cycle racing in the Pyrenees, Luz Ardiden would be a good place to start.

There's another image from Luz Ardiden indelibly etched on the minds of cycle racing fans: a photograph from the 2003 Tour. In it the yellow jersey of Lance Armstrong lies sideways on the ground, to his right is Iban Mayo, clad in bright orange, and behind them in turquoise green is Jan Ullrich. It's the sort of picture that art historians dream about, with so much symbolism and meaning to be inferred. The Texan is still awkwardly fixed to his bike – an odd position that suggests he hasn't quite realized what has happened to him, or refuses to accept it. His fragile Basque rival Mayo is flailing on the ground while Ullrich, riding behind on his all-black bike with a look of unbridled panic, is straining with every sinew to avoid the catastrophe.

Getting caught on the strap of a spectator's bag, which is what caused the crash, was the latest incident in a Tour which steadfastly refused to go Armstrong's way. Nevertheless, having stared down the barrel of the gun, Armstrong ultimately sealed his victory. That day, after dragging himself back up off the ground and chasing somewhat frantically to rejoin Ullrich, who out of respect had ridden a steady tempo rather than attacking, Armstrong then stuck in the knife and claimed 40 seconds on the German with a solo stage win. It was more than half of his final margin in Paris of 70 seconds, which was the closest Armstrong ever got to being beaten in any of his seven Tours – although the titles were stripped from him in 2013.

The climb's character is a good fit with Armstrong's: it is tough and unrelenting from start to finish. After riders have descended slightly out of Luz Saint Sauveur, the 14.7km ascent has an average gradient of 7.6% and a maximum of 12% in places. Unlike many climbs nearby, the gradient remains relatively constant the whole way up, hovering between 7 and 8% almost all the way to the top.

The climb has featured eight times in the Tour since 1985, the year of its first visit, and since the road doesn't lead anywhere other than the ski station it has always been a summit finish. It invariably comes after a long day on the mountains too; in order to get here riders will have climbed either the Col du Tourmalet to the west or the Col d'Aubisque to the east. Befitting of its place as one of the Tour's toughest climbs, Luz Ardiden has plenty of substance to go with its style.

Opposite: Fans fight for every last inch of space on the upper slopes of Luz Ardiden in anticipation of the arrival of the Tour de France.

Solférino c hapel

1	680m	-3.7
Km	Alt.	Grad. %

2	750m	5.8
Km	Alt.	Grad. %

3	800m	5.0
Km	Alt.	Grad. %

4	875m	7.5
Km	Alt.	Grad. %

START ▶	N	710m
		Alt.

Luz Saint Sauveur

Sazos

FINISH ■

	1715m	
	Alt.	

14	1669m	7.2
Km	Alt.	Grad. %

5	961m	8.6
Km	Alt.	Grad. %

6	1031m	7.0
Km	Alt.	Grad. %

8	1219m	8.9
Km	Alt.	Grad. %

9	1287m	6.8
Km	Alt.	Grad. %

13	1597m	5.8
Km	Alt.	Grad. %

12	1539m	7.9
Km	Alt.	Grad. %

10	1375m	8.7
Km	Alt.	Grad. %

11	1460m	8.5
Km	Alt.	Grad. %

7	1130m	9.9
Km	Alt.	Grad. %

Grust

Cureille Dessus

Google Earth

159

Route to the Summit

Having made its debut in 1985, Luz Ardiden is a relatively recent arrival on the scene at the Tour de France. However, this Pyrenean peak has quickly established a reputation as a scenic, perfectly located and of course gruellingly tough summit finish.

◀ Finish

Luz Ardiden might not have the snowy grandeur or sheer scale of some of its older, bigger neighbours. But what it lacks in height and heritage it more than makes up for in the stunning aesthetic of the road as it nears the 1,715m high summit. Rising out of the trees and into the open fields, the final few kilometres of road enter a natural amphitheatre and snake in and out of the mountainside's natural contours to create a stunning environment for a stage finish. On race day much of the roadside is filled with campervans and motorhomes, little white boxes tracing the route back down the mountain, although this doesn't detract from the fresh green hue to the vista. Across the horizon lies the Pic de Léviste, but the real visual treat is watching riders creep their way up in the distance on their passage to the summit. Of course if you're a rider yourself, looking ahead fills you with a very different type of anticipation, as you see just how far there is to go and realize how much suffering it will take to get there.

Left: Luz Ardiden is a natural amphitheatre.

Solférino chapel

The very first section of the road from Luz Saint Sauveur actually heads downhill; it's not until the road crosses the bridge over the Gave de Gavarnie river, precisely one kilometre out of town, that the climbing truly begins. This bridge is overlooked by the Solférino chapel, a simple stone church built with solid proportions and unfussy Romanesque architecture by Napoleon III to commemorate victory over the Italians at the Battle of Solférino in 1859. The actual town of Solférino is hundreds of miles away near Lake Garda in northern Italy.

Opposite: Like a bull to a red flag, Samuel Sanchez of the Basque Euskaltel team charges towards the Basque flag on Luz Ardiden in 2011. His stage win sent the local fans crazy.   Above left: The 2003 Tour and Lance Armstrong and Iban Mayo are brought down by a spectator's bag strap as Jan Ullrich swerves to avoid the carnage. The Texan would remount and win the stage.   Above right: The little town of Luz Saint Sauveur is the starting point for the climb to Luz Ardiden.

◀ Luz Saint Sauveur

Luz is derived from the word for light, and the town sits in a triangular confluence of three valleys, affording it a lot more sun and warmth than its surrounding environment. However, in the summer of 2013 the town was affected by devastating floods cascading down the valley, sweeping away many of the main valley roads and causing extensive damage. The town has a long history of hosting the Tour de France, although usually as a brief bypass on the way up or down the Col du Tourmalet, to the east via Barèges, or the Col d'Aubisque further away to the west. From the Tourmalet, a common approach to Luz Ardiden, the road takes a sharp left in the very centre of town, heading on a brief and gentle downhill where the mountain about to be climbed is visible dead ahead. With over 1,000m of vertical ascent, it's a sobering sight for riders of the Tour.

Left: Luz Saint Sauveur is a bright crossroads in the Pyrenees.

Sazos

The first few kilometres of Luz Ardiden are almost dead straight, apart from a turn by the Solférino chapel, but at the hamlet of Sazos the first hairpin bends appear. The road also shifts up a gear, turning for two kilometres from a tough but manageable 6.5% to a distinctly tricky 8%. While the first few kilometres of the climb are surrounded by trees, entering the settlement affords the first views over towards the Hautacam to the northwest or back east towards the valley leading to the Col du Tourmalet.

Grust

At the village of Grust, which sits 999m above sea level, comes the first leg-breaking section of the climb. Hitting 10% average for a kilometre (but with sections on the tight hairpin bends nearing 12%), the stretch is enough to start cracking the weaker riders in the field – although by this point riders who aren't climbing specialists will already be in quite a bit of difficulty. It was here that Lance Armstrong made his stage-winning move in 2003, following and then countering the Spanish climber Iban Mayo on the Basque Euskaltel squad.

Cureille Dessus

Here the road gets steeper once again, nudging a 9% average gradient with just four more kilometres remaining. While the road is two-lane and well-surfaced, because of the steep banks the hordes of lively Basque and Spanish fans in this part of France often spill deep onto the road, creating corridors of noise, with *txapelas* (Basque berets) and the *Ikurriña* (Basque flag) being waved frantically at riders. The narrow file of riders means moving up in the bunch can be very tricky, handing the tactical advantage to riders near the front.

The Mountain Kings

From heralding the changing of the guard in terms of Tour domination to plucky chancers able to exploit the tactics of the overall favourites, Luz Ardiden has provided a jaw-dropping backdrop to some of the most riveting stages in recent Tour de France memory.

1985 Greg **LEMOND**

The rivalry between Greg LeMond and Bernard Hinault has got to be one of the most compelling in the history of cycling, and Luz Ardiden was where it all kicked off. LeMond, a younger team-mate of the four-time Tour winner, was up the road with Stephen Roche after Hinault, suffering from a heavy fall earlier in the week that had left him battered and bruised and with two black eyes, lost contact on the Col du Tourmalet. On the summit finish at Luz Ardiden, LeMond wanted to attack Roche and chase after the lone escapee Pedro Delgago. But his team car drove alongside, telling LeMond to sit on Roche's wheel because Hinault was around 45 seconds behind. "Maybe I misunderstood it and they actually said four to five minutes," LeMond recalled. He eventually realized his team-mate was struggling up the climb a long way back, and that his own chances of winning the stage and potentially the Tour had been taken from him through what he claims was deceit. Delgado won the stage (and Hinault the Tour), and while LeMond's manager always rebuffed claims of lying, the incident would set the scene for one of the great Tours of all time as the pair reprised their rivalry the following year.

1987 Dag Otto **LAURITZEN**

The Norwegian pioneer, a former military man who started cycling to rehabilitate himself from injury, became the first man from his country to win a Tour stage when he won alone on Luz Ardiden in 1987. He did so on the 7-Eleven team, itself the first American squad to ride the Tour and featuring the likes of Andy Hampsten and Davis Phinney. Lauritzen attacked on the final climb of Luz Ardiden after approaching from the Col d'Aubisque to the west. Lauritzen wasn't exactly a mountain climber born and bred, but he benefited from the games of cat and mouse being played by the Tour's overall favourites Charly Mottet, Pedro Delgado and eventual winner Stephen Roche on the road behind him. Clearly overcome with joy as he crossed the line (the less said about Lauritzen's headband, the better), a stage win on Bastille Day changed Laurizen's life. He now works as a pundit on the Tour de France for Norwegian television. It changed cycling in Norway too; the next generation of its riders, who were at most just small boys when Lauritzen took his stage, produced four more Tour stage winners in Kurt Asle Arvesen, Thor Hushovd, Edvald Boasson Hagen and Alexander Kristoff.

1990 Miguel **INDURAIN**

In the 1990 Tour a feisty little Italian, Claudio Chiappucci, found himself in the yellow jersey in the Pyrenees after a stage one breakaway netted him over 10 minutes on the serious overall contenders. If Chiappucci could limit his losses in the Pyrenees, he had a real chance of a Tour podium. However, in a move that was either genius or suicide, he attacked early on stage 16 over the Aspin and Tourmalet in the hope of taking the race to the opposition. It backfired. Greg LeMond, defending Tour champion and world champion, caught up with the Italian in Luz Saint Sauveur thanks to his risky descent and his aerodynamic Scott handlebars (which were later banned). The American then set about extending his lead as much as possible, churning a high gear and bobbing his shoulders in the baggy rainbow jersey of world champion. Tucked on to his wheel was a young Spaniard called Miguel Indurain, who would surge around LeMond and win the stage by six seconds. LeMond made up all but five seconds on Chiapucci that day, and would go on to win the Tour (with the Italian in second). But the stage was an omen of things to come. The following year saw the beginning of Indurain's five-year stranglehold on the Tour, with LeMond finishing seventh.

2001 Roberto **LAISEKA**

Aesthetically speaking, Roberto Laiseka was hard to love. The gaunt Basque climber was one of those riders whose face seldom wore anything other than a pained, drawn expression of fatigue. He was a man who looked 10 years older than he was, who possessed a somewhat ungainly style on the bike, and who had the misfortune of riding his entire professional career in the bright orange jersey of Euskaltel-Euskadi. Nevertheless, Laiseka did enjoy one moment of celebrity in the 2001 Tour de France when he won alone on Luz Ardiden, close to the Spanish border. With the Tours of that era on permanent lockdown by Lance Armstrong and his almighty US Postal team (of course, we now know why they were so powerful), any wannabe stage winners could only be allowed to escape if they were perceived not to be a threat in the GC. Being a pure climber, Laiseka had no chance of threatening the Texan overall and so when he attacked at the foot of the climb he was allowed to break free. It was the biggest win of Laiseka's career, which also included three stages of his home Grand Tour, the Vuelta a España, but true to form Laiseka couldn't quite muster a smile on the podium.

Superbagnères

Often overshadowed by its larger neighbours, Superbagnères is seldom top of the bill when the Tour de France hits the Pyrenees. But this mountain gem combines a testing road with unpredictable conditions to make a summit finish on the cliff-top ski station a rare treat indeed.

❝ The climbers were in paradise, but it was purgatory for the rest. **❞**

Cycling journalist Keith Bingham

Draw up a list of the most famous climbs of the Tour de France and it's unlikely that Superbagnères would make it into the top five. It might not even make it into the top ten.

Perhaps one of the reasons for Superbagnères' lack of superstar status – and part of its charm – is that it is relatively subtle, and certainly not one of the great alpine highways like the Col du Grand Saint Bernard or the Tour's icons like Mont Ventoux. The road to Superbagnères creeps its way up around the back of a medium mountain tucked away in the heart of the Pyrenees, which at 18km and a maximum altitude of 1,800m is neither especially high nor particularly long.

Yet this Pyrenean firecracker really ought to be a lot more famous – and more fêted – than it actually is. It hasn't yet failed to deliver a thrilling conclusion to each of the six stages to which it has been the summit finish, which of course is the whole point of a mountain climb in the Tour.

The road from Bagnères de Luchon to the ski station perched on a cliff overlooking the town (hence the name, "Super" or "Above" Bagnères) is 18.4km long with an average gradient of 6.3%, but as usual these stats only tell half the story. The opening three kilometres take riders along a shallow valley road that heads south out of Bagnères and the remaining 15 kilometres are typically Pyrenean in their unsettled rhythm. Approaching the ski station and the imposing Grand Hotel, sections of 12% are capable of throwing a spanner into the spokes of even the Tour's strongest climbers.

Before 1961 the only way up to the resort was by a nauseatingly steep ratchet railway out of Bagnères de Luchon, and the tarmac road has existed a little over 50 years. It goes without saying that it was built primarily with motor vehicles in mind. The consideration principally went to facilitating the passage of winter sports enthusiasts and not that of the Tour de France riders. They of course would have to deal with it from a much more arduous position than behind a steering wheel.

Even if it is a modern creation, the climb has all the characteristics of its more venerable neighbours. The road through the woodland of the Bois du Mont du Lys is hot, oppressive and claustrophobic in the summer (Superbagnères is on a south-facing slope), while the pastures near the summit experience their own unique microclimate and are frequently exposed to the cold and harshness of the mountain weather.

In 1979 it saw Bernard Hinault, then a 24-year-old Breton whose hot-headed energy and aggression could be seen spilling over like molten iron from a cast, tear up the climb in an individual time trial stage that saw the rare event of the Pyrenees featuring in the opening three days of the race. Hinault, the defending champion and the last true patron or "boss" of cycling, dominated the stage and the overall. It marked the definitive arrival of "The Badger" and his era at the top of his game and the top of his sport.

Seven years later and Hinault rode solo on to the climb once more, this time after a long day in the Pyrenees that had approached Superbagnères via the Col de Peyresourde in the 1986 Tour. In a show of bravado, he had a sizeable advantage on the rest of the field at the bottom of the climb but as he laboured up its slopes he was reeled back in and passed by his younger team-mate Greg LeMond, the man who had helped Hinault win his fifth Tour a year before but who would stop him winning a sixth this time around.

The time of Hinault, the last Frenchman to win the Tour, had come to an end. Superbagnères had defined an era in the way that only the greatest Tour climbs can.

Opposite: **The first man to win five Tours de France, Jacques Anquetil approaches the summit at Superbagnères during an individual time trial up the climb in the 1962 Tour.**

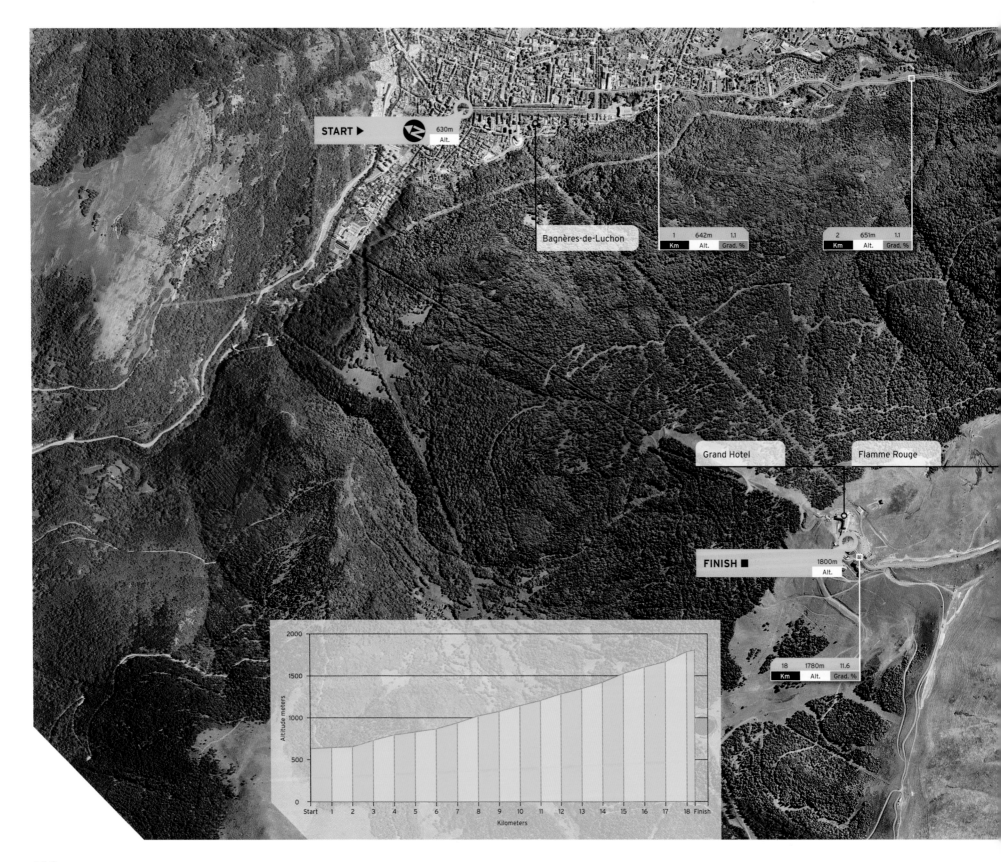

START ▶ 630m Alt.

Bagnères-de-Luchon

1	642m	1.1
Km	Alt.	Grad. %

2	651m	1.1
Km	Alt.	Grad. %

Grand Hotel

Flamme Rouge

FINISH ■ 1800m Alt.

18	1780m	11.6
Km	Alt.	Grad. %

2000

1500

1000

500

0

Altitude meters

Start 1 2 3 4 5 6 7 8 9 10 11 12 13 14 15 16 17 18 Finish

Kilometers

3	730m	7.7
Km	Alt	Grad %

4	795m	3.5
Km	Alt.	Grad. %

5	829m	3.3
Km	Alt.	Grad. %

6	865m	3.9
Km	Alt.	Grad. %

15	1519m	8.4
Km	Alt.	Grad. %

12	1279m	7.3
Km	Alt.	Grad. %

16	1595m	8.2
Km	Alt.	Grad. %

13	1340m	7.7
Km	Alt.	Grad. %

La Carrière

17	1661m	6.4
Km	Alt.	Grad. %

7	936m	8.1
Km	Alt.	Grad. %

11	1200m	7.1
Km	Alt.	Grad. %

14	1415m	7.4
Km	Alt.	Grad. %

8	1018m	7.4
Km	Alt.	Grad. %

Bois du Mont du Lys

10	1139m	6.8
Km	Alt.	Grad. %

9	1071m	5.7
Km	Alt.	Grad. %

Pont de Ravi

Google Earth

167

Route to the Summit

Superb by name, superb by nature, the climb of Superbagnères features the very best that the Pyrenees has to offer: thick woods, open meadows, skittish and unpredictable changes in gradient and weather, and a finish at a small, esoteric ski station dominated by the vast Grand Hotel.

◀ Grand Hotel

Perched on the ledge of the Pic d'Aspe and overlooking the town of Bagnères de Luchon, the summit and ski station of Superbagnères sits at 1,800m. Dominating this little square of tarmac on the side of the mountain is the Grand Hotel, an enormous grey pile that was built in 1922 to cater for the burgeoning Pyrenean tourism industry. The building of the hotel was a feat in itself, even in the early twentieth century; at that point the only way to the top was via a steep ratchet railway from Bagnères. Its imposing, square form is a blend of alpine refuge with Parisian art nouveau, and it remains a charmingly incongruous addition to this day, visible in miniature silhouette form from the town below. At this altitude and prominence, and caught where valleys meet from different directions, the summit is particularly exposed to stormy weather whipped up when winds from the west and the north collide.

Left: Grand Hotel, a solid edifice of the nascent Pyrenean tourist industry.

Pont de Ravi

After the road has gone south, then west in a backwards L-shape from Bagnères de Luchon, it reaches the Pont de Ravi bridge and crosses to the northern side of the River Lys and begins to climb the escarpment. The road's character changes instantly, with three relatively shallow hairpins coming in quick succession after another steep section that takes riders to the westernmost point of the climb. The nearby Mont du Lys and the Pic de Céciré peaks enclose the road until it begins to climb more rapidly. Again the road steepens, with a little ramp of 9% a kilometre later.

Opposite: Jacques Anquetil labours at the head of the peloton on Superbagnères in the 1961 Tour de France. Above left: A rider crests the Crête de Sarrat de Cagot during the individual mountain time trial to Superbagnères in 1962. Above right: Bernard Hinault grimaces in the yellow jersey on Superbagnères shortly before getting dropped in the 1986 Tour.

BAGNÈRES-DE-LUCHON

◀ Bagnères de Luchon

A spa town in the Victorian era, Bagnères de Luchon (or "Luchon Spa") still caters to those seeking health and vitality in the fresh mountain air of the Pyrenees. Only these days it's skiing, cycling and hiking rather than taking the waters which draws people in their thousands. Thanks to its proximity to a range of Pyrenean climbs, including the Col de Peyresourde and Port de Balès, the town has played host to the Tour de France ever since 1910 and by 2014 had hosted the start or finish of 52 stages, some of them the most renowned days in the history of the race. Sitting in the shadow of the Pic du Maupas and the border with Spain, the road to Superbagnères heads south out of town on the D125 through the cool, moist pine forests of the Pique valley. The straight road keeps a shallow average gradient to begin with but is marked by occasional descents and steep little ramps, making it a tough little warm-up to the remainder of the climb.

Left: Bagnères de Luchon: Mountain retreat for intrepid health-seekers.

Bois du Mont du Lys

Deep into the Bois du Mont du Lys, 11km in, the road serves another typically abrupt change in gradient. This bit of the climb is a relatively straight, easterly slog, double backing on the road below it, with no hairpins to offer riders any respite. On the south-facing slopes the woods can be hot and oppressive; the deciduous woodland and thick, dark earth banks absorb sunlight and turn the climb into something like a steamy tropical greenhouse. With the road stretching off interminably into the distance, here it can feel like the climb is never going to end.

La Carrière

At 15km comes the toughest section of the climb, at La Carrière. It's a 500m straight of asphalt at a 12% gradient, a stretch that confronts riders head on like a wall. With around 3km remaining to the summit it can provide the perfect springboard for an attack or be the final nail in the coffin for a rider struggling on up the slopes. Half a kilometre or so later, the road emerges from the trees and into pastures at the Crête de Sarrat de Cagot. It then offers fine views out across the surrounding valleys, but Tour riders will scarcely have time to enjoy them.

Flamme rouge

After six hairpins up the last part of the south-facing slope, riders emerge on to the table-top plateau that serves as the base camp for the ski activities. The final kilometre is actually one of the most difficult, with an average of 9%. With 500m to go there's a further kick in steepness, and without the mountainside to block the wind or the foliage to filter the rain, riders here face the full brunt of any inclement weather at the top. Indeed the uppermost part of the climb is totally exposed to bright sunshine and winds swirling from every direction.

The Mountain Kings

The relative scarcity of trips by the Tour de France may explain why Superbagnères is in the rare position of being a climb without a dud visit. The Tour first climbed its slopes to a summit finish in 1961 and most recently in 1989, and there has been a gripping tale to tell at the end every time.

Opposite top left: A sodden José-Manuel Fuente on his way to a solo stage win in the middle of a storm on Superbagnères in 1971.

Opposite top right: An over-geared Tom Simpson, followed by his support car, is about to lose the yellow jersey of the 1962 Tour de France on a time trial to Superbagnères.

Opposite bottom: Pedro Delgado fends off an over-enthusiastic spectator near the summit in the 1989 Tour. Robert Millar (r) is poised to nip around the Spaniard to win the stage.

1961 Ken LAIDLAW

The first rider onto the slopes of Superbagnères in the summer of 1961 was not one of the greats of the era but a little-known Scot, Ken Laidlaw, riding on the Great Britain team. Aged 25 and riding his first Tour in the year he turned professional, Laidlaw had descended off the Col de Peyresourde with the lead group on stage 18 from Toulouse, but broke clear on the lower slopes out of Bagnères de Luchon in a solo bid for victory. His team was down to three riders from the 12 who started, and Laidlaw's move was invaluable in terms of the prestige and plaudits it brought the unheralded riders from "Blighty", but it had no bearing on the outcome of the Tour. Sadly, Laidlaw began to tire as he reached higher, and the riders he had dropped out of Bagnères – Charly Gaul, Imerio Massignan and eventual overall winner Jacques Anquetil – caught and overtook him. Massignan went on to win the stage in a biblical thunderstorm, with dust from the new road swirling around in the wind and rain rolling in off the Bay of Biscay. But Laidlaw's efforts netted him universal respect and the prize of the day's most aggressive rider. He finished the 1961 Tour in 65th, an achievement in itself given that the first Brit to finish the Tour, Brian Robinson, had only done so six years earlier.

1962 Tom SIMPSON

A new British star was born at Superbagnères in 1962. Stage 13 was a time trial up the climb, beginning in Bagnères de Luchon. Last off the start ramp was 24-year-old Tom Simpson, the first ever Brit to wear the yellow jersey, having taken the race lead the day before as the race entered the Pyrenees by tactically infiltrating a successful breakaway composed of riders behind him in the general classification. On the Gitane team, Simpson was already riding his third Tour but perhaps still suffered from some youthful naivety. He was reportedly over-geared for the unrelenting climb, where a low gear allowed for a high cadence and a more comfortable adjustment to the changes in gradient and pace. He was also probably suffering from his previous day's efforts on a particularly gruelling 208km stage over four giant climbs. After struggling his way up the climb to Superbagnères he finished 31st behind stage winner Federico Bahamontes and lost his yellow jersey to the Belgian Jef Planckaert, who had beaten him into second in the week-long Paris–Nice earlier in the season It was the only time Simpson wore yellow, yet despite a crash in the final week on an alpine descent he finished sixth in Paris, his best ever overall result in the Tour.

1971 José-Manuel FUENTE

On stage 15 in 1971 the rain was pouring down in buckets, and the Tour was in the stunned aftermath of a tempestuous Pyrenean stage that saw race leader Luis Ocaña, the only man ever truly capable of giving Eddy Merckx a run for his money, crash out on the Col de Menté. What followed was no less dramatic; on the shortest road stage in Tour history – 19.6km from Bagnères de-Luchon to Superbagnères – the Tour rode flat out in an experimental mass-start mountain climb. There was no yellow jersey in the stage either; Eddy Merckx, who was racing second overall behind Ocaña, refused to wear it out of respect for his rival. He had even considered abandoning the Tour, but was talked out of it by race organizers. However, as Merckx continued, it was another Spanish rider who seized the day: José-Manuel Fuente. The mountain specialist had won the previous stage into Bagnères-de-Luchon and, riding in the iconic blue and yellow KAS jersey and on a stripped back, super-light road bike with no bottle cages, took off on the tough section in the woods with around 7km to go. Behind him, Merckx suffered but shadowed his closest remaining rivals Lucien Van Impe, Bernard Thévenet and Joop Zoetemelk to finally don the yellow jersey at the summit.

1989 Robert MILLAR

The tenth stage of perhaps the most exciting modern Tour de France had all the hallmarks of a classic day in the mountains. The battle for the overall classification saw gripping hostilities between the two main protagonists, Greg LeMond and Laurent Fignon. The American led Fignon by five seconds but the Frenchman, who suffered and laboured his way through the long, hot stage over the cols of the Tourmalet, Aspin and Peyresourde, took 12 seconds off his rival to take the yellow jersey. Over the next fortnight it went back to LeMond, then back to Fignon, and finally LeMond held it by just eight seconds in the most famous finish in Tour history. Ahead of Fignon and LeMond on that day to Superbagnères, a trio of Pedro Delgado, Charly Mottet and Robert Millar had moved clear. To date it is the last time that the Tour has visited Superbagnères, and appropriately, in an echo of the first visit 28 years earlier, it was a Scotsman who stole the show. Millar won the stage from Delgado in what would be the final Tour stage win of his career. And it was done in some style. The 1984 King of the Mountains, riding in the famous cartoon colours of the Z-Peugeot team, he was first man over all four of the day's climbs and pipped Delgado in a two-up sprint to the line.

Hautacam

1520m

Length: 14.9km
Start: 455m
Ascent: 1065m

The cursed climb of the Tour de France, or so they say, given its history. Whether it's the swirling Pyrenean mists, the crazed Basque fans, the diabolic and ever-changing gradients or the characters who have won on its slopes, there's an enduring and unique character to the Hautacam.

> **" An incredible performance there. It was amazing the way he just rode away from everybody else. "**
> *Cycling commentator Paul Sherwen on Bjarne Riis (1996)*

It's easy to miss the Hautacam. It's far from the highest summit in the Pyrenees, if indeed you can call it a summit at all. It's a dead-end climb, culminating in a small ski station that gives the climb its name. The exact finish line of the Tour de France varies – its most recent appearances in the race have seen it finish at a car park at 1,520m in altitude, a few kilometres shy of the very top (and around 115m lower) – but it always finds itself situated in a shallow mountain meadow in the Pyrenean foothills rather than surrounded by soaring peaks.

Away from race day the 14.9km road used by the Tour, which starts in the village of Ayros Arbouiox, is particularly hard to find. It skirts around the hillside, with tributaries and distributaries linking little hamlets, chalets and farmsteads with the main valley road, which leads to the nearby Col du Tourmalet and the town of Lourdes.

Frankly, it's a hard climb to love too. It's not an unpleasant environment, but compared to the majestic ribbons of tarmac cutting through the snowline and the scree slopes deeper into the mountains, Hautacam is an ugly relative with a nasty side and a sordid, if compelling, reputation. Its first appearance in the Tour was just over two decades ago, in 1994, and it suffers from the lack of a link to the charm of thr early years of the Tour de France. It's the Mr Hyde to the picture postcard Dr Jekyll, but

what it lacks in charm it more than makes up for in character.

Its 7.8% average profile belies a vicious and erratic gradient that steepens to 13% in places and makes it one of the toughest climbs in the Tour. It's when leaving the village of Artalens, nine kilometres from the summit, that the Hautacam really sinks its teeth in. The road steepens in a three-kilometre section where the thin tarmac doesn't drop below 9%. It's a mountain made for the pure climbers, one which suits riders who are able to vary their pace and gearing at the click of a finger. It punishes those with diesel engines who prefer to cruise at a high tempo.

Like Robert Louis Stevenson's dark, Victorian alter ego, it's a climb that has exposed to the world the very worst side of cycling. Its place in the Tour de France was, until 2014, inseparable from the greed and illicit excesses of the EPO generation.

In 1996 it was where Bjarne Riis defied the formbook and the laws of gravity to shift into overdrive and surge clear of five-time Tour winner Miguel Indurain, taking the stage and cementing his yellow jersey. Later, after his career had ended, the balding, turbo-charged Dane revealed that it was a cocktail of EPO, growth hormone and cortisone that fuelled him to such heights.

Some Pyrenean climbs are high enough that the Tour can ride through and above the mountain chain's notoriously fickle weather, yet on the lower slopes of the Hautacam the mist and rain can linger. In the damp gloom of the 2000 Tour, Lance Armstrong seemed to skim across the standing water while his rivals wallowed; the Texan obliterated the opposition on the first summit finish of the Tour to stamp his authority on the race. In 2008, the duo of Leonardo Piepoli and Juan José Cobo broke clear on the lower slopes with the two team-mates taking a stage one–two. Piepoli would test positive for EPO later in that Tour.

Vincenzo Nibali is the latest rider to win on the Hautacam, taking a solo stage win on the final summit finish of the 2014 Tour in emphatic fashion. Yet, conscious of the reputation of what he'd just accomplished on his way to overall victory, the Sicilian was at pains to point out that his time up the climb was much slower than in previous editions. Perhaps the Hautacam has finally found redemption in the form of its latest conqueror. It's about time.

Opposite: The backmarkers of the peloton find comfort in numbers as they tackle the Hautacam on the 18th stage of the 2014 Tour de France.

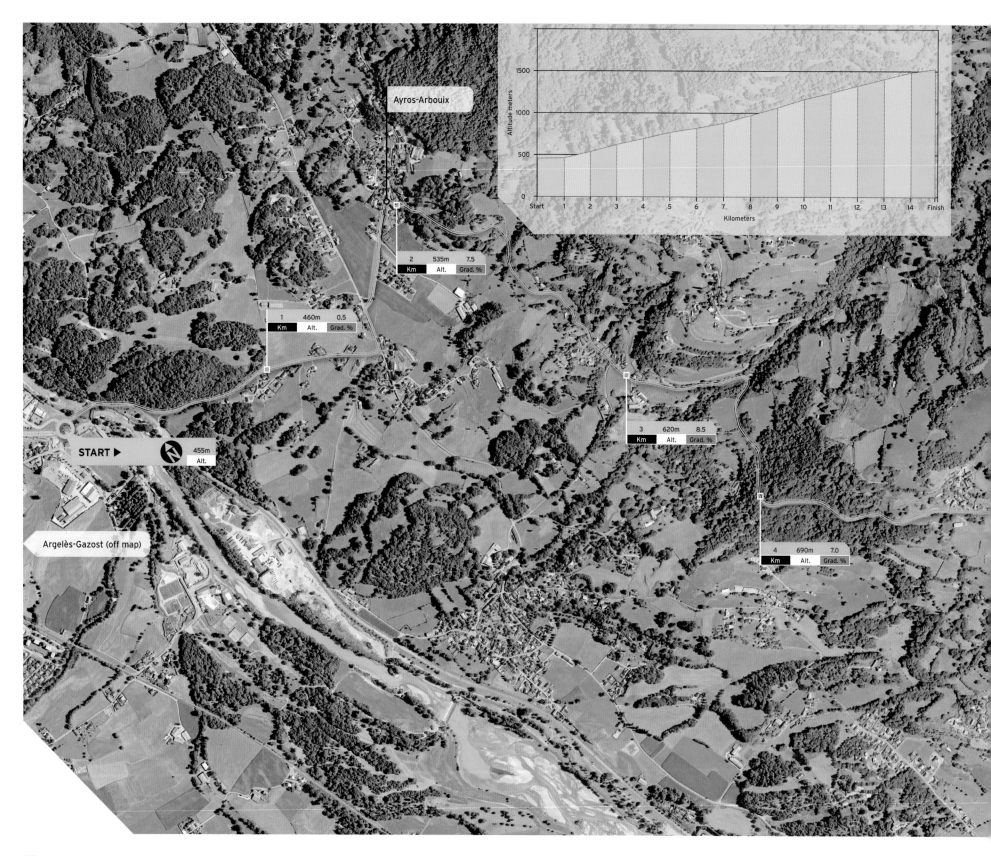

Ayros-Arbouix

2	535m	7.5
Km	Alt.	Grad. %

1	460m	0.5
Km	Alt.	Grad. %

3	620m	8.5
Km	Alt.	Grad. %

START ▶

	455m
	Alt.

Argelès-Gazost (off map)

4	690m	7.0
Km	Alt.	Grad. %

Saint-André

9	1060m	9.0
Km	Alt.	Grad. %

14	1480m	8.0
Km	Alt.	Grad. %

FINISH ■ 1520m
Alt.

11	1235m	7.5
Km	Alt.	Grad. %

10	1160m	10.0
Km	Alt.	Grad. %

13	1400m	8.0
Km	Alt.	Grad. %

8	970m	9.5
Km	Alt.	Grad. %

Ruisseau de
Couyéou de Mates

5	765m	7.5
Km	Alt.	Grad. %

7	875m	6.0
Km	Alt.	Grad. %

12	1320m	8.5
Km	Alt.	Grad. %

6	815m	5.0
Km	Alt.	Grad. %

Artalens

Google Earth

Route to the Summit

An erratic and irregular road, the climb of Hautacam alternates from claustrophobic to expansive, from steep to shallow, and from straight to switch-backed. Starting at the foot alongside the Gave de Pau, the low-altitude route skirts past streams, springs and ditches that are the hallmarks of the lower slopes of the Pyrenees.

◄ Finish

The "summit" of the climb to Hautacam isn't really a summit at all. The road continues upward for another 1.5km and 115m in altitude to the Col de Tramassel. However, the trappings of the modern Tour de France – VIP tribunes, team parking, podiums and broadcast infrastructure among other things – demand that the finish of the Hautacam is here. It's an otherwise arbitrary point on the road, one wide enough to accommodate the vehicles and temporary structures but which leaves the amateur cyclist (who has slogged away for an hour or so) with more than a slight sense of bathos upon arrival. The setting is tranquil and bucolic; the quiet mountain air rings with cowbells, and horses often wander onto the road and stand staring sardonically at cyclists. On a clear day the views west towards the Col d'Aubisque can be quite something, yet the top is often shrouded in mist. It's unfortunate for the cyclo-tourist, but when it descends on the finish of the Tour de France it adds a sense of drama and intrigue seldom found elsewhere in France.

Left: Hautacam, a faux summit in tranquil surroundings.

Argelès-Gazost

The town of smart architecture, narrow streets and water fountains sits at the foot of the Hautacam, perched on a little rocky outcrop beside the Gave de Pau river. It's a crossroads in the Pyrenees – linking the town of Lourdes to the north with the road to the cols of the Tourmalet and Aubisque. In fact the latter begins in the town, ascending the steep outcrop to the west and heading off out of sight. However, the Tour skips the town when it approaches the Hautacam from the Tourmalet, crossing the river further south outside Pierrefitte Nestalas.

Opposite: Fans form a noisy corridor at the start of the climb to Hautacam. Above left: Cadel Evans leads the peloton through the Basque crowds in 2008. Above right: Luxembourg's Kim Kirchen (l) loses the race lead and the yellow jersey as he cracks on the Hautacam in 2008 Tour.

◀ Ayros Arbouix

The village of Ayros Arbouix marks the proper start of the climb after a flat and fast approach along the valley floor. There's no easy introduction, as on some other climbs in the Pyrenees; the road starts climbing straight away at a gradient of between 6% and 10%, already featuring the sort of schizophrenic changes in severity that characterize the climb in its entirety. There's a dense, enclosed feel to the climb at this point; houses surround the road and the accompanying eclectic mix of road furniture and obstacles – including low stone walls, drain covers and potholes – require focus. This is not the sort of place that affords riders the time and freedom to let their minds wander in the cool mountain air and expansive views. It's where the fog of war descends as riders jostle for position in the bunch amid the visual clutter and the actual fog of the all-too-common bad weather.

Left: Ayros-Arbouix, the claustrophobic municipal start to the climb proper.

Artalens

Usually, on the Tour's *hors catégorie* climbs, the steepest sections of road provide the best point for the strongest riders to attack and win the stage or put time into their rivals. However, in 2014 it was a tiny section of downhill near the hamlet of Artalens, where the first stretch of road meets its first serious hairpin and heads north, that allowed Vincenzo Nibali to put in his final and stage-winning dig, distancing veteran American Chris Horner. The climb of the Hautacam is sprinkled with timeless little hamlets of this size all the way to the top.

Saint André

A generally flowing road of shallow bends makes a second sharp 180-degree turn at the village of Saint André, changing its angle to a more direct route east up the mountain. It is the start of the hardest two kilometres on the climb; kilometres of 10.3% and 11.3% average gradient that are so severe as to warrant the colour black in the official Tour de France Roadbook profile, reserved only for the toughest sections of the race. This is where the climb of the Hautacam begins to bite, where even the fastest riders have to use their bottom gear.

Final ramp

The final steep ramp of 10.4% average for a kilometre comes with around four kilometres to the summit at an altitude of 1,200m, just as the fastest riders pass the 30-minute mark for the climb (although the back markers will take a lot longer). The road crosses the Ruisseau de Couyeou de Mates, performs a tight twirl through a pair of hairpins, and then traverses the Ruisseau d'Estibos. By this point steep cuttings in the slope have opened out into Pyrenean meadows and riders can be grateful for a refreshing breeze, if no let-up in the gradient.

The Mountain Kings

The Hautacam has seldom been far away from courting controversy in the five times the Tour de France has been to visit since 1994. Of course the Tour loves to make characters out of its mountains and locations, and every good story needs an antagonist; the exploits of many of the sport's antiheroes has led some to call Hautacam the "cursed climb".

1994 Luc **LEBLANC**

Emerging through the mist to become the first-ever stage winner atop Hautacam, 13 July 1994 was the continuation of a purple patch for Luc Leblanc. The Frenchman, who had already won the mountains classification in the Vuelta a España, would go on to place fourth overall in that year's Tour and end his season by becoming world champion. At the end of a monster 263.5km stage Leblanc, after six hours and 58 minutes, chipped away from the wheel of Miguel Indurain to cross a finish line that was barely visible on the TV cameras placed just a few dozen yards beyond it. The size of the effort showed on his contorted body and the thousand-yard stare on his wide eyes. His win sent the French commentators into raptures; the Tour's home support delighted in the triumph of a Frenchman over the impregnable fortress Indurain on the eve of Bastille Day. Sixteen seconds behind Indurain, Marco Pantani found himself wanting on the Hautacam on the first of two visits in his career; six years later he would have no answer to another dominant rider of his generation, Lance Armstrong.

1996 Bjarne **RIIS**

The story of Bjarne Riis on the Hautacam is a story of illusion and deceit. Riis had fitted a smaller chainring to his bike in advance of the stage; when he made his decisive move, flying past his opponents inside the final 10km, he did so in the big ring. It was a psychological killer blow to his rivals. And it was done with the braggadocio of a serial cheat who had the temerity to glide back through the peloton, inspect his fellow riders, and stick the knife in with *sang froid*. His rivals knew that they had no chance of catching him, and Riis knew it too. Indeed the image of Riis from that day, sunken cheeks, baggy jersey and arms in the air after 34 minutes and 38 seconds of climbing, is a haunting symbol of the transformative powers of performance-enhancing drugs and the darkest days of the Tour. There's something quite horrifying in the Dane's enormous eyes and body that had been stripped back almost to the bone. In truth that yellow jersey never did fit him. When he won his Tour he was 32, after a cycling career that had been mediocre at best. The lies unravelled and in 2007 he confessed to cheating.

2000 Javier **OTXOA**

The sole survivor of an early breakaway group over the nearby climbs of the Col d'Aubisque and Col du Marie Blanque, young Basque climber Javier Otxoa took the biggest win of his career atop the Hautacam on a day that was long remembered for its apocalyptic conditions and the seismic statement from defending champion Lance Armstrong. Suffering from the fatigue of the day's efforts, Otxoa held off a rabid and determined Armstrong (who attacked from the peloton behind). A lead of 12 minutes at the foot of the mountain was cut to just 42 seconds. It was a momentous ride for the fact that someone had successfully managed to give Armstrong the slip in the high mountains, and equally momentous for that fact that Armstrong had ridden so fast to destroy the field and almost ensure that they didn't. It was the pinnacle of Otxoa's tragic career; the following spring he and his twin brother Ricardo, 26, were hit by a car on a training ride. Ricardo died and Javier emerged disabled from a long coma that few thought he would survive. However, he later went on to win gold medals in the 2004 and 2008 Paralympic Games.

2014 Vincenzo **NIBALI**

The Italian Vincenzo Nibali had no reason to hold back on the Hautacam, the final summit finish of a Tour which saw him dominate from start to finish across the hills of Yorkshire, the cobbles of northern France and the mighty climbs of the Alps. After the peloton had traversed the Col du Tourmalet and descended the valley of the Gave de Pau, Nibali upped the tempo with his Astana team-mates, swept up the remnants of the breakaway, followed a speculative attack by the veteran American Chris Horner, and took off alone with 9.5km to go. With nothing but the gradient and the wayward elbow of a spectator threatening to get in his way, the peloton crossed the line in dribs and drabs behind him, scuffling for the minor placings. It was vindication for Nibali in a Tour where his dominance was diluted by the absence of Alberto Contador and defending champion Chris Froome, who had both abandoned to injury earlier in the race. Yet Nibali's time, three minutes slower than Riis 12 years before him, dismissed suggestions that his performance would not stand up to scrutiny in years to come.

Col de Peyresourde

1569m

Length: 15.2km
Start: 630m
Ascent: 939m

With gentle surroundings that are more tranquil than terrifying, the Col de Peyresourde is a bit of a wolf in sheep's clothing. Behind its bucolic landscape is a difficult climb that has been integral to the passage of the Tour de France ever since its debut in 1910.

> **❝** It has a soft grass carpet that makes you want to lie down among the cows and the sheep. **❞**
>
> *Jean-Marie Leblanc, former Tour director*

The Col de Peyresourde has a distinction that can never be taken away: on 21 July 1910, it became the first high mountain pass in the Tour de France.

The Tour had visited the mountains of the Vosges in 1905, beginning with the Ballon d'Alsace, yet it was not until five years later that it first entered the Pyrenees. It did so on a stage from Bagnères de Luchon to Bayonne, a staggering 326 kilometres, and first up on the menu without further ado was the Peyresourde.

The climb is a fearsome proposition in its own right: 15.2 kilometres long from Bagnères de Luchon with an average of 6.3% (again, like most climbs in the Pyrenees, it climbs at an irregular rate and regularly reaches 10%). It is 10km and 6.6% from Avajan to the west. Yet because of its proximity to other Pyrenean giants, principally the Col du Tourmalet to the west, it has never quite escaped their shadow. Sitting at the eastern end of a chain of passes beginning with the Col d'Aubisque known as the "Circle of Death", it often comes as an aperitif to a hard day's slog or the final digestif after the equivalent of a heavy three-course meal. Occasionally it has played a role as the climb just before a summit finish at Superbagnères, or the Tour has traced just a small portion of its slopes before turning right at Trébons de Luchon and up to the Port de Balès.

Author Daniel Friebe has described the Col de Peyresoude as rising out of Bagnères de Luchon "like aroma from a kitchen", and there is a homely, comfortable quality to the climb. Visually it isn't threatening; riders don't feel they could drop off the edge of a vertigo-inducing precipice if the wind picks up. Surrounding the pass, there are pleasant meadows and a line of trees at regularly intervals along the roadside that would look more suited to bordering a Parisian boulevard than a *hors catégorie* mountain climb. Jean-Marie Leblanc, a former racer turned Tour de France director, famously said it was the sort of climb that made riders want to lie down in the fields among the cows rather than battle tooth and nail against each other.

The col has likely been used for millennia (which helps reinforce that imagery of a traditional, rural utopia) but the road was widened and took its present form in the eighteenth century. Yet with all this imagery, the Col de Peyresourde can trick riders. It can lull them into complacency, tempting them to over-exert themselves before other climbs later in the stage or to suffer at the end of a hot day in the mountains. In 1969, shortly before Eddy Merckx's now legendary solo ride, his team took control on the Peyresourde (the first climb of the day) and set a fast but steady tempo precisely because

there were so many over-enthusiastic riders attacking early and increasing the likelihood that the peloton would fracture and some riders would miss the time cut.

Approached from either east or west, the Col de Peyresourde has more often than not provided a convenient route for the Tour to get from one climb to another. It has done so 65 times. Yet 2012 was perhaps the year when the Peyresourde finally got its chance to shine. Stage 16 traversed four huge climbs and finished with the Peyresourde and a fast run into Bagnères, won by Thomas Voeckler. The following day the climb got as close as it could get to hosting a summit finish, having never done so before. The Tour ascended from Bagnères and turned left just after the col in the direction of the ski station at Peyragudes. It wasn't quite a continuation of the Peyresourde: past the improbably high Peyresourde-Balestas airport, the soft meadows gave way to barren rocky slopes. But the climb that has so often played the pretty bridesmaid finally got to be the bride. After 102 years, the Col de Peyresourde got the time in the limelight that its long and illustrious history deserved.

Opposite: Rolling meadows dotted with trees and carpeted by wild flowers make for a deceptively bucolic setting on the Col de Peyresourde.

1	670m	6.7
Km	Alt.	Grad. %

2	721m	3.9
Km	Alt.	Grad. %

3	750m	4.0
Km	Alt.	Grad. %

START ▶ | 630m |
| Alt. |

4	774m	7.4
Km	Alt.	Grad. %

Trébons-de-Luchon

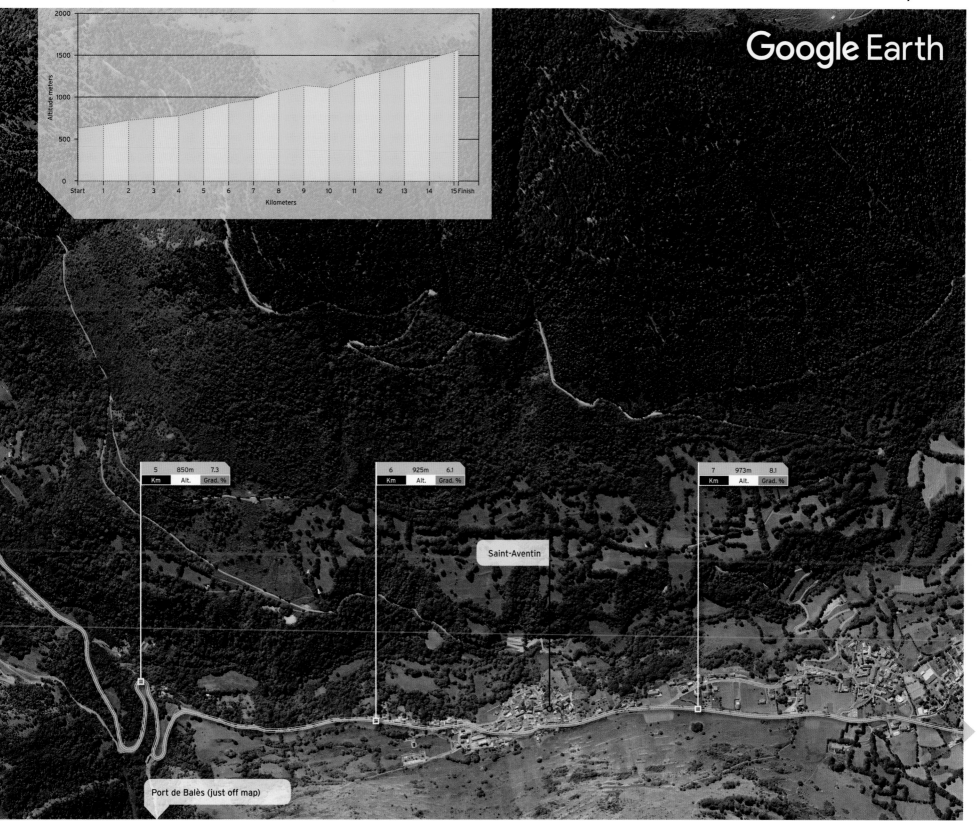

Google Earth

Km	Alt.	Grad. %
5	850m	7.3

Km	Alt.	Grad. %
6	925m	6.1

Km	Alt.	Grad. %
7	973m	8.1

Saint-Aventin

Port de Balès (just off map)

Image © Landsat © Google 2014

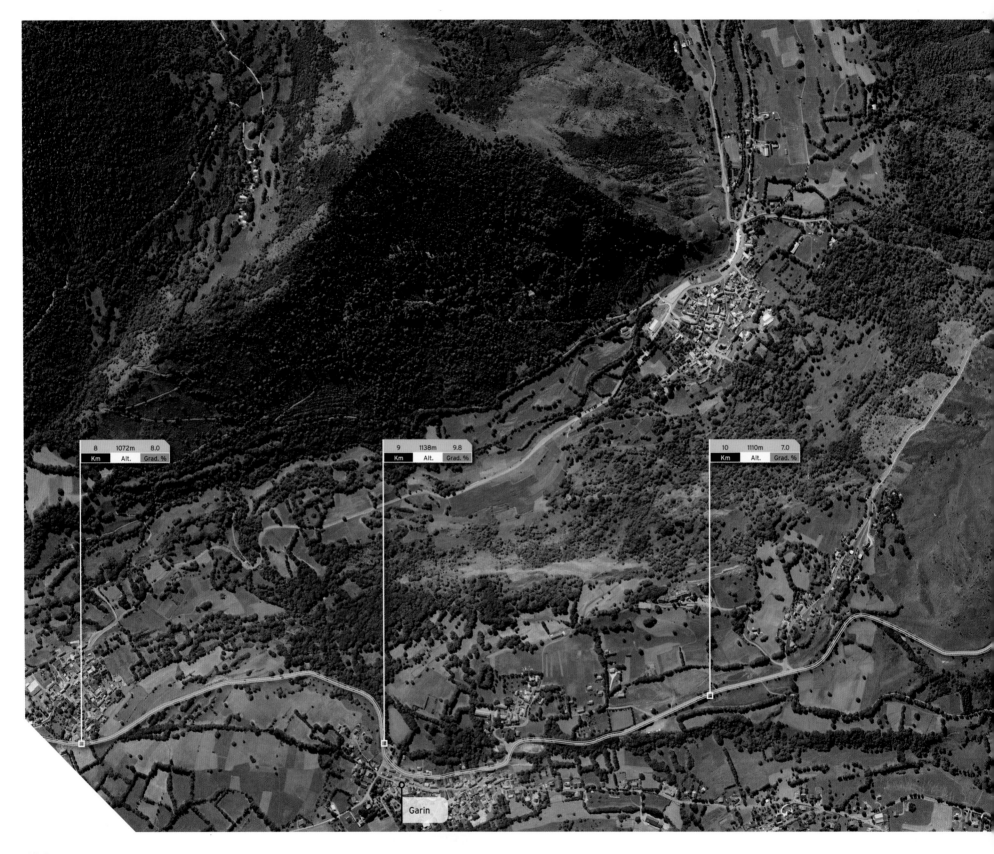

8	1072m	8.0
Km	Alt.	Grad. %

9	1138m	9.8
Km	Alt.	Grad. %

10	1110m	7.0
Km	Alt.	Grad. %

Garin

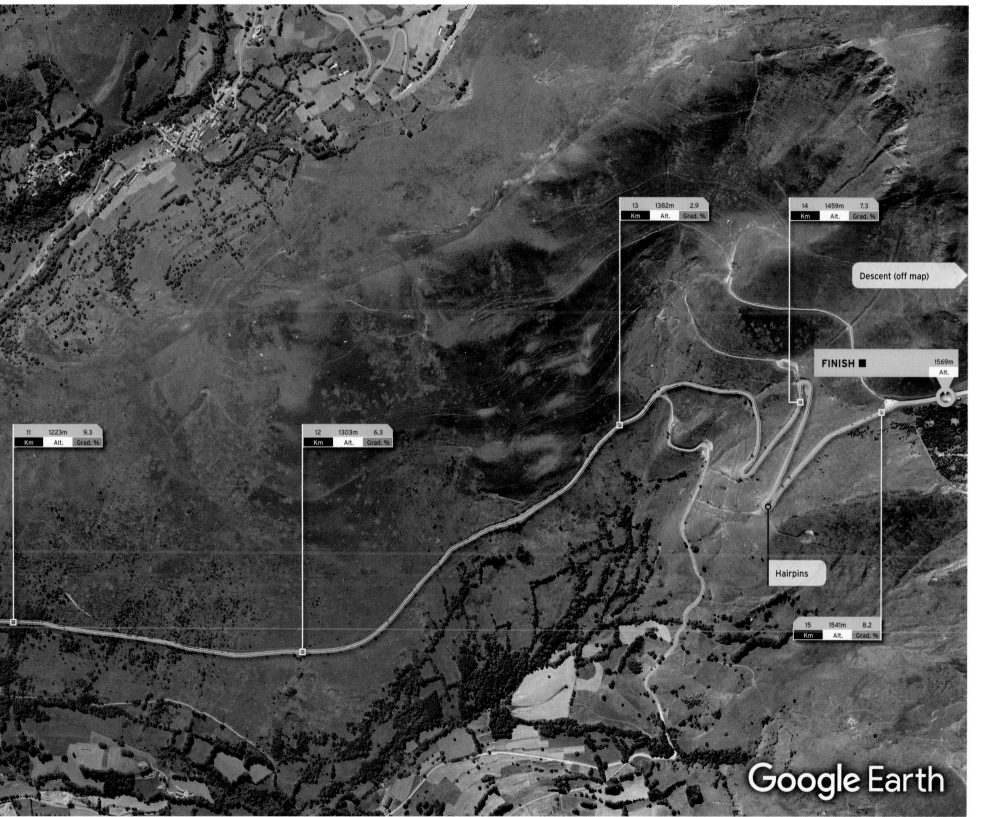

13	1382m	2.9
Km	Alt.	Grad. %

14	1459m	7.3
Km	Alt.	Grad. %

Descent (off map)

FINISH ■ | 1569m |
| Alt. |

11	1223m	9.3
Km	Alt.	Grad. %

12	1303m	6.3
Km	Alt.	Grad. %

Hairpins

15	1541m	8.2
Km	Alt.	Grad. %

Google Earth

Route to the Summit

As the link between Bagnères de Luchon to the east and the Aure valley to the west, the Col de Peyresourde has regularly been climbed from both sides by the Tour de France. The eastern ascent from Bagnères just edges the west in terms of number of crossings and is home to the climb's best-known features.

FINISH

◀ Finish

The Col de Peyresourde is a col in the truest sense of the word; it is a V-shaped notch in the chain of peaks running north to south, which act as a border between the French *départements* of the Hautes-Pyrénées and the Haute-Garonne. The pass is bordered by steep grassy slopes and sits in the centre of a brief stretch of flat road, but either side of the col the road drops down as if running down the flanks of a saddle. A few hundred metres to the west of the pass, the road forks south and continues uphill to Peyragudes, the ski station at 1,605m that was created in 1988 (and named by eliding the names of the two existing stations at Peyresourde and Agudes). It was this route that the 2012 Tour took on stage 17, heading out of the gentle meadows and on to the barren ski slopes on a spur overlooking the pass. In doing so they passed the aerodrome at Peyresourde-Balestas, a sloping airstrip that demands pilots perform the exciting and spectacular manoeuvre of landing on an uphill runway.

Left: The Col de Peyresourde passes through a narrow notch in the landscape.

Garin

This tiny settlement at 1,000m altitude can barely even be called a hamlet – fewer than 150 people live in the parish. It marks the halfway point of the climb from Bagnères de Luchon but achieves more column inches than its worth due to the winner of the first ever Tour de France, Maurice Garin. The man himself never got to ride through his namesake; the rider they called the *ramoneur* or chimney sweep (his former profession), was disqualified from the 1904 Tour for cheating and never raced it again.

Opposite: **Early crossings of the Col de Peyresourde regularly forced riders off their bikes and onto their feet.**   Above left: **Jan Ullrich was famously caught out while descending the Peyresourde in 2001.**   Above right: **The gentle slopes of the Peyresourde provide ample parking for the white swarms of motorhomes that descend on the Tour every summer.**

◄ Port de Balès

With four kilometres ridden from Bagnères de Luchon the regular shallow turns of the D618 are interrupted by three hairpins in quick succession. The D51 juts off the final tight bend at right angles to the road in order to head north and uphill towards the mighty Port de Balès. A *hors catégorie* climb in its own right, the Port de Balès is a mishmash of gradients steep and soft on a road that within 16 kilometres of the turning climbs to 1,755m. Its descent leads further downstream of Bagnères in the Pique valley, which for a long time meant it was little more than a scenic siding that didn't take people anywhere they couldn't already get to. It wasn't until 2007 that the Tour climbed it for the first time after race organizers arranged for the 1980s tarmac road, which had fallen into a sorry state over just 15 years, to be resurfaced. The race was back again in 2012, ascending from the north before linking up with the Peyresourde at the turn and climbing westwards to a summit finish at Peyragudes.

Left: **The Port de Balès was surfaced specifically for the Tour de France.**

Hairpins

By and large a straight road on the eastern flank, the climb to the Col de Peyresourde suddenly features a series of three hairpins shortly before it reaches the pass as if it's performing a little jig. The notches in the hillside afford spectacular views to the east back down the climb and across the Pique valley and their tree-lined curves bordered by soft meadows and carpets of wild flowers form a beautiful finale to the ascent. However, the final 2.2 kilometres remain between 7% and 10%, making them some of the toughest.

Descent

Four and a half kilometres from the pass on the west is the final tight right-hand hairpin, a bend which achieved notoriety in 2001 when it caught out Jan Ullrich on the way down. Startled by the first serious bend on the descent, and one with a particularly steep approach, the German entered the corner far too quickly and almost failed to turn at all, riding somewhat comically over the edge and down through a field, clinging on to his handlebars as if he didn't know what else to do. He emerged a few moments later, unscathed.

Saint Aventin

The little hamlet marks the point where the road, which has up till now sliced through the gorge of the One river, emerges into the open fields and pastoral landscape that characterizes the Col de Peyresourde. The scars of glacial moraine – where in the last Ice Age glaciers gouged out lateral cuts and deposited material from further up the valley – border the road and run east to west like little wrinkled terraces in the earth. However these are well hidden from the road and are more visible from the air.

The Mountain Kings

The heroes of the Peyresourde aren't always the biggest superstars in the Tour de France. Whether they are attackers, stage win specialists or just clinging on for survival, this climb offers opportunities to the riders that don't often get to enjoy the limelight.

1910 Octave **LAPIZE**

In Tour history the very first Pyrenean stage, and thus the very first high mountain stage, was a slog from Bagnères de Luchon to Bayonne: 326 kilometres on rutted, muddy tracks which included five enormous climbs. The Col de Peyresourde was the first one. Octave Lapize, riding on the Alcyon team of defending champion François Faber, took off alone on the lower slopes and stayed away over the Peyresourde, pushing his single-speed bike on the trickier sections. He led still over the next climb, the Col d'Aspin, but was caught on the Col du Tourmalet. No matter: he had enough left in the tank to pip Pierino Albini in the Basque port town after more than 14 hours in (and out of) the saddle. Time mattered little in those days since the Tour was essentially a gargantuan, outdoor version of a points race on the track. Lapize used his Pyrenean escapade to lay the foundations of his Tour win, overhauling Faber in one of the very first instances of intra-team rivalry, a recurring theme that would re-emerge with Coppi and Bartali, Hinault and LeMond, and Wiggins and Froome. Lapize lost his life in the First World War, shot down in 1917 while serving in the French air force.

1947 Jean **ROBIC**

The 1947 Tour winner Jean Robic was a short man with a short temper. One of the Tour's great characters, he was colloquially christened "Old Leatherhead" owing to his habit of wearing a leather crash helmet after breaking his skull in a crash in 1944. He also reportedly liked to pick up water bottles filled with lead at the top of mountain climbs in order to give his 60kg bodyweight a helping hand from gravity on the descents. Also nicknamed "Little Goat", and blessed with a climbing physique, Robic led over the Peyresourde for three years in a row between 1947 and 1949. On that first occasion, Robic dragged himself back into contention for the Tour title with a solo attack that led to him winning the stage by over 10 minutes (while picking up a further five bonus minutes for crossing the day's climbs first). However, the little Frenchman eventually won the Tour with a bizarre and rare attack with a small group on the final day of the race, moving clear of the yellow jersey Pierre Brambilla on a small climb and finding by the end of the stage that he had gained 13 minutes. In doing so he won by three, and became the first rider to win the Tour without having worn the yellow jersey.

2010 Jens **VOIGT**

The exploits of Jens Voigt on stage 16 of the 2010 Tour provide a good illustration of how the German workhorse obtained modern-day cult hero status. He crashed on the descent of the Col de Peyresourde at a time when his team leader Andy Schleck was a long way up the road and all of their Saxo Bank support vehicles with the spare bikes were following Schleck and the main bunch. In fact Voigt was so far behind the peloton that even the neutral service bikes had left him. Having quit the Tour to a serious crash on the Col du Petit Saint Bernard 12 months earlier, Voigt wasn't about to give in. He got hold of a miniscule bike that had apparently been used for a kids' event earlier in the day and was following the race in convoy. It was far too small and had toe clips on the pedals, but Voigt hopped on and made the fast descent down the Peyresourde with his bloody, bruised body contorted into all manner of awkward shapes. Word reached his team boss Bjarne Riis up the road, and the Dane left a spare bike in the care of a *gendarme* and radioed to Voigt that it would be waiting for him. It was, the policeman handed over the bike and Voigt lived to fight another day, finishing the stage and the Tour.

2012 Thomas **VOECKLER**

The French *baroudeur*, or firebrand, is perhaps the most expressive rider of modern Tour history. He wears clear lenses in his sunglasses, it has been suggested, to allow him to make eye contact with his adoring public watching him on the television. Shy and occasionally bashful off the bike, he wears his heart on his sleeve while riding and often gurns his way through the Tour at the head of a breakaway, pulling all manner of faces and poking his tongue out towards the TV cameras at every opportunity. So it was in 2012 where Voeckler led the race over four Pyrenean climbs on stage 16, cementing his lead in the King of the Mountains classification that he would go on to win in Paris. Not content with that, he dropped his companions on the final climb of the Col de Peyresourde from Loudierville to the west and solo'd his way to the pass, his tongue poking out of his mouth, his thighs (in his trademark brief shorts) stamping on the pedals and his back looking almost uncomfortably straight. Voeckler then bombed down the descent to Bagnères de Luchon to take his second stage win of that year's Tour in the spa town's leafy boulevards in the late afternoon heat.

4
CLASSIC CLIMBS OF THE REST OF FRANCE

Not all great climbs of the Tour de France are found in the Alps and the Pyrenees. Beyond the borders of these two great mountain chains lie climbs in the Massif Central, the Vosges and, in the case of Mont Ventoux, on its own and right where it wants to be. These are unique places with unique roles in the history of the Tour de France. Outliers from the mainstream, they come with an additional guarantee: if the Tour has sought them out, you know that they will be worth the effort.

Opposite: The barren slopes of the "moonscape" on Mont Ventoux form one of the most famous mountain finishes in the history of the Tour de France.

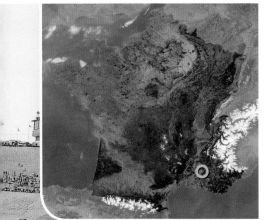

Mont Ventoux

1912m

Length: 21.8km
Start: 309m
Ascent: 1603m

A remorseless cauldron of heat, noise and wind; of all the climbs in the Tour de France, Mont Ventoux strikes the most terror into the hearts of riders. Deriving, some say, from an ancient Provençal word meaning either "windy" or "far peak", the very name of this mountain is capable of conjuring up fear.

> " The heat, the fans, it's overwhelming. There are steeper climbs in the Tour but none so difficult. The Ventoux is unique. "
>
> **Bernard Thévenet**

Mont Ventoux is a climatic and geological anomaly, a wave-shaped ridge oriented west to east with a peak reaching nearly 2,000m, set deep in the heart of the rolling vineyards and lavender groves of Provence. Its white peak can be seen for dozens of miles, a monolith in the rolling hills of the south of France. Exposed to the mistral winds, in six months the now iconic observatory that marks out the mountain's summit can go from baking in the 40°C Mediterranean sun to sitting submerged deep in drifts of snow. The weather station has recorded winds of 200mph.

The mountain is often colloquially known as the Giant of Provence, though Antoine Blondin, one of the pioneering journalists of the Tour, called it a "sorcerer's cauldron". There are stories of riders of the ilk of Eddy Merckx being given oxygen at the summit, and the tale of Jean Malléjac collapsing and losing consciousness on the climb's second appearance in the race in 1955. Andy Schleck, who rode the climb on the penultimate stage of the 2009 Tour, called it "the hardest climb of the Tour de France".

There are three ways to the summit but the climb up the south face from the town of Bédoin is the most common and the most difficult. At 21.8km in length with an average gradient of 7.43%, Ventoux is actually the sort of climb where riders would do better to ignore the averages. After a gentle start, the gradients soon ramp up to 5% and 6% as riders leave behind the fields and enter the forest. By the halfway mark the pitted and bumpy road surface has tilted to an average into double figures, but it does so on a choppy road with ramps and bends where the steepness approaches the high teens.

The climate here is hot and the thick, broiling forest is heady with the scent of pine and cedar. Yet as the trees begin to thin and a fresh chill stabs at riders' sweaty bodies, they emerge past Chalet Reynard and into its famous bleached, barren limestone moonscape. Ventoux is almost unique in the Tour in that riders climb to the very summit, as opposed to a col, the lowest point between two peaks. The cone of the mountain looks like year-round snow cover but is in fact exposed rock and loose stones at an altitude where the climate is too harsh for plant life to survive. It's intimidating, even in a car. The wind blows and barks and at times the views over the surrounding landscape, around a mile lower in altitude, give the impression that you could be swept up and blown off in an instant.

From Louison Bobet to Eddy Merckx and Marco Pantani, there are few riders who can claim to have got the better of Ventoux. Indeed it's the human toll of the mountain that overshadows its physical hostility.

During the 1967 Tour, Tom Simpson collapsed three kilometres from the summit as the alcohol and amphetamines in his blood catalysed his body's exhaustion from the exposure and fatigue. He climbed back on his bike before falling again shortly after. He was taken by helicopter to hospital but it was later confirmed that he died on the mountainside. The demise of Simpson has become one of the most infamous moments in cycling and a memorial now sits at the spot where he fell, a site where amateurs pay tribute with bottles and caps and Tour riders take off their helmets as a mark of respect.

The French philosopher Roland Barthes once wrote that, to cyclists, Mont Ventoux was "a god of evil", something "to which sacrifices must be made". Even today, 65 years on from its first appearance, there is no place that encapsulates the physical extremities, and the heavy toll, of the Tour de France better than Mont Ventoux.

Opposite: **The finish line is in sight as Chris Froome, accompanied by a television helicopter, enters the final kilometre of the climb through the famous "moonscape" of Mont Ventoux during the 2013 Tour de France.**

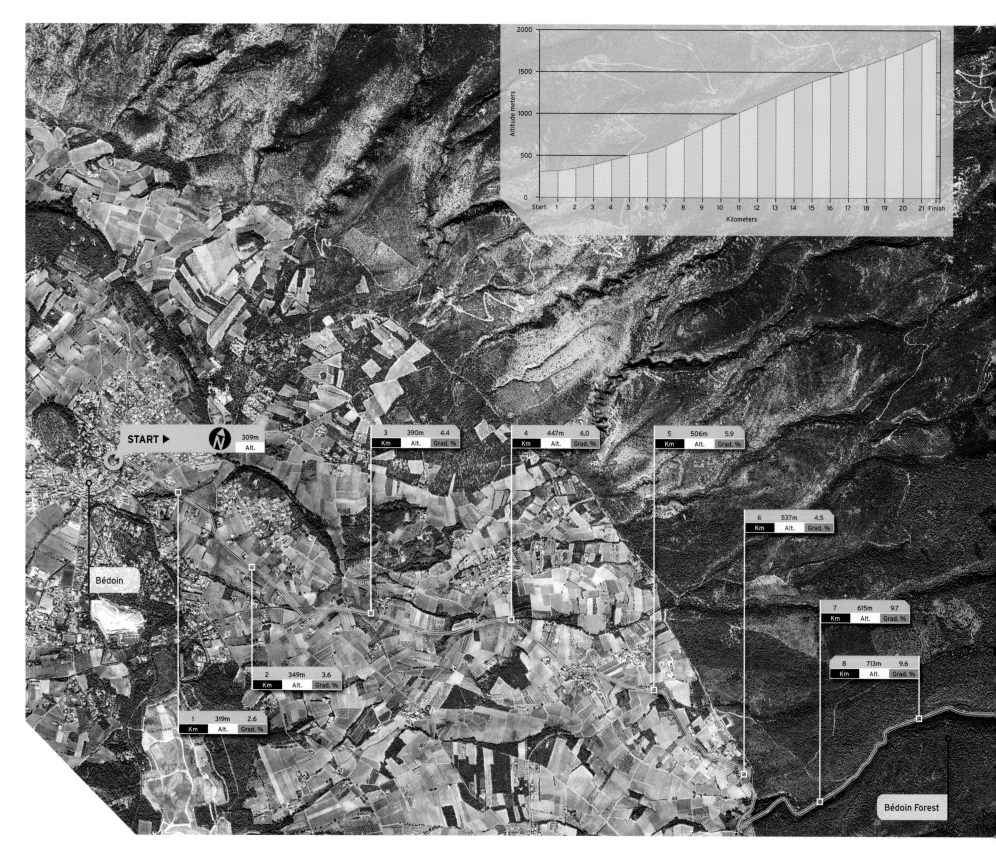

START ▶

309m
Alt.

Bédoin

1   319m   2.6
Km   Alt.   Grad. %

2   349m   3.6
Km   Alt.   Grad. %

3   390m   4.4
Km   Alt.   Grad. %

4   447m   6.0
Km   Alt.   Grad. %

5   506m   5.9
Km   Alt.   Grad. %

6   537m   4.5
Km   Alt.   Grad. %

7   615m   9.7
Km   Alt.   Grad. %

8   713m   9.6
Km   Alt.   Grad. %

Bédoin Forest

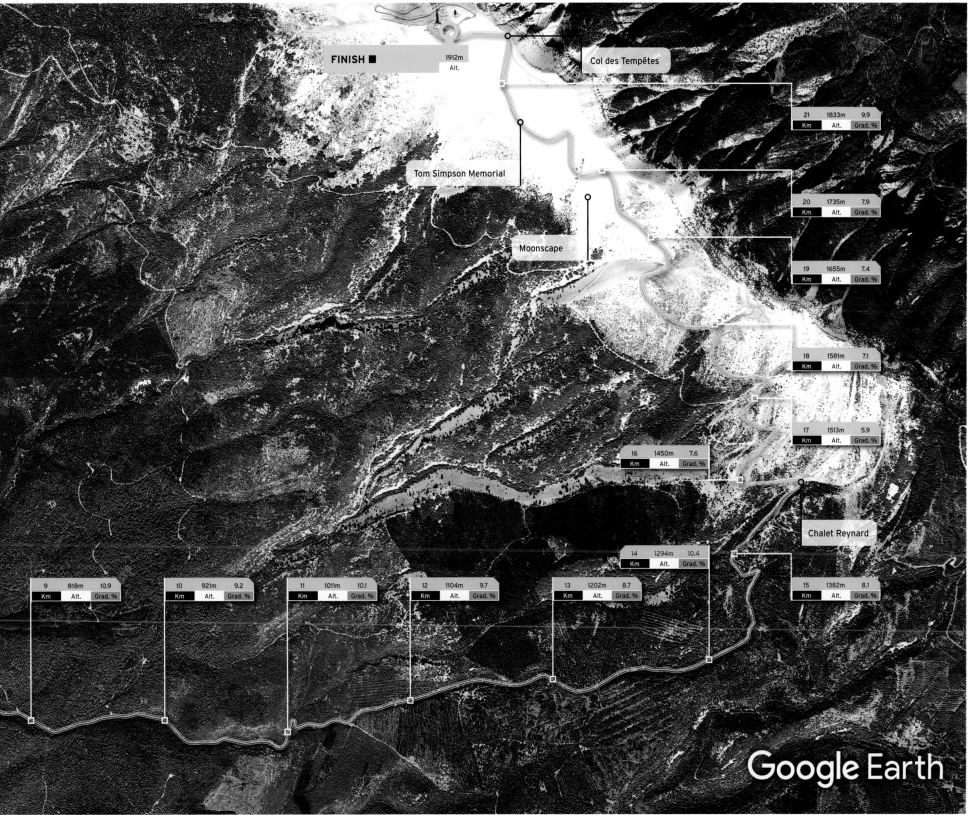

FINISH ■   1912m
Alt.

Col des Tempêtes

Tom Simpson Memorial

Moonscape

21	1833m	9.9
Km	Alt.	Grad. %

20	1735m	7.9
Km	Alt.	Grad. %

19	1655m	7.4
Km	Alt.	Grad. %

18	1581m	7.1
Km	Alt.	Grad. %

17	1513m	5.9
Km	Alt.	Grad. %

16	1450m	7.6
Km	Alt.	Grad. %

Chalet Reynard

14	1294m	10.4
Km	Alt.	Grad. %

9	818m	10.9
Km	Alt.	Grad. %

10	921m	9.2
Km	Alt.	Grad. %

11	1011m	10.1
Km	Alt.	Grad. %

12	1104m	9.7
Km	Alt.	Grad. %

13	1202m	8.7
Km	Alt.	Grad. %

15	1382m	8.1
Km	Alt.	Grad. %

Google Earth

Route to the Summit

"The climb comes in two parts," says famous French rider Thomas Voeckler. "The section through the forest is the toughest part; then you're faced with the wind. The Ventoux doesn't allow even a moment's relaxation."

◀ Bédoin Forest

Locals apparently razed the woods of Ventoux to the ground in centuries gone by, so the forest that now marks the end of the vineyards and lavender groves and the beginning of the climb proper is a modern creation. It is populated with oak, cedar and pine, and the climatic conditions around Ventoux combine to create a unique ecosystem, though Tour de France riders care little for the flowers and insects as they enter the trees 5km out of Bédoin. It's a double-edged sword; the leaves do shade the Tour from the omnipresent sun, but they also trap in the hot air like a muggy greenhouse, deflecting any breeze. At the St Estève corner the road suddenly jumps up to 8.5% and for five miles it doesn't dip below 9%. If this abrupt change of pace doesn't do for any frontrunners hung out to dry on the sweltering approach to the climb then the jolts of 11% or 12% certainly will. It's here that true Tour contenders make their statements of intent; just as the farmers of Provence did years ago, it won't take long for the Tour de France peloton to be swiftly cut down under the pressure.

Left: Bédoin Forest: Arboreal haven before the ordeal commences in earnest.

BÉDOIN FOREST

Tom Simpson memorial

Erected in 1968 with support from club cyclists, family members and donations from readers of *Cycling* magazine back home in Britain, the simple stone memorial at the point where Simpson died in 1967, 1.5 kilometres from the summit, has become an unofficial shrine to the man and a place of pilgrimage for disciples of the sport. In 1970 the Tour's race director laid a wreath at the memorial as frontrunner Eddy Merckx, a former team-mate of Simpson, raced past in the first Tour to return to Ventoux since 1967.

Opposite: Riders pay tribute to Tom Simpson at his memorial on the uppermost slopes of Mont Ventoux. Above left: The Schleck brothers lead the 2009 Tour de France through the Ventoux moonscape. Above right: Chris Froome takes a solo stage win on Ventoux while in the yellow jersey during the 2013 Tour.

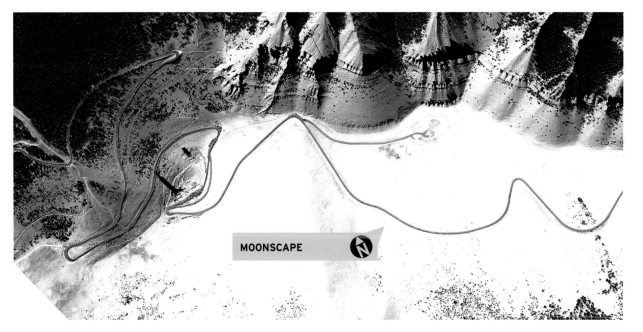

Left: Mont Ventoux Moonscape: Parched expanse to test the nerves.

◀ Moonscape

They call it the "moonscape", but "brick kiln" might be more apt; underneath the unshielded sun the bleached white rocks that surround the peak of Mont Ventoux reflect the sun's rays and fry to a crisp anything exposed for too long. The real Tour fans brave enough to await the race on the upper slopes are rewarded with a natural amphitheatre, a gladiatorial arena where the few remaining front riders exchange blows, whether it's Lance Armstrong versus Marco Pantani in 2000, Stephen Roche versus Pedro Delgado in 1987, or Chris Froome versus Nairo Quintana in 2013. "There's no air, there's no oxygen," said Armstrong in 2000. "There's no vegetation, there's no life … it's more like the moon than the mountain." The road curves gently in and out of bowls in the mountainside but never enough for a rider to get out of sight of the chasers, while the wind brings a shocking chill and seldom blows favourably.

Châlet Reynard

A small bar and restaurant at 1,450m marks the point where the road from Bédoin, 15km downhill, and that from its neighbouring village of Sault join up and head to the summit together. It's close to where Chris Froome upped the tempo in 2013, shedding all but Nairo Quintana before going on to win the stage. "So much of it is on feeling. I like to think that in those moments I can feel when it's hard. I can feel I'm hurting, and I hope the others are hurting at that point," he said after he'd received oxygen at the summit.

Bédoin

Glance at the nature of the opening kilometres of the Mont Ventoux climb leaving Bédoin and you wouldn't know it to be a mountain ascent. Surrounded by buzzing fields, riders approach on a gentle gradient between 3 and 5% for the opening six kilometres.. But the flat surroundings of Ventoux mean riders tackle the climb after a long, hot, flat approach, and one which doesn't give them the chance to find their climbing legs. Bédoin signals that things are going to get a lot worse before they get better.

Col des Tempêtes

The 1,841m Col des Tempêtes is 70m below the road's high point. A small stone wall with a sign gives way to breathtaking views to the north. When riders round the final right-hand bend, there are just 100m to the finish line. It can mean a joyful final surge to victory as the observatory comes back into view, or a tactical pinch point where the stage – or vital seconds - can be won or lost. The adjacent car park provides enough flat asphalt to be a nice place for amateurs to survey the view, reflect on their achievement, and eat sweets from the souvenir shop.

The Mountain Kings

Whether it is the searing heat, the relentless gradients, or the reputation of the climb itself, Mont Ventoux has been driving riders to the very edge of their physical and mental limits for more than 60 years. A stage including the Ventoux never fails to provide fireworks to light up the Tour and set victors well on their way to sporting stardom.

Previous pages: Mont Ventoux and its iconic observatory dominate the landscape of Provence.

Opposite top left: A sweat-drenched Eros Poli approaches the foot of a broiling Ventoux on his epic solo breakaway during the 1994 Tour.

Opposite top right: British cyclist Tom Simpson on his fateful climb of the Ventoux in 1967.

Opposite bottom: Charly Gaul, the "Angel of the Mountains", rides through his own personal torment on his way to setting a 31-year record for the climb in the 1958 Mont Ventoux time trial.

1955 Ferdi KÜBLER and Jean MALLÉJAC

Mont Ventoux had made its debut in the Tour in 1951, when five riders, including Raphaël Géminiani and Louison Bobet (an eventual Tour winner), braved the mountain together. But it was in 1955 when the Ventoux first left its mark on the Tour on a dramatic 198km stage from Marseille to Avignon. As the peloton approached Bédoin, Ferdi Kübler, the brash Swiss winner of the 1950 Tour, dismissed Géminiani's warning and bragged in broken French about conquering the mountain. He attacked 10km from the summit, but it went horribly wrong; foaming at the mouth, shoulders sagging and head bobbing, he criss-crossed the road and crashed several times on the descent. While he made it to Avignon, his injuries and the mental toll of the day caused him to quit the Tour and he never raced it again. Behind Kübler, things were much worse for the Frenchman Jean Malléjac, who had collapsed on the side of the road and received oxygen from the Tour's doctor. It is likely he had sought excess chemical assistance to prepare for the Ventoux. Malléjac, however, always insisted that he had been drugged. Bobet won the stage and carried on to Paris where he became the first man to win the Tour three times in a row.

1958 Charly GAUL

Nicknamed the "Angel of the Mountains", slight and slim Luxembourger Charly Gaul flew up the slopes of Ventoux during an individual time trial in 1958. It laid the foundations for his only overall Tour de France victory. Followed by his support car and a reporter's motorbike and with the hot sun of Ventoux casting sharp shadows over his face, Gaul heaved at his bike with its saddle lowered right down to the frame in order to accommodate his tiny legs, which pedalled furiously over the hour-long effort in his typical toes-down, fluid style. It speaks volumes of Gaul's climbing talent that his time of one hour, two minutes and nine seconds from Bédoin, ridden on poor road surfaces and a heavy, steel-framed bike, stood for 31 years until Jonathan Vaughters, an American on the US Postal team of Lance Armstrong, took it in 1999. Indeed the record up Ventoux has been something of a blue riband marker in professional cycling. The current time of 55 minutes and 51 seconds was set by the Spanish climber Iban Mayo in 2004 – which, given the era and Mayo's subsequent two-year doping ban, must be taken with a fistful of salt. On his way to the stage win in the yellow jersey in 2013, Chris Froome recorded a time of 59 minutes on the nose.

1967 Tom SIMPSON

The year tragedy struck on the slopes of Mont Ventoux. Tom Simpson, the charming Englishman known as "Mister Tom" and the first British rider to win the world championships road race, collapsed and died on the barren slopes close to the summit. In the searing heat, Simpson began to weave across the road before falling to the ground. At the time he was erroneously reported to have shouted "Put me back on my bike" (Simpson's words were "On, on, on" according to his mechanic Harry Hall, who helped him remount). Regardless, he rode on for a few hundred metres before collapsing again. Mouth-to-mouth resuscitation from the Tour's doctor, who had treated Malléjac 12 years earlier, couldn't revive Simpson who died on the mountain before a helicopter took him to hospital. Half empty tubes of pills were found in his jersey pocket and accounts suggest Simpson had consumed brandy during the stage. Simpson's death is now marked by a stone memorial paid for and maintained by cyclists in Britain. Another one of Simpson's lasting legacies is that of mandatory tests for performance-enhancing drugs, which were introduced the following season.

1994 Eros POLI

They don't come less suited for the high mountains than Eros Poli. Tall, broad and fast on the flat, the Italian was suited to crossing mountain climbs on his own, but at the back of the peloton, not at the front. However, without his usual team leader Mario Cipollini to look after, Poli set off on a bold solo breakaway on the 231km 15th stage of the 1994 race, a stage ending in Carpentras after visiting Ventoux. Poli knew that even all the time in the world might not be enough for him to make it over the final, fearsome climb in the lead, but after riding his own personal purgatory to escape from the bunch and keep them from chomping at his heels, he reached the foot of the climb with a staggering 25-minute lead. An hour of heaving and hauling later, Poli was up and over the top – drenched in sweat and exhausted by the effort. When the rest of the field crossed the summit they were still four and a half minutes down, and Poli knew it would be enough. He swooped down the tight bends and high-speed straights with the skills he was used to deploying while fighting for position in the final few kilometres of a sprint stage, and went on to take a memorable victory, one which ensured his cult hero status in the sport.

Puy de Dôme

1415m

Length: 14.0km
Start: 368m
Ascent: 1047m

Featuring arguably the toughest finish to a mountain climb in Tour de France history, the Puy de Dôme is a truly legendary ascent, which modernity and changing times have conspired to consign to the history books.

❝ If the photo had not been taken then the legend would never have existed. ❞
Raphaël Géminiani

The Puy de Dôme is a mountain climb caught in time. The ancient volcano, which sits as the jewel in the crown of the Chaîne des Puys range overlooking the industrial town of Clermont-Ferrand, is a hall of fame of iconic moments and images of the Tour de France.

It's where the French stars of the 1980s Laurent Fignon and Bernard Hinault came of age and proved their credentials as victors in their nation's biggest sporting event. It's where Eddy Merckx was captured clutching his side in pain in a locker room after being punched by a fist striking out from the banks of fans in 1975. It was a moment that brought about the beginning of the end for the hitherto unbeatable Belgian. "The only regret in my career is that I finished the '75 Tour de France after the punch," Merckx said in 2015. "Afterwards, all my problems came from that."

The history of the mystical and alluring mountain stretches back to before the time of the Romans, with a temple on the peak dating to the time when the Celts ruled modern-day France. The Puy de Dôme was also where local scientist Blaise Pascal carried out his experiments on atmospheric pressure during the 17th century. Today the peak is home to a weather station and observatory.

The climb, rising for 14 kilometres in a spiral around a perfect peak topped with a radio antenna, is now an icon in itself. But none of the images taken of the Tour de France on the Puy de Dôme are as famous as that of the duel between Jacques Anquetil and Raymond Poulidor in 1964.

The two great rivals are contorted over their bikes at the end of a long, hot stage, almost knocking heads as they battle for every last inch of road. Anquetil is a picture of exhaustion, his wide eyes staring hollowly out of his pale, gaunt, greyhound-esque face. Behind them surges an almighty wake of motorbikes, reporters, fans and the faint landscape of the Auvergne.

Did Poulidor have the wrong bike? He claimed in a later interview that he should have fitted a 25-tooth rear sprocket, rather than a 24, and that because of the pull of the lucrative criterium circuit he didn't reconnoitre the climb before the race. He won the stage but didn't gain enough time on the yellow jersey of Anquetil to take the race lead. Did his hesitation cost him his best ever chance of Tour victory? It's one of the sport's great "what ifs", and all part of the legend of the climb.

Nowadays photographs and memories are all that remain of the Puy de Dôme as a Tour location. The road was closed to cars and cyclists between 2010 and 2012 while works were completed on a narrow-gauge railway that wound its way up the peak on a track adjacent to the road. The size of the trains means that the tarmac is now only wide enough for one emergency vehicle access lane. Other vehicles are now banned from driving or riding up to the top, although if you believe what you read in internet forums, many cyclists still do make it to the peak, often getting up early to ride up and down before the first train leaves the station at the bottom.

If they do, they're in for the hardest climb in the region and one of the hardest in the Tour. It's not the longest or the highest by a long way, but the final five kilometres climb almost 600m at an average gradient that hardly ever drops below 11%.

It was the only *hors catégorie* climb in the Massif Central. Was, rather than is, because sadly the Tour outgrew the Puy de Dôme even before the arrival of the railway. The summit is simply not large enough for all the finish-line infrastructure of the modern race. The Tour de France on the Puy de Dôme is extinct; lava last flowed from the peak in around 6,000BC and the Tour last visited in 1988.

However, it is a tribute to the climb that in 13 visits by the Tour there were so many exciting stages; indeed there was never a dull moment, which is a characteristic shared by only a handful of climbs. It might never return, but the Puy de Dôme will live long in the memory of the Tour.

Opposite: Jacques Anquetil (l) and Raymond Poulidor almost touch wheels as they fight for every last inch of road in one of the most famous duels to have ever taken place on the Puy de Dôme.

START ▶

368m
Alt.

Clermont-Ferrand

1	377m	0.9
Km	Alt	Grad %

2	414m	3.7
Km	Alt	Grad %

3	461m	4.7
Km	Alt	Grad %

Altitude meters

1500
1200
900
600
300
0

Start 1 2 3 4 5 6 7 8 9 10 11 12 13 Finish

Kilometers

4	539m	7.8
Km	Alt	Grad %

5	616m	7.7
Km	Alt	Grad %

6	694m	7.8
Km	Alt	Grad %

7	721m	2.7
Km	Alt	Grad %

Google Earth

La Font de l'Arbre

8	759m	3.8
Km	Alt	Grad %

9	847m	8.8
Km	Alt	Grad %

Entrance

First bend

11	1091m	12.7
Km	Alt	Grad %

12	1199m	10.8
Km	Alt	Grad %

Summit

Temple of Mercury

10	964m	11.7
Km	Alt	Grad %

FINISH ■

	1415m
	Alt.

13	1317m	11.8
Km	Alt	Grad %

Google Earth

Route to the Summit

From the busy streets of Clermont-Ferrand to the windswept peak at the top of the ancient volcano in the Chaîne des Puys, the road to the Puy de Dôme took riders of the Tour de France from hustle and bustle to wilderness in just 10 kilometres.

FINISH Ⓝ

◀ Finish

Instantly recognizable thanks to the TV antenna that stands tall on its summit, the Puy de Dôme sits in a long line of volcanic peaks running roughly north to south and known as the Chaîne des Puys. It is remarkable less for its height (1,485m) than its prominence; the conical peak stands tall among its surroundings, looking like what you would get if you asked primary school children to draw a mountain. Like a miniature, rounded version of Mont Ventoux, the peak is devoid of trees. But unlike "the bald mountain" to the southeast, scrub and grass give this one a soft green cloak. The views are equally spectacular, though, extending right across to Limousin region to the west, the Alps (on a clear day) to the east and the volcano chain north and south. The mountain has a rich human history, too. In 1908, local industrialists the Michelin brothers put up a prize for the first aviator to fly a plane from Paris and land it on the peak. The feat was achieved by Eugène Renaux three years later.

Left: An observatory sits on top of the Puy de Dôme.

Entrance

The entrance to the Puy de Dôme used to be like the raising of a giant curtain on a theatre, with a full orchestra of fans in the background. Approaching the climb from the main road, the summit and the travails awaiting the riders would be in full view, dominating the skyline. These days the approach road to the Puy de Dôme swings off to the left towards the car park and there's little more than a simple sign forbidding entry to all except emergency vehicles.

Opposite: **The perfectly conical peak of the Puy de Dôme looms over the riders of the Tour de France in 1964.** Above left: **The mercurial Luis Ocaña emerges from the fog clinging to the Puy de Dôme in 1971 to take a solo stage win.** Above right: **Joop Zoetemelk is cheered by happy fans as he strains his way to victory on the summit of the Puy de Dôme at the end of a mountain time trial stage in the 1978 Tour de France.**

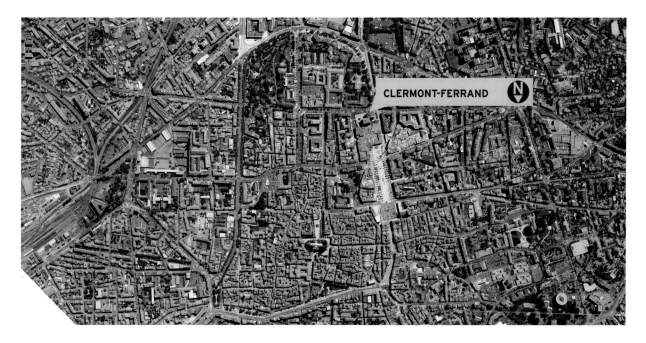

◀ Clermont-Ferrand

The biggest city in the Massif Central and a former industrial powerhouse, Clermont-Ferrand marks the beginning of the climb to the Puy de Dôme. The mountain itself is just 10 kilometres away as the crow flies, and the bald peak overlooks the city's streets. You don't have to look far for evidence of the region's volcanic past; the enormous cathedral in the centre of Clermont-Ferrand has been built from local black volcanic rock, and from the air the array of white, terracotta and black buildings makes the city look like the scattered contents of a bag of licorice allsorts. The city has particularly strong links to cycling. Michelin, the company which invented the removable and glue-less pneumatic bicycle tyre, was founded in the city in 1889 and for many decades was the city's biggest employer, at one point directly providing jobs more than 30,000 people. The town has tended to provide a start point for the stage after the summit finish on Puy de Dôme. However, the town has hosted relatively few visits for its size: just two finishes, seven starts, and nothing at all since 1988.

Left: **Clermont-Ferrand is the industrial home to Michelin tyres.**

La Font de l'Arbre

One of the first villages outside the city limits of Clermont-Ferrand, the settlement of Font de l'Arbre marks the point where riders leave the main road and turn right towards the foot of the Puy de Dôme. Sitting in the Volcans d'Auvergne regional park, the village is home to a spring where early Tour riders would have filled their bottles and taken one last drink before the ascent. It's good stuff; nearby is the town of Volvic, famous for its bottled water.

First bend

Shortly after the entrance to the private road, the tarmac hits a steeper section of the mountainside and immediately swings left to start its spiral ascent to the summit. Here the road becomes very tough indeed, rising to 12% gradient and staying there until the penultimate kilometre. This is the most southern facing section of the climb; as the road climbs the steep sides it is brutally exposed to the burning sun, with no trees to offer shade but a hot rock wall to reflect heat.

Temple of Mercury

The summit of the Puy de Dôme is home to the remains of a large Gallo-Roman temple built in the second century AD to honour the Roman messenger god Mercury. It was discovered in 1873, and excavations carried out early in the twenty-first century have revealed a series of different buildings that had been covered up by the creeping soil and passage of time. Probably humans have found spiritual significance in this remarkable mountain for millennia.

The Mountain Kings

Having hosted 13 summit finishes in its relatively short history, with first blood going to Fausto Coppi in 1952, for 36 years the remorselessly steep and notoriously difficult Puy de Dôme was a regular proving ground for four generations of Tour de France greats.

1964 Jacques **ANQUETIL** and Raymond **POULIDOR**

The 1964 battle on the Puy de Dôme was the brightest clash of swords during the four-year war between two of the home nation's greatest ever Tour de France riders: Jacques Anquetil and Raymond Poulidor. Anquetil, winner of four previous editions of the Tour, came into the 1964 race already fatigued from winning the Giro d'Italia earlier in the season. Nevertheless on the morning of the stage to Puy de Dôme, with four stages to go, the wily old fox held a 56-second lead on Poulidor. Predictably the two were the last remaining riders at the front of the race as the Tour hit the slopes of the climb. Accompanied by a petrol-powered flotilla of press vehicles riding in their wake, the duo fought tooth and nail, with a dog-tired Anquetil clinging to the inside line, doing all he could to keep Poulidor on the outside and hide the cracks in his armour from his fresher but more reluctant younger rival. Poulidor took 42 seconds by the finish but it was not enough to take the yellow jersey. Anquetil, relieved to have survived the final mountain test, thrashed "Poupou" in the final stage time trial through Paris and won his fifth and final Tour.

1975 Eddy **MERCKX**

1975 was the year when the Tour de France's unbeatable rider was finally beaten. Quite literally, it transpired, on the Puy de Dôme. As Belgian rider Lucien Van Impe (who would win the Tour the following year) took off to win the stage from Bernard Thévenet, 49 seconds down the road Merckx was punched in the abdomen by a roadside spectator shortly before the summit. Merckx made it to the finish, threw up, and rode down the hill to identify the culprit, who claimed it was an accident. It was the start of a nightmare fortnight for Merckx, who had to battle stomach painkillers, blood thinners and a rival, Thévenet, riding the Tour of his life. He famously cracked on Pra-Loup on stage 15 and crashed hard early on stage 17, a fall which broke his cheekbone and jaw and from that evening on limited his intake to liquids only. Remarkably Merckx still clung on to second place overall in Paris, having gone on riding to ensure he and his team earned the financial rewards that a podium would bring, but the toll that the effort took on his body was far greater than even he anticipated. He would not win the Tour again.

1983 Laurent **FIGNON**

Tendinitis kept the current champion Bernard Hinault away from the 1983 Tour de France but his absence opened up the door to France's next great Tour champion: Laurent Fignon. The rider nicknamed "The Professor" couldn't have been more different from Hinault, the man to whom he was previously understudy and domestique on the iconic Renault team. Hailing from the Parisian suburbs, he was tall with a blond ponytail and wore geeky glasses. His quiet, private nature often came across as arrogance and conceit. Hinault was a feisty, stocky, salt-of-the-earth rural man from Brittany. The stage 15 time trial from Clermont-Ferrand to Puy de Dôme was the stage that brought Fignon within striking distance of the yellow jersey, Pascal Simon. The steep slope of the Puy de Dôme was where Simon cracked, riding with a broken shoulder and finishing well off the pace behind the stage winner Angel Arroyo. Although Fignon didn't win the stage, he finished 10th and took three and half minutes from Simon to sit just 52 seconds behind his rival. He eventually took the lead on Alpe d'Huez on stage 17 when Simon finally abandoned due to his injuries.

1988 Johnny **WELTZ**

Stage 19 at the end of the 1988 Tour de France was the last ever stage to climb the Puy de Dôme. Sadly it wasn't a vintage Tour for the climb to go out on. The 1987 champion Stephen Roche was absent through injury, and the winner Pedro Delgado would have his victory tarnished after testing positive for probenicid, a steroid masking agent which was about to be banned by the international cycling federation later that year. Still, the stage to Puy de Dôme at least provided one last hurrah before being consigned to the history books. *Baroudeurs* (a French term for plucky riders who chance their luck from breakaways) Rolf Golz and Johnny Weltz had broken clear during the stage and held an advantage of more than 15 minutes on the peloton with 50 kilometres to the finish. Weltz dropped his breakaway companion on the steep slopes of the Puy de Dôme to take a solo win by 43 seconds, showing once again that it's not always the thoroughbred climbers that take the glory in the high mountains. Behind them, a dominant Delgado took off from the favourites to finish third and strengthen his stranglehold on the overall fight for the yellow jersey.

Ballon d'Alsace

1178m

Length: **9.5km**
Start: **552m**
Ascent: **626m**

The Ballon d'Alsace was the first true mountain climb of the Tour de France. Making its debut in 1905, it quickly demonstrated the majesty and possibilities of the high mountains and opened the door to bigger climbs and the modern Tour as we know it.

> **"** Not only am I asking them to climb a mountain of over 1,000 metres, I am asking them to do it right under the eye of the enemy! **"**
>
> *Henri Desgrange*

These days the climb of the Ballon d'Alsace earns a first or even second category ranking by the Tour de France. From the more frequently used northern approach via Saint Maurice sur Moselle the road, which dates from the 1700s, climbs 9.5km at an average of 6.3% to a summit of 1,178m. From Malvaux to the south the pass is 12.5km at 5.2% and from Sewen it is 13.2km at 5.1%. It's difficult, but hardly the stuff of nightmares.

Yet there's a reason why climbing up and over the Ballon d'Alsace remains significant, even if the Tour has only visited nine times since the end of the Second World War. The initial ascent in 1905 was the first time in the history of the Tour de France that a climb had been picked out and incorporated into the route purely because of the challenge it presented to riders and the narrative it added to the race. It began our modern-day obsession with the mountains; the hype that surrounded the Ballon d'Alsace in 1905 would have been no different to the hype around the showdown on Alpe d'Huez on the penultimate stage of the 2015 Tour, 110 years later.

Ballon is French for "ball" and it is a term given to many of the surrounding climbs in the Vosges Mountains in the very east of France, whose ancient peaks have been eroded and rounded by the slow work of the weather. Nearby are the climbs of the Grand Ballon ("Big Ball") and Petit Ballon ("Little Ball"), and you can tell from the place names that all of them sat right on or over the German border after the Franco-Prussian War of the 1870s until the 1918 Armistice handed Alsace-Lorraine back over to France. The landscape is soft and green and on a good day the views from the Ballon d'Alsace stretch right down to the snow-capped peaks of the Bernese Alps, a reminder that this is a very different environment altogether.

As the Tour has become shorter and deviated more from its original route template (which was a circular tour of France in a very literal sense), the frequency with which the race has returned to the Ballon d'Alsace has slowly declined like the steady slopes of the climb itself. Indeed after 1905 the Tour went on to bigger and better things – the Pyrenees in 1910 and the Alps a year later – and it's those high, snowy cols that have shaped our obsession with the mountains ever since.

Yet the Ballon d'Alsace has hosted some iconic moments in Tour history: the first ever climb in the King of the Mountains competition in 1933, the arrival of Gino Bartali on the scene in 1937, and in 1969 the first stage win of Eddy Merckx (who would win 33 more on his way to becoming the greatest cyclist ever seen).

The climb featured in 2005 as the last summit on a medium mountain stage to Mulhouse, marking 100 years since the first ever visit. Michael Rasmussen launched a solo attack to sweep up the mountains points, while have-a-go hero Jens Voigt took the yellow jersey after he and Christophe Moreau used the climb as a springboard to break clear of a six-strong chase group. And while it has only been crossed once this millennium, the Vosges are coming back into vogue thanks to the modern-day Tour director, Christian Prudhomme, with his innovative route planning and tendency to feature the smaller climbs to the east of the country.

It will never regain its status as the celebrity climb of the Tour de France, but the continued presence of the Ballon d'Alsace more than 110 years after it first featured serves as a pleasing reminder of the Tour's distant origins.

Opposite: (l-r) Lucien Aimar, Jan Janssen, Tom Simpson and Franco Balmamion ride eyeballs-out on the Ballon d'Alsace in the 1967 Tour.

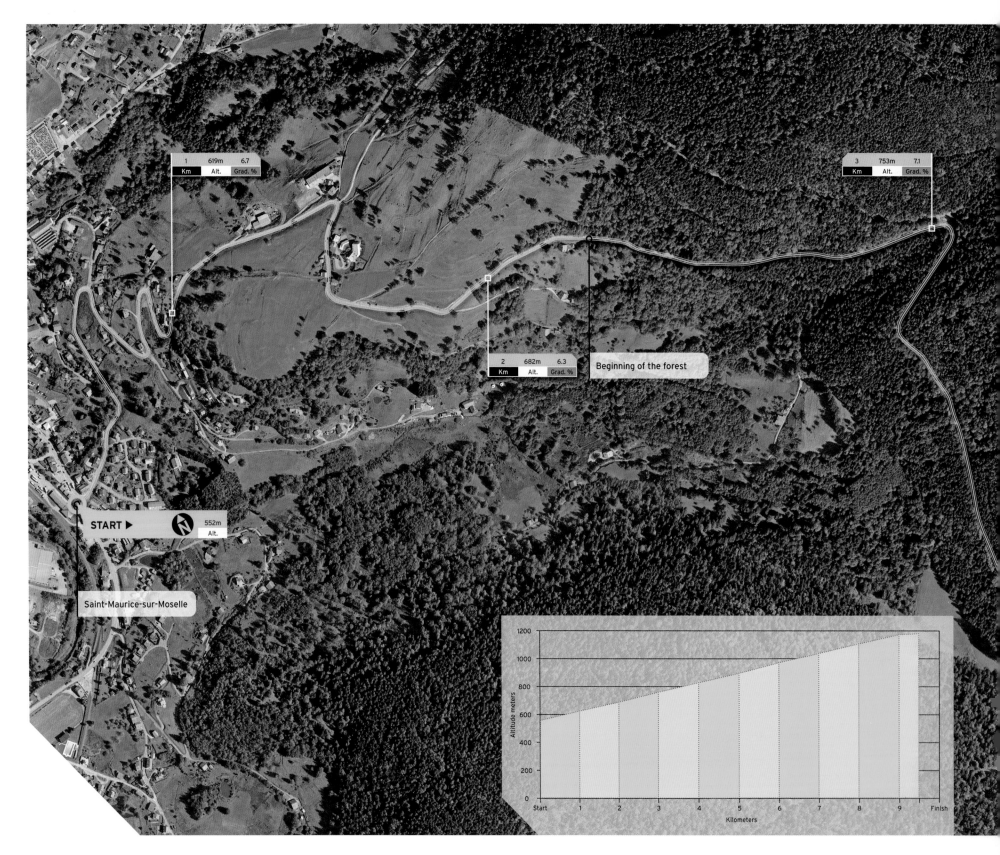

1	619m	6.7
Km	Alt.	Grad. %

3	753m	7.1
Km	Alt.	Grad. %

2	682m	6.3
Km	Alt.	Grad. %

Beginning of the forest

START ▶	552m
	Alt.

Saint-Maurice-sur-Moselle

5	888m	6.7
Km	Alt.	Grad. %

7	1030m	6.7
Km	Alt.	Grad. %

La Jumentérie

9	1164m	7.8
Km	Alt.	Grad. %

Plateau Road

4	821m	6.8
Km	Alt.	Grad. %

Plan du Canon

6	963m	7.5
Km	Alt.	Grad. %

8	1098m	6.5
Km	Alt.	Grad. %

FINISH ■　　　　　1171m

Alt.

Google Earth

Image © Landsat © Google 2014

Route to the Summit

The Ballon d'Alsace is a fairly straightforward climb for riders of the Tour de France, although the muddy, gravel tracks of its early days will have made the nine kilometres much more difficult than they are today. It's a scenic and picturesque road, popular with tourists, but offers enough of a challenge on two wheels for riders to get stuck in and shake up the race.

FINISH

◀ Finish

The Ballon d'Alsace is well connected to civilization; French cities of Strasbourg, Mulhouse and Metz are nearby while those in the Rhine valley aren't far away either. The very top of the climb at 1,178m is high enough to feel significant but low enough to feature a number of permanent cafés, bars and souvenir shops to cater for the hikers, skiers, campers and motorcyclists who make trips to the top, along with the cyclists. There's a simple memorial to the first cyclist of the Tour de France to make it this far, René Pottier. It's just a square granite column with a sepia photograph of the man standing proudly with his machine. The summit offers remarkable views in every direction over wild flowers and grazing animals. On the horizon, 100km to the southeast, lie the high Alps of Switzerland, whose snowy peaks are visible on a clear day. The Alps are on the horizon figuratively as well; for riders in the Tour the Ballon d'Alsace generally heralds the start of a journey south and on to steeper, sterner tests.

Left: Ballon d'Alsace: Finish amongst the tourist traps.

Saint Maurice sur Moselle

The start of the climb to the Ballon d'Alsace is a fairly unremarkable turn from the *route nationale* running through the village of Saint Maurice sur Moselle, right next to the tourist office. The River Moselle streams from a source on the western flank of the climb, before trickling down through the town and onwards to the vineyards of Germany and its confluence with the Rhine.

Opposite: The Réné Pottier Memorial on the Ballon d'Alsace.   Above left: Dark clouds greet the 2005 Tour peloton near the top of the climb.   Above right: The Discovery Channel team guard Lance Armstrong up the climb, also in 2005.

PLAN DU CANON

◀ Plan du Canon

The very name hints at the area's military significance during the wars between France and Prussia (later Germany) during the nineteenth and twentieth centuries; when the early Tours visited the climb it was as much a symbolic statement of French national longing for the Alsace-Lorraine, annexed by Prussia, as it was about finding a mountain to climb. The modern-day forest road, however, is tranquil and peaceful. The approach to the Plan du Canon with 5km to the summit features a slight softening of the gradient before a sharp left-hand hairpin signifies the start of the toughest section of the climb. It's a subtle but significant change; the road moves from gradients of 7% and under to 7% and over, enough to take the wind out of the sails of any riders hanging on and offering an opportunity for climbers to utilize their strengths and break free. From a relatively straight road with sweeping bends, the arrival of the hairpins also gives attackers the opportunity to get around the corners, into the trees, and out of sight of their chasers.

Left: Plan du Canon, the belligerent rampart of yesteryear.

Beginning of the forest

The opening 2.3km of the climb is surrounded by fields and the outskirts of Saint Maurice but it's not long before the road delves deep into the forest and passes 700m in altitude. It becomes clear from this point on that there is a tough core of granite underneath the Ballon d'Alsace; grey stone walls overgrown with greenery border the road, which itself is made of a distinctive pale grey tarmac.

La Jumentérie

A jumentérie in French is a horse stable, and these rather grandiose buildings have been home to horse breeders for centuries. They also mark the end of the hairpins and the beginning of a long straight stretching out for a mile. By this point the road has also emerged from the trees and is bordered by lush green fields. It goes without saying that riders might be able to spot the odd horse, too.

Plateau road

The final push to the summit climbs steadily but relatively steeply, and once over the crest the road descends through idyllic high downs and grassy fields, a bald patch on the mountain surrounded by forest like a monk's tonsure. Henri Desgrange wasn't lying when he said he would be sending his riders right under the noses of the enemy; the road sits adjacent to what was in 1905 the border with Germany.

The Mountain Kings

From the first mountain climbing pioneers to the advent of the King of the Mountains and the greatest cyclist that ever lived, the Ballon d'Alsace might not be the toughest climb in the book, but it has borne witness to pivotal moments in Tour de France history.

Opposite top left: Rudi Altig only just clings onto an unstoppable Eddy Merckx in the 1969 Tour de France.

Opposite top right: René Pottier, a man not to be messed with during the 1905 Tour de France and the first victor on the Ballon d'Alsace.

Opposite bottom left: "Big Gun" Raphaël Géminiani during his 130km solo breakaway that would land him a stage win in Mulhouse.

Opposite bottom right: Vicente Trueba, the Spanish climber who was the first ever "King of the Mountains", climbs the Ballon d'Alsace in 1933.

1905 René **POTTIER**

The diminutive, moustachioed Frenchman was first over the summit of the Ballon d'Alsace in 1905 as part of Tour boss Henri Desgrange's latest publicity ruse, but in doing so became the first real mountain climber of the Tour de France. Unfortunately the feat didn't bring him much luck; his Tour was over 24 hours later. He had punctured a number of times on the rough roads on the descent of the Ballon d'Alsace and then the following stage he abandoned to a crash. But Pottier was back a year later, once again riding hell for leather on the climb with such a devastating impact that *L'Auto* newspaper reported that he "hadn't reached the first hairpin before the group was torn apart". He led over the climb for a second year in a row, but this time it was on his way to winning the overall Tour de France. However, Pottier's tale ends in tragedy; he committed suicide at the age of 27 in the January of the following year, reportedly after discovering that while he was winning his debut Tour, his wife was having an affair. Desgrange erected a memorial to his first mountain champion on the Ballon d'Alsace later that year.

1933 Vicente **TRUEBA**

Thirty years after the first Tour and its founder and boss Henri Desgrange decided to spice things up again, this time with the introduction of the King of the Mountains classification to reward riders for crossing classified mountain summits first. The Ballon d'Alsace had been the Tour's first classified climb and was now the first to count in the Tour's new competition; first over the top was the Spanish rider Vicente Trueba. Trueba was a *touriste-routier*, an independent rider without what would now be called a professional team, who turned up and rode the Tour while taking care of his own sustenance and lodging. With most stages over 200km and held on very basic roads, it was quite some achievement. Trueba, a true mountain climbing specialist nicknamed "The Flea", reached nine of the 16 classified summits before anyone else to claim the first classification, although it was many more years before the now iconic polka dot jersey was introduced. He didn't win any stages – reportedly because he was as bad at descending as he was good at climbing – but did manage to cling on to sixth overall, second of the *touriste-routiers*.

1952 Raphaël **GEMINIANI**

A five-time finisher in the top ten of the Tour de France, Raphaël Géminiani was one of a number of talented riders of his generation who had the misfortune to see their careers coincide with those of Fausto Coppi and Louison Bobet. Yet "Big Gun" (so named because of his larger than life personality and his beak of a nose) was still capable of tremendous feats in the race, including on stage eight of the 1952 Tour. The skinny Frenchman took off on a solo move that lasted 130km, leading over four cols deep in the Vosges mountains including the Ballon d'Alsace to win alone in Mulhouse. Géminiani got a second stage that Tour, inside the final week as the race hit the high mountains of the Pyrenees, but Coppi would go on to win overall by a mammoth 28 minutes. Although he would never taste overall Tour success as a rider, Géminiani moved on to be one of the sport's most successful managers. His team, somewhat narcissistically named "St Raphaël", would be home to five-time Tour winner Jacques Anquetil during the 1950s and holds a special place in British cycle racing as the team of the country's first Tour stage winner Brian Robinson.

1969 Eddy **MERCKX**

The Ballon d'Alsace was where the Tour de France got its first taste of Eddy Merckx, the man who would go on to win five titles and 34 overall stages, a record that stands to this day. The cycling world already knew what to expect from the prolific Belgian, then just 24, but the manner in which he dismantled the field on the sixth stage, the second of four summit finishes to have taken place on the Ballon d'Alsace, was jaw-dropping nonetheless. By the foot of the climb he had already managed to distance all but one of the rest of the field, which included previous Tour winners Felice Gimondi, Lucien Aimar, Roger Pingeon and Jan Janssen. Only the German powerhouse Rudi Altig had managed to stick to Merckx's wheel, but he didn't last long after the road had turned uphill. Merckx, slim and supple next to the colossal German, effortlessly put more than four minutes into the previous four overall Tour winners, ripped the yellow jersey from the shoulders of Désiré Letort, and never looked back. This was Merckx at his effortless best. Later that year, Merckx was inolved in a serious crash during a track race, after which he said he was "never the same again".

The Tour's First Mountain

Born of cheating riders, rising nationalism and one man's endless quest for ever more theatrical challenges. But how did this humble mountain in the pretty hills of the Vosges become the first true mountain climb in the history of the Tour de France?

The Ballon d'Alsace was the first climb of the Tour de France. Or was it? Before answering that question, let's consider the situation of the Tour in 1905. Henri Desgrange, the flamboyant and some might say slightly sadistic newspaper editor and creator of the Tour, had seen his new invention descend into farce. He had disqualified the top four from the 1904 race, its second edition, following Dick Dastardly acts of sabotage and cheating, including the completion of parts of the route by train. Most came to the conclusion that the miscreants had probably been at it in 1903 too. Desgrange had to do something to save his Tour.

All the while, France was rubbing shoulders with its increasingly militaristic German neighbours to the east, and the area around the Vosges Mountains, at that point straddling the border between the two countries, became an object of national infatuation. Desgrange, ever the innovative showman, decided to take the Tour as close to the border as he dared while, in a typical act of hyperbole, he inflated the scale of the challenge facing the riders to crest the mountain. In short, the Ballon d'Alsace was to become the embodiment of France's enemy, ready to be conquered through the strength and valiance of its brave cyclists. Never mind that they all cheated the year before.

Desgrange is perhaps guilty of over-egging things – the Ballon d'Alsace is nowhere near the scale of the high mountain passes in the Alps and the Pyrenees. Nor, to answer the initial question, was it technically the first climb the Tour had scaled. On the very first stage of the very first race in 1903, riders had

ridden over the 759m Col du Pin-Bouchain on the way from Paris to Lyon. The following day, they went over the 1,151m Col de la République near Saint Étienne.

But on stage two on 11 June 1905, as a result of Desgrange's promotion, the levels of anticipation and enthusiasm around the Tour hit fever pitch. Six lead riders approached, climbed off their single-speed bikes to remove their back wheels, flipped them around to engage their climbing sprockets, and charged at the dusty road up the Ballon d'Alsace. René Pottier was the first over the top after around 40 minutes following a scrap with Lucien Petit-Breton and Henri Cornet; Hippolyte Aucoutrier, Émile Georget and Louis Trousselier were all dropped on the way up. It wasn't quite the slog that Desgrange was after, but it didn't matter. One reporter symbolically, and presciently, wrote that Pottier was "king of the mountains".

Later that Tour, riders would cross the Côte du Laffrey and the Col Bayard on the way from Grenoble to Toulon. Desgrange was delighted, the public was delighted, and the Ballon d'Alsace became a regular feature in the following decade, even being climbed twice in the 1914 Tour just months before Europe descended into war.

Although it has been less popular in recent decades, the Ballon d'Alsace is where the first chapter of the mountains in the Tour de France was written. The story now runs froms the humble Côte de Jenkin Road in the suburbs of Sheffield that hosted stage two of the 2014 Tour to the mighty Col du Galibier in the high Alps – but it starts here. The Ballon d'Alsace is genesis.

Index

Page numbers in *italic* type refer to pictures; numbers in **bold** type refer to main entries

Picture credits

The publishers would like to thank the following sources for their kind permission to reproduce the pictures in this book.

Corbis: /Gilles Lansard/Photononstop: 89TL

Getty Images: /Agence Zoom: 172; /Harry Engels: 198-199; /Eric Feferberg/AFP: 78TR; / Bernard Jaubert: 119TR; /Ezra Shaw: 112; /Universal Image Group: 6R, 7TR, 7B; /Koen van Weel/AFP: 20

Offside Sports Photography: /Excelsior: 189TR; /L'Equipe: 4, 8, 9, 12, 13, 14, 15, 16, 24TR, 25TL, 25TR, 26-27, 29T, 29BL, 29BR, 30, 31, 32, 39TL, 43TL, 51TL, 53L, 53TR, 53BR, 61TL, 63TL, 63TR, 63B, 64, 70TR, 71TR, 73TR, 73BR, 79TL, 79TR, 83T, 83BL, 83BR, 89TR, 91BR, 101BR, 111BR, 121TR, 122-123, 124, 128TR, 129TL, 129TR, 130-131, 133T, 133BL, 133BR, 134, 141TL, 141TR, 142-143, 145B, 145TR, 152TR, 155TL, 155TR, 155B, 156, 161TL, 163L, 163TR, 164, 169TR, 171TL, 171B, 177TL, 179TL, 179TR, 187TL, 189TL, 189B, 190-191, 192, 196TR, 197TL, 197TR, 201TL, 201TR, 201B, 202, 208TR, 209TL, 209TR, 211L, 211TR, 211BR, 212, 217TL, 219TL, 219TR, 219BL, 219BR, 220, 221, 224; /Parisien: 171TR; /Pressesports: 3, 10-11, 17, 18-19, 38TR, 39TR, 40-41, 43TR, 43B, 44, 45, 46, 50TR, 51TR, 54, 61TR, 62TR, 71TL, 73L, 74, 80-81, 88TR, 91L, 91TR, 92, 98TR, 99TL, 99TR, 101T, 101BL, 102, 106TR, 107TL 107TR, 108-109, 111L, 111TR, 118TR, 119TL, 121L, 121BR, 140TR, 145TL, 146, 147, 148, 153TL, 153TR, 160TR, 161TR, 163BR, 168TR, 169TL, 176TR, 177TR, 179B, 180, 186TR, 187TR, 216TR, 217TR

PA Images: /Peter Dejong/AP: 84

Special thanks to Charlotte Wilson and Mark Leech at Offside for their expert knowledge and assistance researching the photography for this project.

Every effort has been made to acknowledge correctly and contact the source and/or copyright holder of each picture and Carlton Books Limited apologises for any unintentional errors or omissions that will be corrected in future editions of this book.

Left: 2014 King of the Mountains Rafal Majka takes a solo stage win on Pla d'Adet.